S.M. Bhardwaj and G. Rinschede (eds.)
Pilgrimage in World Religions

GEOGRAPHIA RELIGIONUM

Interdisziplinäre Schriftenreihe zur Religionsgeographie

Herausgegeben von
M. Büttner, Bochum
K. Hoheisel, Bonn
U. Köpf, Tübingen
G. Rinschede, Eichstätt
A. Sievers, Vechta/Bonn

in Zusammenarbeit mit der
KATHOLISCHEN UNIVERSITÄT EICHSTÄTT

Dietrich Reimer Verlag
Berlin

GEOGRAPHIA RELIGIONUM
Interdisziplinäre Schriftenreihe zur Religionsgeographie
Band 4

S.M. Bhardwaj and G. Rinschede (eds.)

Pilgrimage in World Religions

— presented to Prof. Dr. Angelika Sievers
on the occasion of her 75th Birthday —

Dietrich Reimer Verlag
Berlin

Anschriften der Herausgeber der Reihe:

Prof. Dr. Dr. Dr. M. Büttner
Kiefernweg 40
D-4630 BOCHUM

Prof. Dr. K. Hoheisel
Merler Allee 68
D-5300 BONN 1

Prof. Dr. U. Köpf
Liststraße 24/I
D-7400 TÜBINGEN

Prof. Dr. G. Rinschede
Ostenstraße 26
D-8078 EICHSTÄTT

Prof. Dr. A. Sievers
Römerstraße 118/3308
D-5300 BONN 1

Schriftleitung:
GEOGRAPHIA RELIGIONUM
AR Thomas Breitbach
Ostenstraße 26
D-8078 EICHSTÄTT

CIP-Titelaufnahme der Deutschen Bibliothek
Pilgrimage in World Religions: presented to Prof. Dr. Angelika Sievers on the occasion of her 75th birthday / S.M. Bhardwaj and G. Rinschede (eds.) — Berlin : Reimer, 1988.
(Geographia Religionum; Bd. 4)
ISBN 3-496-00959-4
NE: Bhardwaj, Surinder M.; Sievers, Angelika: Festschrift; GT

Gedruckt mit Unterstützung der Katholischen Universität Eichstätt

ISBN 3-496-00959-4

Gesamtherstellung: Dietrich Reimer Verlag, Berlin
Printed in Germany 1988

Preface

The task of the editors of this volume is twofold:

– To publish recent studies and ideas on pilgrimage, including papers delivered at a session titled *"Pilgrimage"*, organized by them at the "83rd Annual Meeting of the Association of American Geographers" held at Portland, Oregon U.S.A. The authors include Geographers and an anthropologist from the United States, Canada, and the Federal Republic of Germany. They examine the geography of pilgrim systems in different cultural regions of the world, study several new dimensions of the pilgrimage place and process, and reveal the influence of pilgrim streams. Methodological and empirical aspects of pilgrimage and pilgrim tourism examined in this volume may spawn further studies.

– Conjointly, to honour a researcher who has made a particularly important contribution to geography of religion: ANGELIKA SIEVERS. Belonging to the school of Carl Troll, she turned her attention to religio-geographical themes in South Asia with a socio-geographical study on "Christianity and geographic environment in Southwest Ceylon" (1958), a mission-geographical study on "The Christian groups in Kerala (India), their geographic environment and the problem of Christian Unity" (1962 and 1964), inspired by fieldwork in South India and Ceylon/Sri Lanka which resulted in a socio-geographical monograph on Ceylon (1964), including chapters on the socio-religious background. She shows how the Christians in various different periods divide into distinctive groups and also how the caste structure passed to the Christian groups. Together with other geographers such as Deffontaines, Fickeler, Troll, Hahn, Fehn, Schwind, Zimpel and Wirth among others, she applies the functional method particularly to religio-geographical investigations.

Within the framework of her socio-geographical works on "Tourism in Sri Lanka/Ceylon" (1981/1983) she also directs her attention to religio-geographical problems, primarily the problems of pilgrim tourism. Since 1985 she is co-editor of the interdisciplinary scientific series on geography of religion "Geographia Religionum". In her most recent articles she deals with the "Significance of pilgrimage tourism in Sri Lanka (Ceylon)" (1985/1987) and with the "Pilgrimage phenomenon in socio-geographical research" (1985/1987). On the occasion of her 75th birthday these last two articles were published in an Indian "Festschrift to Angelika Sievers" (1987) and a "Homage to David Sopher" (1987) edited by R. L. Singh and Rana P. B. Singh.

We wish Angelika Sievers continued success in her work, especially on the geography of religion with its regional research emphasis on South Asia, and look forward to the keen insights she has always provided.

Publications (selection)

- Christentum und Landschaft in Südwest-Ceylon: eine sozialgeographische Studie. — In: Erdkunde, Archiv f. wiss. Geogr. 1958, 107 – 120.
- Die Christengruppen in Kerala (Indien), ihr Lebensraum und das Problem der christlichen Einheit. Ein missionsgeographischer Beitrag. — In: Zeitschr. f. Missionswiss. u. Religionswiss., 1962, 161 – 187.
- Ceylon. Gesellschaft und Lebensraum in den orientalischen Tropen. Eine sozialgeographische Landeskunde. = Bibl. Geogr. Handbücher, Steiner: Wiesbaden 1964.
- Distribution and socio-economic structure of Christian groups in Kerala (India). — In: Abstracts of Papers. 20th Internat. Geogr. Congress, London 1964, 289.
- Südasien und andere ausgewählte Beiträge aus Forschung und Praxis. (= Kleinere geographische Schriften, Bd. 4) Reimer: Berlin 1982.
- Der Tourismus in Sri Lanka (Ceylon). Ein sozialgeographischer Beitrag zum Tourismusphänomen in tropischen Entwicklungsländern, insbesondere in Südasien. (= Erdkundl. Wissen, Heft 62). Wiesbaden 1983.
- Zur Bedeutung des Pilgertourismus in Sri Lanka (Ceylon). — In: Grundfragen der Religionsgeographie, Geographia Religionum, Band 1, Berlin 1985, 257 – 286.
- Das Pilgerphänomen in sozialgeographischen Untersuchungen. — In: Grundfragen der Religionsgeographie, Geographia Religionum, Band 1, Berlin 1985, 183 – 193 (jointly with G. Rinschede).
- The pilgrimage phenomenon in socio-geographical research. — In: National Geographical Journal of India, Vol. 33 (3), 1987, 213 – 217 (jointly with G. Rinschede).
- Significance of pilgrimage tourism in Sri Lanka (Ceylon). — In: National Geographical Journal of India, Vol. 33 (4), 1987, 430 – 447.

The editors wish to thank the President of the Katholische Universität Eichstätt, Prof. Dr. Nikolaus Lobkowicz and its chancellor, Mr. Carl Heinz Jacob, for the financial backing which made the publication of this fourth volume possible. The editors also wish to thank Ms. Maria Bernecker for producing the setting copy, as well as Dipl.Ing. Karl-Heinz Schatz und Mr. Reinhard Geißler for the cartographical work. We also thank the editors of "Geographia Religionum" for the inclusion of these contributions in Volume 4 of the series.

The editors finally wish to thank Mr. Thomas Breitbach for the editorial revision of this volume and Ms. Gabriella Collard for proofreading.

February 1988

Surinder M. Bhardwaj
Gisbert Rinschede

Contents

		page
Preface		5
Bhardwaj, S. M. and G. Rinschede:	Pilgrimage — A World Wide Phenomenon	11
Tanaka, H.:	On the Geographic Study of Pilgrimage Places	21
Nolan, M. L.:	Pilgrimage and Perception of Hazard in Western Europe	41
Rinschede, G.:	The Pilgrimage Center of Fátima/Portugal	65
Stoddard, R. H.:	Characteristics of Buddhist Pilgrimages in Sri Lanka	99
Oberdiek, U.:	Sādhus in Gaṅgotrī	117
Bhardwaj, S. M. and Madhusudana Rao:	Emerging Hindu Pilgrimage in the United States: A Case Study	159
Prorok, C.:	Patterns of Pilgrimage Behavior Among Hindus of Trinidad	189

Surinder M. Bhardwaj and Gisbert Rinschede

PILGRIMAGE — A WORLD-WIDE PHENOMENON

1. Pilgrimage in the World Religions (Fig. 1)

Pilgrimages to holy places have taken place since early days in the history of mankind. They, however, attained great significance with the emergence and development of the great world religions (Hinduism, Buddhism, Judaism, Christianity, and Islam). They may be considered among the oldest forms of *circulation* based upon non-economic factors, although they were greatly facilitated by the contemporary trade routes. During the course of history pilgrimage activity has gone through a very varied development in the different religions. Conditions of relative tranquility, and the turmoils due to wars resulted in many peaks and troughs in the pilgrimage flows. Despite a general tendency toward secularization in the modern world and other religious changes, pilgrimages have been experiencing a world-wide boom during the last few decades, thanks to the modern means of mass transportation and the increasing use of the automobile.

The World Christian Encyclopedia (1982) estimates that altogether about 130 million people take part in pilgrimages every year. Of these approximately 90 million are Christians, and the remainder 40 million are Hindus, Buddhists, Jews, Moslems, and others. However, our calculations suggest that well over 200 million pilgrims must be participating annually in international, national, and regional pilgrimages; about 150 million Christians, and over 40 million Hindus, Buddhists, Jews and Moslems. As many as 40 million Christians alone converge on their twenty most prominent pilgrimage centers. Likewise, fifteen major Islamic holy places attract over ten million Moslem pilgrims; Mecca alone accounts for three million of the faithful.

Large *Christian places of pilgrimage* belonging almost exclusively to the Roman-Catholic church are to be found not only in Europe, but also in Latin America and Anglo America (Figure 1). Of great international significance here are above all Rome, Jerusalem, Lourdes and Fátima. Typical national pilgrimage

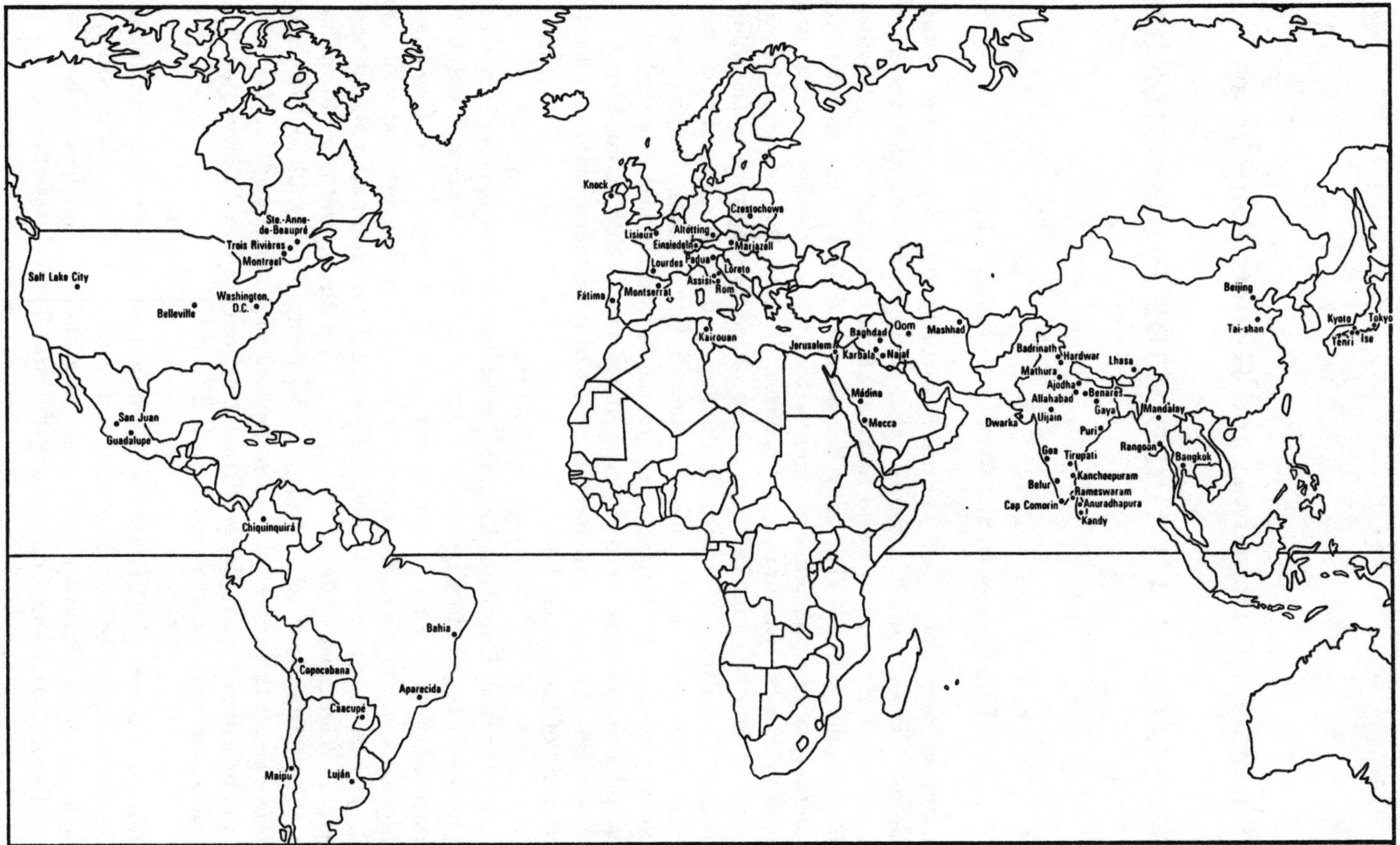

Fig. 1: Pilgrimage places of national and international importance

Prod.: Bhardwaj/Rinschede

centers are Czestochowa in Poland, Knock in Ireland, St. Anne-de-Beaupré in Canada, Washington D.C. in the USA, Guadalupe and San Juan in Mexico, Chiquinquira in Columbia, Copacabana in Bolivia, Maipu in Chile, Lujan in Argentina, Caacupé in Paraguay and Aparecida in Brazil. Within the "Church of Jesus Christ of Latter Day Saints" (the Mormon Church) Salt Lake City is of national and international importance. Christian pilgrimage centers are virtually absent in Black Africa probably because the veneer of Christianity is thin and the influence of its own nature religions still profound.

The primary pilgrimage centers of *Islam* are the two religious nuclei, Mecca and Medina in Saudi Arabia, with Mecca, the focus of *hajj*, as the most important pilgrim destination for all Moslems. Other major Middle Eastern Moslem pilgrimage centers include Baghdad, Karbala, and Najaf (An Najaf) in Iraq, as well as Qom and Mashhad in shiite Iran. Jerusalem (al-Aqsa mosque) is also of great significance for Islam. Many places associated with Muslem saints in India and Pakistan have also become popular pilgrimage (*ziarah*, or *ziarat*) centers.

For *Hinduism*, in the South Asian cultural realm, the particularly noteworthy pilgrimage centers include among others, Benares (Varanasi), Allahabad (Prayag), Mathura, Hardwar, Gaya, Ayodhya, Ujjain, Dwarka, Puri, Tirupati, Rameswaram, and Badrinath (in the Himalaya).

In *Buddhism* in South-East and South Asia, Mandalay, Rangoon and Bangkok, but also Anuradhapura and Kandy in Sri Lanka are of nationwide significance. In Tibet Buddhism in the particular form of Lamaism has its most important place of pilgrimage at Lhasa. Sarnath and Buddha Gaya in India attract Buddhist pilgrims from many countries.

Shintoism and Buddhism have numerous places of pilgrimage in Japan, of which the most important are to be found in Tokyo, Ise and Kyoto. The centre and pilgrimage place of a new religion known as Tenrikyo is the town of Tenri.

After Buddhist pilgrimages in communist China had completely disappeared and many places of pilgrimage were largely destroyed during the cultural revolution, the old forms of pilgrimage to the religious centers in Peking and to holy mountains, for example Tai-shan, have been once again revived.

2. Definition and Characteristics of Pilgrimage

Pilgrimage is an important form of religiously motivated spatial behavior. In contrast to the regular visits to services taking place daily, weekly or even at various times during the year mostly in nearby local churches, temples, shrines and other religious places of worship, pilgrimage signifies the visit to a distant religious center once or a few times in the life of a believer. Of course, smaller regional centers may be regularly visited, possibly even once a year (German: Wallfahrt). Thanks largely to the modern means of mass transportation, pilgrims have come closer timewise to the pilgrimage centers, so that the great centers of world religions may no longer be visited only once in one's life, but perhaps several times within a few years.

There are some differences with regard to length of time, frequency and regularity of pilgrimages among the different world religions. The *hajj* to Mecca certainly holds a special position here, since it is one of the five decrees (*arkan*) of Islam which every Muslem is expected to uphold. If he is bodily and mentally capable of doing so, if his economic situation allows it and if the journey is not made impossible by a great political danger, he should make the pilgrimage to Mecca at least once in his life. In other world religions, however, pilgrimage is considered to be a voluntary act of special devoutness.

In addition to the periodic pilgrimages to one or more holy places (tours), there are, for example in India, uninterrupted pilgrimages, which constitute a means towards perfection in life.

The destination of every pilgrimage is a holy object. These can be natural phenomena, such as mountains, rivers, trees and animals; cultural phenomena such as churches, temples, graves, pictures, relics, icons, statues or similar things, as well as human individuals. Thus, in Japan the holy Fujısan mountain is visited, in Varanasi the river Ganges, in ancient Germania holy oaks of the God Donar, and in all high religions places of cultural interest are the focal points of pilgrim- tourism. In antiquity there was also, within the sphere of Christianity, the phenomenon of the pilgrimage to a living individual, a hermit or miracle worker, who even in his lifetime attracted many pilgrims. The same is true in Hinduism today; some holy men attract millions of pilgrims.

Undergoing pain, exertion and effort seem to have always been an essential part of pilgrimages. The difficulties of the journey were a way of securing and increasing the blessing on the pilgrimage.

Even nowadays the considerable *distances* which are covered to get to a shrine constitute an important essence of pilgrimage. The further the destination, the greater the success of the pilgrimage, and on the whole the pilgrimage is considered to be more meritorious.

In the past the pilgrimages were made primarily on foot; the strains of travel were particularly great to far off destinations. The great pilgrimage centers such as Rome, Palestine, and Santiago de Compostela, were reached partly on foot, and in part on horseback by the nobles. Muslem pilgrims had to cross seas and deserts on the way to Mecca, and while doing this were often attacked by pirates and bandits. In Buddhism, Hinduism and Lamaism, the pilgrims had to endure similar strains.

In all world religions strict and ardent pilgrims attempt to increase the normal strains and privations of the sacred journey in order to achieve an even greater spiritual satisfaction. Numerous practices of maceration have developed from this conviction. As was customary in the past, particularly in the Middle Ages, many pilgrims in Italy, Portugal, Spain and France still today cover the last part of the way to the shrine moving along on their knees. Some Hindu pilgrims inflict upon themselves the abstinence from speaking and eating. Many measure the distance to the shrine also with their body length and cover great distances in this arduous manner.

In modern industrial societies (Europe, America, Japan etc.) the pain and effort endured on a pilgrimage have greatly decreased or virtually disappeared. Great distances are speedily covered with modern means of mass transportation which bring the pilgrims to their destination within hours or a few days, where earlier several weeks, months, or even years would have been needed. Thus, one of the fundamental ingredients of the pilgrimage process has undergone profound changes. The implications of this technological component for the very nature of pilgrimage are far reaching but have not been adequately examined. We feel that new research on pilgrimages and the nature of their development is necessary.

An attempt to continue reflection and research on pilgrimage phenomenon resulted in the organization of a session on pilgrimage at the meeting of the Association of American Geographers, at Portland, Oregon in April 1987. Some of the papers given at that meeting and additional recent research on pilgrimage in Asia, Europe, North America and the Caribbean forms the subject matter of the present volume of *Geographia Religionum.*

3. About the Contributions

HIROSHI TANAKA identifies and develops four geographically significant themes for the study of pilgrimage places; *evolution, location and distribution, landscape*, and *circulation*. He thus provides a methodological framework in which he is able to not only examine the nature of major contributions made so far, but also suggests the directions that pilgrimage studies might take in the future. He cautions, however, against methodological pitfalls while using the experiential approaches. Although his insights emerge from his many studies of Buddhist pilgrimages in Japan, they help to provide guidelines for the geographic study of pilgrimage in other cultural traditions as well.

MARY LEE NOLAN posits that pilgrimage to holy places in the Western European context is an ancient and widespread religious strategy for coping with hazard. Nolan identifies eight categories of "hazard cults", based upon 1665 hazard related pilgrimages. The large data base allows her to compare the relative significance of different hazards in generating pilgrimage behavior. She shows that pilgrimage is a positive way of coping with hazards, giving people a sense of control. Her conceptualization, rooted in hazard perception literature, supports other pilgrimage studies related to Hinduism and Roman Catholicism. Her study shows how intimately human wellbeing has been connected with the health of the livestock, thus leading to the development of a well defined "veterinary cult".

GISBERT RINSCHEDE studies the evolution of Fátima, in Portugal, from its beginning as a remote Marian apparition site to an internationally famous Roman Catholic center of pilgrimage. Detailed field data on land-use have been mapped to reveal the growth of this settlement and its various morphological components. This paper shows how several economic functions have followed the religious beginnings of Fátima. The nature of pilgrimage flows shows not only the fluctuations, and overall enormous growth in the number of pilgrims, but also brings out the significance of the Portuguese family in relation to pilgrimages. The impact of the modern means of mass transportation has also been examined. Fátima's pilgrimage study suggests that we should evolve our terminology related to pilgrimage studies, and recognize terms such as pilgrim-tourism.

ROBERT STODDARD examines the characteristics of Buddhist pilgrimages in Sri Lanka with three basic questions in mind. These are, the concept of distance decay, temporal changes in the geographic pattern of pilgrimage, and the issue of greater pilgrim social interaction. He finds evidence for the applicability of distance decay idea to the pilgrimage centers analogous to travel behavior related to other nodal places. He also finds that people now travel longer distances than previously, due to greater information availability about sacred places, and due to the fact that people now consider themselves as part of a larger socio-economic and political system. Thus, the spatial changes in pilgrimage pattern have occured. The answer to the third question appears to be negative — STODDARD does not find that pilgrimage creates greater social interaction among participants than at non-pilgrimage centers. Like TANAKA, STODDARD also argues that more sound *generalizations* about pilgrimage behavior await further studies in a variety of contexts.

ULRICH OBERDIEK has presented the first detailed study of Gaṅgotrī and a group of its sacred specialists. He examines Gaṅgotrī in its mythological, historical, and geographic dimensions as a major sacred site, and removes many confusions about the source of the sacred Gaṅgā river. OBERDIEK then focuses upon detailed interviews with a selected group of *sādhus* who are permanent residents of Gaṅgotrī, and who live a solitary lifestyle. Ethnographic details about the *sādhus* give an insight into the relationships between them and this sacred place. His structural perspective shows that search for *sānti* (inner peace) has brought several of them to this otherwise remote sacred place. Like STODDARD, OBERDIEK argues for more research and concrete data before further generalizations can be formulated.

SURINDER BHARDWAJ and MADHUSUDANA RAO focus upon the development of pilgrimage activity centered on the Sri Venkateswara (S. V.) Temple in the United States, as a part of the broader transference process of Hindu religious behavior. They suggest that temples with Southern Indian roots are more likely to become centers of pilgrimage than those built with Northern Indian communities' initiative. Their argument is based on the centrality of the iconic temples in the Dravidian cultural tradition in India. Whether the S.V. Temple will become a symbol of broader Hindu ethnic identity or remain a symbol of Southern Indian cultural tradition in the United States remains an open question. What is not in doubt is that pilgrimage patterns resembling some of the Indian homeland are taking shape. Strong ties of the Asian Indians in the United States with India have ensured that many religious behavior patterns from India may be transferred more easily than was the case with the indentured Indians of the nineteenth century to the "sugar colonies".

CAROLYN PROROK examines the nature of pilgrimage type behavior among the Hindus of Trinidad, thus contributing to the growing genera of literature on the expatriate communities. Although typical pilgrimages to sacred centers, resembling those of the Indian homeland are not developed in Trinidad, ritual bathing in the sea is a clear transference of fluvial bathing fair tradition so widespread in India. The quasi-pilgrimage behavior expressed in the practice of *jag* shows some characteristics of Victor TURNER's "communitas", which were absent in the Buddhist pilgrimages in Sri Lanka. PROROK's essay thus brings out the special circumstances in which selective and modified aspects of traditional Hinduism got transferred to this "sugar colony". Increasing links with the old homeland may yet change this picture.

4. Looking Ahead

The contributions indicate a continuing, even intensifying, interest in the study of religious travel since the conference "Pilgrimage ... The Human Quest" organized by E. A. MORINIS, held at Pittsburgh (U.S.A.) in 1981. Evidence of this interest is the fact that in April, 1988, two full sessions have been organized on pilgrimages at the Phoenix meeting of the Association of American Geographers. Similarly, from May 5 – 8, 1988, the Interdisciplinary Working Group on Religion/Environment-Research has organized the symposium "Religion and Environment" at the Katholische Universität Eichstätt (FRG) in which one full session will be devoted to Pilgrimage and several research projects on pilgrimages will be discussed.

The recently published Encyclopedia of Religion (ELIADE 1987) contains ten articles on pilgrimage, including two by contributors to this volume of Geographia Religionum. Recently, a journal, exclusively devoted to the study of religious travel (*Peregrinologia*) has been announced by Rana P. B. SINGH of Banares Hindu University, India. Geographers focusing on pilgrimage phenomenon are increasingly realizing that in addition to the study of *places* of pilgrimage, the *process* of religious travel must be more clearly understood within the broader and dynamic context of contemporary developments in religion and changing religious concepts. These changes themselves are happening in the varied political, economic, and circulation contexts of different nations. Thus, the transformation of pilgrimage from an arduous journey on foot to a relatively comfortable experience using modern means of transportation needs to be examined afresh.

Although assertions about the social and cultural role of pilgrimage have been made in the literature, evidence to support them has been limited. Contributors to this volume find contradictory evidence, thus indicating the need for more studies especially focused on these aspects.

It is a point worth noting that the phenomenon of pilgrimage, certainly *religious travel*, has intensified parallel with the great advancements in science and technology and the diffusion of education. Therefore, religious travel cannot be considered merely an activity of the ignorant or superstitious people whether in the Orient or the Occident. This points up the need to explore some deeper structural dimensions of this human quest called pilgrimage. Positivistic methodologies, though useful in the analysis of several aspects of pilgrimage behavior, cannot address the experiential dimensions. Therefore, philosophical positions giving centrality to emotive and idealist aspects may be found useful, if applied with due cautions. Manfred BÜTTNER's ideas, on the history and philosophy of geography of religion can help to open up or develop new research themes, several identified by TANAKA, in this volume. Likewise, the directions suggested by RINSCHEDE and SIEVERS (1987) can yield a much wider variety of pilgrimage-tourism studies than have been hitherto done.

All the contributions in this volume, explicitly or implicitly, express a need to explore the deeper developments in religion and their relationship with religious travel. The contributors bring perspectives and insights on a phenomenon of worldwide import, and bring together ideas with their roots in different intellectual traditions, and cultures. They indicate the progress being made, and suggest new directions that need to be developed. In the modern world context, concepts such as *"pilgrim- tourism"* and *"religious travel"* are needed to complement the classical *pilgrimage*. There is also the clear need to fully explore the similarities and differences between the various religious journeys described by specific terms such as *Hajj, Ziarat, Yatra, Wallfahrt, Juneri* and others.

Bibliography

BHARDWAJ, S. M. (1973): Hindu Places of Pilgrimage in India: A Study in Cultural Geography. University of California Press, Berkeley.

BHARDWAJ, S. M. (1987): Hindu Pilgrimage. In: Eliade, M. (ed.), The Encyclopedia of Religion. Macmillan and Free Press, London, Vol. 11, pp. 353 – 354.

BÜTTNER, M. (1985): Zur Geschichte und Systematik der Religionsgeographie. In: Geographia Religionum, 1, Berlin: Dietrich Reimer, pp. 13 – 121.

ELIADE, M. (Editor in Chief) (1987): The Encyclopedia of Religion (sixteen volumes). Macmillan and Free Press, London.

RINSCHEDE, G. (1986): The Pilgrimage Town of Lourdes. Journal of Cultural Geography, 7:1, pp. 21 – 34.

RINSCHEDE, G. and SIEVERS, A. (1987): The Pilgrimage Phenomenon in Socio-Geographic Research. The National Geographical Journal of India, 33, pp. 213 – 217.

SINGH, R. L. and RANA P. B. SINGH (1987): Trends in the Geography of Belief Systems — Festschrift to Angelika Sievers. The National Geographical Society of India, Research Publication Series: 34, 128 p.

Hiroshi Tanaka

ON THE GEOGRAPHIC STUDY OF PILGRIMAGE PLACES

I. Introduction

Common to many cultural traditions is the concept of man as a pilgrim and life as a pilgrimage, for it accords with the "myth of the celestial origin of man, of his 'fall' and of his hopes of being restored to the celestial realm" (CIRLOT 1971, 255). Whether it is this view of life as a pilgrimage that lends pilgrimage its special significance or not, the institution of pilgrimage, a journey to some sacred place or places undertaken as an act of devotion, seems to exist in all major religions.

The ubiquitous phenomenon of pilgrimage functions in a variety of ways within human life. "From pilgrimage man hopes for property and prosperity, fulfilment of desires, annulment of sin, admission to the divine world and external bliss" (VAN DER LEEUW 1967, II, 401). A pilgrimage reassures its participants that the troubles and uncertainties of daily life will be overcome. Anxieties are dispelled and fears lessened through the psychological comfort attained. It offers avenues for spiritual and physical healing and renewal. Pilgrimage provides validation and reinforcement of values and strengthens the preference for particular modes of behaviour. It also serves to reinforce the human bond within the particular cultural group as it provides the opportunity for expression and communication of shared religious beliefs.

That pilgrimage is complex and diverse in its nature and function is evidenced by the widely varying viewpoints adopted by scholars in their attempt to understand and appreciate its existence. Its many aspects are acknowledged in the consideration of it within religious, sociological, psychological, economic, ethnographical, and historical contexts. An overview of pilgrimage from all these viewpoints is presented in Sources Orientales, Les Pèlerinages (1960).

Efforts to classify pilgrimages from particular disciplinary viewpoints have been made, for example, from religious, anthropological, and geographical perspectives respectively by KITAGAWA (1967), BHARATI (1970), and STODDARD (1981).

Among the many types of religious expression, pilgrimage has the greatest geographical significance (DEFFONTAINES 1948; SOPHER 1967). What contribution can we, as geographers, make to the understanding of this phenomenon? Considering the geographic significance of the institution of pilgrimage, the collective contribution of geographers towards its understanding has been modest. BHARDWAJ (1978, 1981) and SOPHER (1982) provided overviews of geographic studies related to pilgrimage.

Despite the diversity of pilgrimage there are a number of shared elements in this cross-cultural phenomenon including pilgrims, pilgrimage places, and the journey itself. The contribution of geographers, in my mind, rests on the conscious recognition of the geographic expression of pilgrimage and the distinctive geographic perspectives applied to the examination of this place-bound religious phenomenon.

There are two dominant interrelated foci of study: pilgrimage circulation and pilgrimage places. Geographic studies centering on the former have been undertaken. For example, RUTTER (1929) made geographical observations and recorded pilgrimage volume to Mecca in relation to the regions of origin of the pilgrims. SHAIR and KARAN (1979) analyzed the evolution of the pilgrimage pattern to Mecca and the contemporary pilgrim flows from various parts of the world. They also attempted to regionalize the Moslem world on the basis of pilgrim flows and surveys of religious attitudes. Through the analysis of field data, SOPHER (1968) conducted a spatial analysis of Gujarati pilgrim traffic and touched on the broader questions of "how pilgrimages may widen the horizons of country folk and serve to integrate regions such as Gujarat as well as the whole of India."

BHARDWAJ (1973, 225, 9) recognized that "the character of places and spatial organization lie at the core of geography" and so justified his consideration of "the nature of circulation generated by sacred places ... as a problem in geography." Through a "combination of the historical-geographic approach and the synchronic study of religious circulation" he attempted to "understand the nature of interconnections between the Hindu sacred places of different levels and their pilgrimage fields."

With regard to studies focused on pilgrimage places, however, our contribution has not been strong, despite our interest in places related to human life as the subject of geographic inquiry. While a variety of places functioning diversely in human existence manifest certain distinctiveness, perhaps the distinctiveness is nowhere as explicit and as clearly expressed as it is among "religious places." Among religious places, holy places of pilgrimage have been of particular attraction to geographers. The distinct contribution of geographers to the understanding of pilgrimage places may be said to be the explicit recognition of the significance of pilgrimage within the framework of place-bound phenomena.

The purpose of this paper is to offer a framework for the geographic study of pilgrimage places taking into account the contributions of pilgrimage studies conducted to date. This paper, however, is not a comprehensive literature survey. Its focus is the identification of research themes and it reflects my keen interest in the investigation of Buddhist pilgrimage places in Japan.

The first identified research theme focuses on the dynamic nature of pilgrimage places, their emergence, humanization, and evolution. The second theme focuses on the spatial expression of pilgrimage places and includes their location, distribution, and spatial connections resulting from pilgrimage circulation. The third theme focuses on the landscapes of pilgrimage places as an expression of the meaning of pilgrimage and as a source and focus of religious activity. The fourth and final theme focuses on the relationship between the pilgrims' behaviour and the ritual setting comprising the pilgrimage site or sites and the pilgrimage path. For ease of identification these research themes are referred to hereafter as the history of pilgrimage places, the spatial expression of pilgrimage places, the landscape of pilgrimage places, and the "ecology" of pilgrimage places.

II. History of Pilgrimage Places

Pilgrimage places, like other places, emerge, develop, some disappear, some revive again. Pilgrimage sites emerge and develop through the process of the humanization of places. On some occasions this occurs through divine instruction and on others through the belief that the divine spirit is accessible at certain places and the attempt is made to sanctify these sites. In the first instance, human beings place themselves under the power of the supernatural. In the second, the attempt is made to harness supernatural powers. The process of the sanctification of geographic sites is an important cultural geographic theme, yet it is not well understood.

When and where and how and through what process given pilgrimage sites emerged and developed requires attention. In reality, historical fact and legend are intertwined and clarifying the historical process of the establishment of pilgrimage places is often difficult. In some cases, archaeological records suggest that certain contemporary pilgrimages have ancient roots. For example, two major Andean pilgrimages, one to Copacabana on the shores of Lake Titicaca and the other to Motupe in the coastal desert of northern Peru, are two such pilgrimages. Both regions are associated with major traditions of pre-Hispanic pilgrimages for which archaeological evidence abounds (VREELAND 1981).

To identify the roots of pilgrimage places often requires investigation into the prehistoric cosmology and the reconstruction of the sacred environment together with the way it was perceived in ancient times. If the data uncovered is insufficient for the interpretation and explanation of the origin of the pilgrimage place we must remain largely in the realm of speculation. One possible avenue is to study pilgrimage sites which have been "transferred" from and/or copied after original sacred places. Santiago de Compostela, El Pilar, and Montserrat in Spain, Walsingham in England and Loreto in Italy, for example, are the outcome of the transfer of sanctity from Jerusalem. The sanctity of Lourdes in southern France has been transferred as far as western Japan. Imochigaura Lourdes on Goto Island has been attracting Catholic pilgrims since the turn of the century.

In Japan, there are also numerous Buddhist pilgrimage centres, the sanctity of which was transferred from other original Japanese pilgrimage sites. NAKANO (1978) has identified over one hundred pilgrimage systems throughout Japan the majority of which are patterned after the Shikoku eighty-eight place or Saikoku thirty-three place pilgrimages. Pilgrimage to the original Shikoku and Saikoku sacred places demanded time, money, physical strength, family cooperation, and the continuation of livelihood activities for the duration of the journey. Stringent political controls on inter-regional domestic travel during the medieval period combined with the aforementioned personal constraints to contribute to the emergence of miniature pilgrimages throughout the country.

Among new world pilgrimage sites there were usually some nuclei which made these sites strong candidates for selection. For example, Guadalupe, Chalma, and Ocotlan in Mexico are newly emerged sites. These places were originally supported by symbols of native belief. Catholic symbols later replaced or were added to these symbols rendering these sites contemporary Christian pilgrimage centres. In fact, as NOLAN (1973) and KURODA (1981) point out, the majority of pilgrimage places in Latin America are the outcome of syncretism between the pre-Columbian native religion and Catholicism, with a few exceptions such as Joaseiro in Brazil (DELLA CAVA 1970) and Wirikuta visited by the Huichol Indians of Mexico on the sacred Peyote Hunt (MYERHOFF 1974).

PRUESS (1981) described and analyzed a unique Thai Buddhist pilgrimage the objective of which was to capture the sanctity or sacred power of a remote shrine and transfer it to a second site over three hundred kilometres away. Elsewhere I have described the process of the transfer of sanctity from original Japanese Buddhist sites to new sites (TANAKA 1983). The process of the introduction, adoption, adaption, and integration of symbols and the emergence and maintenance of particular landscape markers, and the popularization of these sites awaits the further attention of geographers.

The dynamic nature of pilgrimage places is expressed in changes in location, pilgrimage volume, pilgrimage circulation routes, catchment area, pilgrimage landscapes, and place names. Behind such evolution are various factors deriving from changes in religious doctrine, national policy, ruler's intention, transportation systems, national and/or cultural boundaries, social values, recreation, and geomorphological settings. A broad perspective which takes into consideration the spatial-temporal context and cultural differences is a prerequisite for understanding the dynamic nature of pilgrimage places.

III. The Spatial Expression of Pilgrimage Places

The number of pilgrimage places world-wide will vary according to the definition of pilgrimage place. Efforts have been made to identify pilgrimage places. For example, in Western Europe, Latin America, and Anglo America respectively, NOLAN (1987) has identified 6,150, 973 and 330 Christian pilgrimage centres. In Japan, numerous Buddhist pilgrimage sites were identified by NAKANO (1978) and SAITO (1980). Hindu pilgrimage sites are countless. It is said that there are thirty-five million sites existing in three worlds: on earth, in the underground world, and in sky and space (JHA 1981). BHARATI (1963) identified major Indian terrestrial pilgrimage sites. Some pilgrimage centres are found beyond their respective, traditional religious areas; Hindu pilgrimage centres in Trinidad and in Pittsburgh are two examples (PROROK 1987 and BHARDWAJ 1978).

Regardless of religious tradition, pilgrimage places are not uniformly distributed. Recognizing this, efforts have been made to answer the questions, "what characteristics exist in the pattern of distribution?" and "why are pilgrimage centres where they are?" Attempts have been made to identify the factors in the natural and social environment influential to the location of these sites. STODDARD (1966) found generalizations about the locations of sacred places to be virtually non-existent in geographic literature and conducted a statistical examination of the distribution of Hindu holy sites in India. The sites were found to be not optimally distributed in relation to Hindu population where optimality is defined in terms of minimizing aggregate travel distance.

Central to the acknowledged sanctity or holiness of a place within a particular cultural context is its recognized association with deities and/or saintly beings. Such association is an essential aspect of the character of pilgrimage places. As NOLAN (1983, 422) points out, early Christian shrines often developed at the tombs of martyrs in Roman cemeteries. The physical remains of the saint, more than any particular topographic feature, were the focus of pilgrim devotions for it was here, where the remains were located, that pilgrims believed they could come in contact with the saint. Even a small fragment of the relics was sufficient to permit conceptualization of the holy person as fully present. Over the centuries, for a variety of reasons, relic fragments came to be widely distributed among sacred places throughout Christendom. In Japan, the particular significance of each of the Shikoku eighty-eight Buddhist pilgrimage places rests on its two-fold association with Kobo Daishi ("Saint Kobo") and a particular deity. The Saikoku pilgrimage to thirty-three stations is associated with Kannon (Avolokiteśvara). The association of the sacred place with deities is attested in the landscape.

In addition to a site's association with deities, sanctity is often derived from the human response towards geographical characteristics such as distinctive landscapes and land forms. Due to variations in perception of the sacred among different cultural groups, generalization about the principles of sacred location is not feasible. Regionally, however, different categories of natural objects have been assigned sanctity by different cultural groups (SOPHER 1967). The association of pilgrimage sites with sacred mountains in Japan (HORI 1966 and KUBOTA 1985) and with sacred rivers — their source, mouth, confluences, etc. — in India (SOPHER 1967, 49) has been noted. In Malaysia there is a marked association of pilgrimage centres with limestone caves as evidenced, for example, by the Buddhist pilgrimage centre of Perek and the Hindu centre, the Batu Cave.

Such geomorphological settings provide conditions appropriate for the accommodation of sacred places yet geomorphological setting alone cannot explain pilgrimage site location as many geographic locations which seem to satisfy the conditions required for pilgrimage sites are devoid of sacred places. If many exceptions exist, these can no longer be considered as exceptions making comprehensive explanations difficult. One approach is to test whether pilgrimage places exist or not by focusing on those sites which satisfy all conditions identified in the explanations. For that purpose further accumulation of data is necessary to support the assumptions of the hypothesis.

In addition to pilgrimages to single sites, there are pilgrimages to multiple places. In the latter case, a group or groups of pilgrimage sites make up a pilgrimage system to multiple sacred places. As JHA (1981) notes: "In India at the four cardinal points stand the four *Dhams* viz. Badridham (north in the deep Himalayas), Puri (in east), Rameshwaram (in south) and Dwarika (in west) and in or around them the four sacred seats of the Adi-Shankar (788-820 A.D.) which every pious Hindu aspires to visit at least once in his lifetime."

The spatial hierarchy of a pilgrimage to multiple sites may reflect the symbolic meaning of the pilgrimage itself. The earthly pilgrimage may be the metaphysical conception of the spatial journey transposed onto geographic space. On the other hand, the conception of the spiritual journey may be rooted in the practice of terrestrial pilgrimage (MORINIS 1984). In Japan, the Shikoku pilgrimage to eighty-eight places consists of various sub-pilgrimages and the practice of visiting all eighty-eight sacred places at one time signifies that the pilgrim will travel over the mandala world, will be freed from the eighty-eight illusions of the mind that distort the truth and will be able to attain enlightenment, will pay homage to the Buddha whose greatness is divided among the eighty-eight temples, and will receive the charity of the Buddha (TANAKA 1983).

Further, within the pilgrimage each of Shikoku's four prefectures symbolically constitutes a Buddhist *dōjō* or holy place of learning and practising the way. Each *dōjō* serves a specific purpose reflected in its name. *Hosshin no Dōjō* (Tokushima prefecture) is interpreted as *dōjō* in which it is determined that supreme enlightenment will be attained, *Shugyō no Dōjō* (Kochi prefecture) as *dōjō* for the purpose of practising that which has been determined, *Bodai no Dōjō* (Ehime prefecture) as *dōjō* for the attainment of wisdom and understanding of life, and *Nehan no Dōjō* (Kagawa prefecture) as *dōjō* for the satisfactory completion of everything (TANAKA 1981).

In proposing the liminality of the pilgrimage experience, TURNER (1973, 1974, 1978) suggested the locational peripherality of sacred places. SOPHER (1981) noted the significance of this statement and questioned the universality of its application. "To Victor Turner's proposition that pilgrimage provides a liminal experience, fostering a temporary dissolution of society's structure and engendering communitas, there is attached a corollary that is of particular interest to geographers. In arguing that the social liminality of the experience involves and indeed seems to require a spatially peripheral location for the pilgrim's destination, Turner appears to have provided geographers with the kind of structural key to the interpretation of spatial pattern for which some, such as Yi-fu Tuan, have long been searching. But does the key really fit?" (SOPHER 1981).

There are many exceptions. Peripherality is seldom an absolute — it depends upon the geographic scale implied. The Shikoku pilgrimage places, for example, have a peripheral location when the country is viewed on the macro-scale. All eighty-eight places are located on the island of Shikoku, away from mainland Honshu where political and cultural functions are concentrated. When the scale is changed from macro to meso and the focus shifts to Shikoku, the distribution of temples over the island roughly corresponds to the distribution of population. At least half of the sacred places are located near the four prefectural capitals. Further examination on the micro-scale, that is, on the prefectural level, reveals that the pilgrimage sites tend to be located on the outskirts of urban centres rather than at the heart. Focusing on Hindu pilgrimage centres in India, SOPHER (1981) questioned the validity of TURNER's proposition. This issue is far from resolved.

The absolute location of many pilgrimage sites is stable. Such continuity contributes to the reality and persistence of such places. On the other hand, noteworthy with regard to location is the existence of pilgrimage sites the locations of which have been changed, sometimes more than once, for a variety of reasons. At least fifteen out of eighty-eight pilgrimage places on Shikoku have been moved. In Europe, an example of multiple locational change is the shrine of the Holy House of the Blessed Virgin at Loreto. "According to the tradition, the building was the house of the Blessed Virgin in Nazareth, made into a church by the Apostles, for which St. Luke made a statue of Mary. After the fall of the Latin Kingdom of Jerusalem (1291), angels transported the church to Tersatto near Fiume (Rieka, Yugoslavia) on May 10, 1291. Not properly venerated there, it was moved by angels on December 10, 1294, to a woods near Recanati. Again not fittingly venerated, it was miraculously transported to another hill on August 10, 1295. For the same reasons, it was moved a fourth time by angels to its present location on December 2, 1295" (GILLETT 1967, 993).

Perhaps the most mobile focuses of pilgrimage are living holy men. Pilgrimages to Hindu holy men such as Sai Baha, Muni Vidyananda, Mahesh Yogi, and Acharya Rajneesh are recognized by BHARDWAJ (1981) as a distinct category of pilgrimage which emphasizes the spatial locational dynamism of pilgrimage activity. The above examples illustrate that the locational properties of sacred places are not necessarily sufficient conditions to designate particular sites as sacred pilgrimage centres. The question of location and sanctity requires further exploration.

The locations of pilgrimage sites exhibit other dimensions when viewed from the behavioural perspective including the pilgrims' geographic origin and the route and direction of their pilgrimage. The eighty-eight places of the Shikoku pilgrimage are located along the circular route on the circumference of the island and, starting from Ryozen-ji, temple one, at the island's east corner, are numbered sequentially in a clockwise direction. Traditionally pilgrims would begin the sacred journey at temple one and proceed in order to temple eighty-eight. When the pilgrimage is made in this fashion, the second temple visited is located 1.5 kilometres away from temple one, the third temple visited is located 4.5 kilometres away (or 3.0 kilometres from the second temple) and so on and the eighty-eighth temple is located 1,318.3 kilometres from temple one, following the pilgrim route. Many pilgrims, however, visit temple one again at the conclusion of their journey before they leave the island, thus Ryozen-ji becomes both the starting point and the destination point of the pilgrimage. In the latter capacity it becomes the temple located farthest from the beginning of the pilgrimage.

In recent years it has become common for pilgrims to begin their journey at temples other than Ryozen-ji and to visit the sacred places out of sequence. When the location of the sacred places is considered from this behavioural perspective their relative location presents a different picture. The first step in the pilgrimage occurs when the pilgrim leaves his residence. For the majority of pilgrims the first temple is therefore located a considerable distance along the pilgrim route.

Another factor to be considered in a discussion of the locational characteristics of sacred places is inaccessibility and the effort required to reach the sites. Hardship is an inherent characteristic of merit attained through pilgrimage. The use of transportation in contemporary pilgrimage, however, has lessened the hardship and, for modern pilgrims, time distance and cost distance have become the immediate concern. Thus the locational properties of pilgrimage places exhibit a variety of dimensions and await serious inquiry by geographers.

IV. Landscapes of Pilgrimage Places

Sacred places are those locations where the sacred manifests itself, shows itself, and thus makes man aware of its presence. The geographic setting of the sacred place is not characterized solely as it exists unaltered by man. Rather it is characterized primarily by the assemblage of sacred symbols and/or landscape markers, both man-made and natural, which have been invested with special meaning. To the religious man sacred places are a kind of "monadnock" in the homogeneous, profane, flat plain. At countless sacred places sacredness or holiness is centred on a temple, shrine, synagogue, church, stupa or some other structure "but the sacred aura [is] diffused over the neighbouring space, everything in it — the trees and the animals — [are] elevated by the association" (TUAN 1974, 147).

The places encompassed by pilgrimages are focal points for particular symbolization and communication through geographic forms, that is, "concrete visible features of landscape, as well as the more elusive spatial structures" (WAGNER 1972, 2). Landscapes of pilgrimage places provide concrete data through which inherent characteristics of the sacred places can be identified. PRUESS (1976) showed, in the Thai Buddhist context, that the spatial features of a pilgrimage centre and the social use of this religious environment reflects the goals and values of the religious tradition that inspired its creation. MORINIS (1984, 285) also pointed out that "sacred places (in West Bengal, as commonly throughout India,) are usually honoured by the construction of temples and shrines to contain (and separate off) the most sanctified of locations. It is well known that the architecture of Hindu temples embodies metaphysical concepts in its design."

The landscape is not only an expression of the meaning of the pilgrimage, it is also a source and focus of religious experience. There are a number of unanswered questions. What is the role of landscape markers in the religious experience of pilgrims at sacred sites and along the pilgrimage path? To what extent does the sacred architecture embody metaphysical concepts? What landscape characteristics reflect pilgrimage centres as sacred places providing a bridge across which the pilgrim may move from the mundane world to the sacred realm? To what extent are regional, historical, and religious differences reflected in the morphological character of the pilgrimage places?

The type, size, form, and frequency of occurence of landscape markers and their orientation together with the associated soundscape and chromaticscape can be more extensively used to identifiy the character of pilgrimage places and their variations. Attention must be given to the various symbols along the pilgrim path including temples, roadside shrines, and sacred wells, trees, rocks, and mountain peaks. Investigation of the symbolic complex of a given pilgrimage system may help to reveal the hidden, essential meaning of the pilgrimage.

Examination of the landscape at pilgrimage sites and along the path also reveals the nature of the impact of pilgrimage on given regions and the character of pilgrimage itself. Settlements, markets, festivals, art forms, plants and animals, architectural and other technologies, and the spread of disease are some dimensions that have been directly or indirectly influenced by pilgrimage. The impact of pilgrimage on Lourdes, for example, in such areas as demographic developments, economic structure, and the distribution of places of worship, hotels, restaurants, and shops selling devotional articles has been studied (RINSCHEDE 1987).

Pilgrimage has played a historical role in the development and maintenance of communities. For example, it would "seem to have contributed to the maintenance of some kind of international community in Christendom, for French, Spanish, German, and Dutch speakers visited the shrine of Thomas-à-Becket at Canterbury" (TURNER 1973, 202). SOPHER (1967, 53) recognized the contribution of pilgrimage to community-building in Christianity and Buddhism but saw it as secondary to that of other organized networks, monastic and ecclesiastical. For Moslems, the impact of pilgrimage on community-building was probably greater. As LEWIS (1966, 37) points out, "the pilgrimage was not the only factor making for cultural unity and social mobility in the Islamic world — but it was certainly an important one, perhaps the most important."

Religious ideas influence social and economic behaviour and thereby affect the landscape in a variety of ways. Pilgrimage is one vehicle which has contributed to the development of collective religious awareness and beliefs. In the Sri Lankan context, HOLT (1981) proposed that "pilgrimage sites are at once the locals in which deep-seated cultural beliefs and practices are maintained by conservative, traditional forces in society. But, they are also the areas which reflect fundamental changes that may not be so apparent in normative societal contexts."

Needless to say, the complex cultural history reflected in the emergence, development, maintenance, and destruction of pilgrimage places is also registered in the landscape. Pilgrims' behaviour observed at the pilgrimage sites and along the way also reveals the inherent nature of pilgrimage and pilgrimage places.

V. The "Ecology" of Pilgrimage Places

To paint a comprehensive picture of pilgrimage places it is necessary to examine not only the stage on which the pilgrimage is carried out, that is, the physical setting, but also to focus on the behavioural dimension of the pilgrimage. One of the significant aspects of places of pilgrimage is that they are the focal points of various ritual activities performed by countless numbers of pilgrims. A pilgrimage place is activated and actualized by pilgrims. Its location may be peripheral in the context of every day life but, activated by pilgrims, it becomes the central place of the religious world. I have tried elsewhere to describe the inherent structural relationship between the physical setting and the pilgrimage ritual in order to conceptualize pilgrimage places as ritual centres (TANAKA 1977).

Wide variations exist in pilgrims' behavioural patterns at sacred places worldwide but generally given pilgrim behaviour is repeatedly linked to specific physical features. The relationships between the particular physical features and specific pilgrim behaviour are supported by both the occurence of the physical features and pilgrims' recognition of and response to the meaning embodied in the features. In some cases the pilgrims' behaviour is rigidly structured while in others it seems more relaxed.

Generally, if the pilgrimage is obligatory prescribed behaviour is demanded. The rituals of Islamic *hajj,* mandatory performance if the pilgrim can afford the rite without bringing hardship upon his dependents, are perhaps among the most highly structured. The *tawaf* (circling the *Ka'bah* seven times) and *sa'y* (running seven times between two sanctuaries) rituals performed in the vicinity of the *Ka'bah* and the subsequent rituals performed at Minā, Arafah, and Muzdalifah are conducted in a prescribed manner. In Japan, wide variations exist in pilgrim behaviour. Pilgrimage rituals carried out by Buddhist priests in training comply with a strict behavioural code while those performed by lay pilgrims are generally less precise. One of the most rigid Japanese Buddhist pilgrimages is Kaihōgyō. This thousand-day pilgrimage of Mt. Hiei has a twelve hundred-year tradition with a complicated set of rites, symbols, and practices originating in ancient esoteric Buddhism and folk religion. Divided into ten one hundred-day terms over seven years, this pilgrimage is extremely severe: nightly forty kilometre pilgrimages around the mountain the first years, sixty kilometre pilgrimages each night in the last two years, and a nine-day period with no food, no water, no sleep, and no lying down. In the Showa period (1926 –) only nine priests have successfully completed this pilgrimage.

Several questions remain unanswered. What is the nature of the symbiotic relationships between the physical setting, pilgrims' behaviour, and their religious experience? What is the institutionally defined minimum ritual activity associated with particular times and places that qualifies behaviour as proper pilgrim activity? What are the characteristics of the ritual process along the pilgrimage path?

Examination of pilgrim behaviour should not be focused only on the pilgrimage centres; it should include behaviour along the pilgrim path as well. Pilgrimage to a single site often involves multiple places of religious significance along the way. The pilgrim path is dotted with countless numbers of roadside shrines and monasteries. These places, physically and symbolically, may mark the pilgrims' passage from the profane to the sacred world. For example, as MILLER (1981) noted, the monastery at Sivananda Hill at Rishikesh prepares pilgrims physically, psychologically, and spiritually for the remainder of their treacherous pilgrimage northward to the Himalayan Hindu sacred places of Badrinath and/or Kedarnath.

As pilgrimage places are characterized by pilgrim visitation, analysis of pilgrims themselves will illumine the nature of pilgrimage places. Variations in pilgrimage volume in relation to a particular pilgrimage site over time indicates the rise and decline of pilgrimage centres and may also reflect such things as political stability and improved accessibility. Variations in pilgrimage volume among the sacred places belonging to a given religious realm within a given time period indicate the relative popularity of the sites.

The collection of accurate data concerning pilgrimage volume is not only of academic interest, it is indispensable to pilgrimage management if the social problems of the recipient region are to be minimized. Without an accurate pilgrimage count preparation of adequate transportation, accommodation, food, and hygiene is hampered. Accurate prediction of pilgrimage volume to Mecca, for example, is an important statistical work of the Saudi Arabian government.

There are several problems associated with accurate determination of pilgrimage volume. Not all of those who participate in a given pilgrimage may accurately be labelled pilgrims. For example, Mansa Musa, king of Mali in West Africa is reported to have made a pilgrimage to Mecca in 1324, with a retinue of 6,000 followers, servants, and slaves (TRIMINGHAM 1962, 65). Should we consider these latter pilgrims? If we ignore the fact that they were servants and slaves, we will be neglecting the qualitative dimension of pilgrimage volume.

In recent times the distinction between pilgrims and tourists has become blurred to the point where the term "tourist-pilgrim" might aptly be applied to many visitors to sacred centres. SOPHER (1967, 54) pointed out that "pilgrim travel to religious shrines has often had the character of tourist travel and recreation. In the Orient as in the West, there is now also a largely secular tourist traffic to places of religious significance that have some historical, architectural, or scenic interest as well." Often pilgrimage centres are centres of monumental buildings and historical areas of interest. Santiago de Compostela is just one example. Here pilgrim-tourists have an opportunity to admire art in all its manifestations: the Romanesque, the Gothic, the Renaissance, the Baroque, and the Neoclassical.

In order to reveal both the points of convergence and the directions of divergence between tourism and pilgrimage, COHEN (1981) attempted to analyze tourism and pilgrimage as social phenomena at three different levels: deep-structured (unconscious in the minds of pilgrims and tourists); phenomenal (motivations and behaviour of pilgrims and tourists); institutional (social institutions that support and regulate these two activities). Geographers who utilize pilgrimage volume for their presentation and arguments must take into account the qualitative nature of the actors in the phenomenon of pilgrimage.

Pilgrimage volume differs according to the year and the season. The annual or Magh Mela pilgrimage at Prayag (Allahabad) has attracted roughly one million Hindus in recent years while the 1977 Kumbha Mela pilgrimage at Prayag (held once every twelve years) attracted five million devotees (CAPLAN 1981). Patterns of seasonality, varying regionally and with the subject of pilgrim devotion, characterize European pilgrimage (NOLAN 1979). Badrinath, considered to be one of the most sacred Himalayan Hindu pilgrimage sites, is snowbound and thus inaccessible for half the year. At many pilgrimage sites the divine power is believed to be more accessible at certain times than at others, times frequently marked by festivals and feast days. The accessibility of power in the Hindu context has been discussed, for example STANLEY (1977). The concentration of pilgrims is greatest on these special days.

Understanding the qualitative dimension of participants reveals the hidden meaning behind the externally observable pilgrimage travel. A frequent phenomenon in India is the existence of regional substitutes for far-off important and meritorious places of pilgrimage, saving pilgrims the hardship of physically visiting the original sites. The landscape of the "substitute" places reflects their function. "Thus, the Ekāmbareśvara Temple at Conjeeveram (Madras) has a little low corridor which is closed by a small metal gate; the corridor is said to be a subterranean connection to Kāsī (Banaras), 1,500 miles away. The gate is not opened at any time nowadays, but the priest told me that if a person insisted on creeping into the passage, circumserpenting the sanctum, he would aquire the same merit as from a pilgrimage to Banares ... Other vicarious shrines also offer to the pilgrim the merit of Banares, that city being a pilgrimage centre par excellence. 'The place is a veritable Kāsī' — is an idiom found on many blurbs of less illustrious shrines and centres" (BHARATI 1963, 165). Careful consideration must be given to when and how data on pilgrimage volume are collected and how they are to be used.

Compared with pilgrimages to a single place, the circulation patterns of pilgrimages to multiple sites is much more complex making an accurate head count and interpretation of this count difficult. A typical example is the Shikoku pilgrimage. Some pilgrims visit all eighty-eight places in one pilgrimage, some visit all the sacred places in one of Shikoku's four prefectures, some visit a smaller group of temples while some visit just one particular temple. This may be one of the reasons why estimates of annual pilgrimage volume range from fifty to sixty thousand to more than ten times that number.

The "quality" of pilgrims differs from place to place, from one time to another, and in some cases is related to the hierarchical level to which the pilgrimage places belong. For example, BHARDWAJ (1981, 10) identified "that there were several levels at which pilgrimage activity differently manifested. Not only was the spatial dimension of the pilgrim fields different, but the sociological make-up as well as the motivational characteristics of the pilgrims participating at each level differed." Thus it is important to recognize differences in pilgrims themselves including their motivation, sex, age, health, religious affiliation, occupation, education, economic status, and place of origin in order to understand the characteristics of given pilgrimage sites but problems exist with observation and data processing.

One approach to the understanding of pilgrimage places and pilgrimage is to examine the pilgrims' experience. Pilgrims, however, are seldom interested in recording for others detailed accounts of their spiritual journeys. In many cases, they lack the conceptual and linguistic skills required for such analytical description thus what is available are first person descriptions and interpretations of these accounts written by scholars and literati (AZIZ 1984; BURTON 1893; HAMSA 1934; KARVE 1962; and MALCOLM X 1968). TURNER (1974, 1978) attempted to analyze pilgrimage processes on a more universal level. A phenomenological approach may be feasible, but methodological dangers remain concerning how to identify various individual experiences and interpret them within the societal context. When the mutual relationship between the pilgrims' behaviour and the pilgrimage places becomes clear in a specified context on the cognitive level it becomes possible to delve into the internal meaning of pilgrimage places.

VI. Conclusion

Over the ages numerous places have come to be recognized as sacred. Among them, particular sacred places, pilgrimage centres, have attracted the faithful in vast numbers. Despite the universal significance of the phenomenon of pilgrimage, our understanding of pilgrimage places remains limited. Studies that focus on the pilgrimage places themselves are a proper facet of geographic inquiry. In order to establish future research guidelines, I have introduced four geographical research themes which I consider to be important to the understanding of the character of pilgrimage places. I have not touched on related research themes focusing on pilgrimage circulation. As geographers, should the ultimate goal of our contribution to the better understanding of pilgrimage be people focused, activity focused, or place focused? Obviously these are interrelated but we need to consciously target our endeavours so that the contribution of geographers can be widely recognized and utilized.

Summary

Towards the better understanding of the character of pilgrimage places, four geographical research themes are identified and discussed: the emergence, humanization, and evolution of pilgrimage places; the spatial expression of pilgrimage places including their location, distribution, and spatial connections resulting from pilgrimage circulation; the landscapes of pilgrimage places; and the relationship between the pilgrims' behaviour and the ritual setting comprising the pilgrimage site and pilgrimage path.

Zusammenfassung:

Zur Geographischen Erforschung von Pilgerorten

Für ein besseres Verständnis des Charakters von Pilgerorten werden vier geographische Forschungsthemen herausgestellt und besprochen: die Entstehung, der menschliche Einfluß, die Entwicklung der Pilgerorte; die räumliche Dimension der Pilgerorte einschließlich ihrer Lage, Verteilung und der sich aus den Pilgerströmen ergebenden räumlichen Verbindungen; das Landschaftsbild der Pilgerorte, die Beziehung zwischen dem Pilgerverhalten und der rituellen Ausstattung der Pilgerorte und Pilgerwege.

Bibliography

AZIZ, B. N. (1984): "Pilgrim's Perspective: On the Personal Dimensions of the Sacred Journey." Unpublished paper.

BHARATI, A. (1963): "Pilgrimage in the Indian Tradition." History of Religions III, 135 – 67.

BHARATI, A. (1970): "Pilgrimage Sites and Indian Civilization." In: J. W. Elder ed.: Chapters in Indian Civilization, Kendall and Hunt, Dubuque.

BHARDWAJ, S. M. (1973): Hindu Places of Pilgrimage in India: A Study in Cultural Geography. University of California Press, Berkeley.

BHARDWAJ, S. M. (1978): "Geography and Pilgrimages." Paper presented at the International Congress of Anthropological and Ethnological Sciences, New Delhi.

BHARDWAJ, S. M. (1981): "Peregrinology and Geography: An Overview." Paper presented at the conference, Pilgrimage: The Human Quest, University of Pittsburgh.

BURTON, R. F. (1893): Personal Narrative of a Pilgrimage to Al-Madinah and Meccah. 2 vols, republished in 1964, Dover, New York.

CAPLAN, A. (1981): "Prayag's Magh Mela Pilgrimage: Sacred Geography and Pilgrimage Priests." Paper presented at the conference, Pilgrimage: The Human Quest, University of Pittsburgh.

CIRLOT, J. E. (1971): A Dictionary of Symbols. Routledge & Kegan Paul, London, 2nd ed.

COHEN, E. (1981): "Pilgrimage and Tourism: Convergence and Divergence," paper presented at the conference Pilgrimage: The Human Quest, University of Pittsburgh.

DEFFONTAINES, P. (1948): Géographie et Religions. Gallimard, Paris.

DELLA CAVA, R. (1970): Miracle at Joaseiro. Columbia University Press, New York.

GILLETT, H. M. (1967): "Loreto." New Catholic Encyclopedia, VIII, McGrawhill, New York.

HAMSA, B. S. (1934): The Holy Mountain. Farber and Farber. London.

HOLT, J. (1981): "Pilgrimage to Kandy: A Relic and its Power." Paper presented at the conference, Pilgrimage: The Human Quest, University of Pittsburgh.

HORI, I. (1966): "Mountains and their Importance for the Idea of the Other World in Japanese Folk Religion." History of Religions, 6, 1 – 23.

JHA, M. (1981): "Structure and Function of Hindu Pilgrimage." Paper presented at the conference, Pilgrimage: The Human Quest, University of Pittsburgh.

KARVE, I. (1962): "On the Road: A Maharashtrian Pilgrimage." Journal of Asian Studies, 22, 13 – 29.

KITAGAWA, J. M. (1967): "Three Types of Pilgrimage in Japan," Urbach, E. E. et al. eds.: Studies in Mysticism and Religion. The Magnes Press, Jerusalem, 155 – 64.

KUBOTA, N. (1985): Sangaku Reijō Junrei. Shinchōsha, Tokyo.

KURODA, E. (1981): "Social and Symbolic Meaning of Pilgrimages — A Review of Latin American Cases with Emphasis on Oaxaca, Mexico." The Japanese Journal of Ethnology, 46, 105 – 14.

LEWIS, B. (1966): "Hadjdj," The Encyclopedia of Islam II, Luzac & Co. London.

MALCOLM X (1968): Autobiography of Malcolm X. Grove, New York.

MILLER, D. (1981): "Hindu Monasteries as a Point Along the Pilgrim's Path: The Sivananda Ashram at Rishikesh." Paper presented at the conference, Pilgrimage: The Human Quest, University of Pittsburgh.

MORINIS, E. A. (1984): Pilgrimage in the Hindu Tradition: A Case Study of West Bengal. Oxford University Press, Delhi.

MYERHOFF, B. (1974): Peyote Hunt: The Sacred Journey of the Huichol Indians. Cornell University Press, Ithaca.

NAKANO, G. ed. (1978): Koji Junrei Jiten. Tokyodō, Tokyo.

NOLAN, M. L. (1973): "The Mexican Pilgrimage Tradition." Pioneer America, I, 13 – 27.

NOLAN, M. L. (1979): "A Time to Make Pilgrimage: Seasonality of Religious Travel in Europe." Paper presented at the Annual Meeting of the Association of American Geographers, Philadelphia.

NOLAN, M. L. (1983): "Irish Pilgrimage: The Different Tradition," Annals of the Association of American Geographers, 73, 421 – 38.

NOLAN, M. L. (1987): "Christian Pilgrimage in the Old and New Worlds: A Comparative Perspective." Paper presented at the Annual Meeting of the Association of American Geographers, Portland.

PROROK, C. V. (1987): "Hindu Pilgrimage in the Caribbean." Paper presented at the Annual Meeting of the Association of American Geographers, Portland.

PRUESS, J. B. (1976): "The Sacred Dimension: The Social Use of Space at a Buddhist Shrine." Paper presented at the Northwest Anthropological Conference, Central Washington State College.

PRUESS, J. B. (1981): "Sanctification Overland: The Creation of a Thai Buddhist Pilgrimage Center." Paper presented at the conference, Pilgrimage, The Human Quest, University of Pittsburgh.

RINSCHEDE, G. (1986): "The Pilgrimage Town of Lourdes." Journal of Cultural Geography, 7:1, 21 – 34.

RUTTER, E. (1929): "The Muslim Pilgrimage." The Geographical Journal, 74, 271 – 73.

SAITO, A. Ed. (1980): Bukkyō Junrei-shū. Bukkyo Minzoku Gakkai, Tokyo.

SHAIR, I. M. and KARAN, P. P. (1979): "Geography of the Islamic Pilgrimage." Geojournal, 3, 599 — 608.

SOPHER, D. E. (1967): Geography of Religions. Prentice-Hall, Englewood Cliffs, N. J.

SOPHER, D. E. (1968): "Pilgrim Circulation in Gujarat." Geographical Review, 58, 392 – 425.

SOPHER, D. E. (1981): "The Goal of Indian Pilgrimage: Geographical Considerations." Paper presented at the conference, Pilgrimage: The Human Quest, University of Pittsburgh.

SOPHER, D. E. (1982): "Geography and Religions." Progress in Human Geography, 5, 510 – 24.

SOURCES ORIENTALES (1960): Les Pèlerinages: Edition de Seuil, Paris.

STANLEY, J. M. (1977): "Special Time, Special Power: The Fluidity of Power in a Popular Hindu Festival." Journal of Asian Studies, 37, 27 – 44.

STEVENS, J. (1981): "Kaihōgyō: The Mountain Pilgrimage of Mt. Hiei." Paper presented at the conference, Pilgrimage: The Human Quest, University of Pittsburgh.

STODDARD, R. H. (1966): Hindu Holy Sites in India. Ph.D. thesis, Department of Geography, State University of Iowa.

STODDARD, R. H. (1981): "Pilgrimages Classified by Geographic Characteristics." Paper presented at the conference, Pilgrimage: The Human Quest, University of Pittsburgh.

TANAKA, H. (1977): "Geographic Expression of Buddhist Pilgrim Places on Shikoku Island, Japan." Canadian Geographer, 21, 111 – 32.

TANAKA, H. (1981): "Evolution of a Pilgrimage as a Spatial-Symbolic System," Canadian Geographer, 25, 240 – 51.

TANAKA, H. (1983): Junreichi no Sekai [The World of Pilgrimage Places]. Kokon Shoin, Tokyo.

TRIMINGHAM, J. S. (1962): A History of Islam in West Africa. Oxford University Press, Oxford.

TUAN, Y-F. (1974): Topophilia: A Study of Environmental Perception, Attitudes and Values: Prentice-Hall, Englewood Cliffs, N.J.

TURNER, V. W. (1973): "The Center Out There: Pilgrims' Goal." History of Religions, 12, 191 – 230.

TURNER, V. W. (1974): "Pilgrimage and Communitas". Studia Missionalia, 23, 305 – 27.

TURNER, V. W. (1974): Drama, Field and Metaphor. Cornell University Press, Ithaca.

TURNER, V. W. and TURNER, E. (1978): Image and Pilgrimage in Christian Culture. Columbia University Press, New York.

VAN DER LEEUW, G. (1967): Religion in Essence and Manifestation. Peter Smith, Gloucester, Mass., Vol. II, trans, by J. E. Turner.

VREELAND, J. M. Jr. (1981): "Pilgrims' Progress: The Emergence of Secular Authority in a Traditonal Andean Pilgrimage." Paper presented at the conference, Pilgrimage: The Human Quest, University of Pittsburgh.

WAGNER, P. L. (1972): Environment and People, Prentice-Hall, Englewood Cliffs, N. J.

Mary Lee Nolan

PILGRIMAGE AND PERCEPTION OF HARZARD IN WESTERN EUROPE[1]

Introduction

Students of human response to *environmental hazard* have found that "an overwhelming majority of the people asked about hazard and disaster in their own localities view the occurence as either unaccountable or as an act of nature or of God (or gods) or some other supernatural force." (BURTON, KATES AND WHITE 1978, 212). As might be expected from these *perceptions of hazard causality*, it is common for individuals and social groups in many different cultures to engage in religious behaviors as means for preventing or alleviating hazard conditions and as mechanisms for social recovery in the wake of disaster. Religious responses to hazards were mentioned in eight of the studies included in a global examination of hazards edited by WHITE (1974). Among these responses, pilgrimage to a holy place is one of the most ancient and widespread *religious strategies for coping* with hazard, disaster and general uncertainty in environment. This means of coping has received very little attention in hazard studies, either as an indicator of hazard perception, or in terms of its possible effectiveness.

This article examines the above themes by considering 1,665 hazard- related pilgrimage traditions in Western Europe. Information on these pilgrimages was collected during the course of a study of contemporary European pilgrimages and shrine traditions (NOLAN and NOLAN in press). Data were obtained from pamphlets and booklets distributed at individual shrines, information sent by European bishops and shrine administrators in response to a mail query, notes taken during 25 months of field work between 1976 and 1984, and published materials describing shrines in particular regions or countries such as the works by ADAIR (1978), ANTIER (1979), CHRISTIAN (1976), CONSEJO SUPERIOR DE INVESTIGACIONES CIENTIFICAS (1978), COUTURIER DE CHEFDUBOIS (1953),

DORN (1975), FISCHER and STOLL (1977 – 79), GABRIELLI (1949), GILLETT (1957), GUGITZ (1956 – 58), HENGGELER (1968), KOLB (1976, 1980), LADAME (1980), LÄPPLE (1983), LAURENTIN (1983), LOGAN (1980), LUSTENBERGER (1978), MCNASPY (1963), MADDEN (1975), MADER (1984), MANFREDI (1954), POCHIN MOULD (1955), SALVINI (1970), SANCHIS (1983), STAERCKE (1954), UTZ (1981) and VINCIOTTI (1960).

For the purposes of this discussion, a *hazard cult* is defined as a pilgrimage tradition that relates specifically to the prevention or alleviation of conditions that threaten human life, individual or group viability, and/or property and usefulness of the resource base. Cults were categorized by *hazard type* including 1) illness, handicap, and epidemic disease; 2) acts of human violence such as war or attack by bandits, 3) natural hazards produced by meteorological and geomorphic events along with those biological hazards not subsumed in the first two categories; 4) problems affecting domesticated animals; 5) problems related to human reproduction, 6) accidents, including fires; 7) bad harvests and famine; and 8) supernatural hazards such as ghosts, demons, devils, and dragons (Table 1).

Table 1: Hazard-Related Pilgrimage Cults

Type of Hazard	Number of Cases	Percent of Cases
Human Illness and Disease	823	49
Threats of Human Violence	243	15
Physical Environmental Hazards	231	14
Livestock Disease and Infertility	134	8
Human Reproduction Problems	99	6
Accidents	79	5
Famine and Bad Harvests	40	2
Supernatural Threats	16	1

Two ideas underlying this discussion are: 1) that the percentage of cults related to a specified hazard condition provides a rough indicator of the relative importance of that hazard in the minds of a region's people, and 2) that the distribution of hazard cults provides a general idea of the *geography of perceived threat.* The latter thesis, however, must be viewed from an historical perspective, because pilgrimages, once established, often endure for long periods of time. Some active shrines are associated with hazards that are no longer significant threats in a specific sense. Modern Europeans, for example, are not especially worried about Bubonic plague or invasions by Turkish armies, although salvation from such problems is still commemorated in areas where these threats once posed major problems and generalized problems related to disease and human violence still prevail.

Over the past few centuries, there has been a decline in the importance of hazard cults related to the agricultural cycle. High densities of such shrines in certain regions apparently indicate areas where types of cultus, once, more widely spread, have survived in fairly large numbers to the present. It should also be considered that important shrines, drawing from extensive regions, typically attract pilgrims for many reasons including desires to give thanks for or seek salvation from hazard conditions representing all or most of the categories given above.

A. Types of Shrines

Christian pilgrimage is not exclusively a response to hazard. Probably a majority of the millions of pilgrimages made in Western Europe each year are undertaken as acts of devotion or contrition. Some of the most important and enduring European shrines, including Santiago de Compostela, Spain, and St. Peter's in Vatican City, are rarely visited in response to hazard conditions. In contrast, some major shrines are associated with salvation from so many different types of hazard conditions that it is difficult to categorize them as having a specific type of hazard cult tradition.

I. Rijeka and Loreto as Examples

Some shrines are primarily associated with specific types of hazards. An example is found at Rijeka, Yugoslavia, in the place where the Virgin's house is said to have rested briefly on a miraculous journey from the Holy Land to Loreto, Italy. The Yugoslav shrine, on the crest of a hill overlooking the harbor, is credited primarily with efficacy in salvation from perils of the sea. Eighteenth and nineteenth century ex-votos, commissioned to painters by survivors of storms at sea, share the walls of a room in the shrine complex with model ships and framed newspaper clippings describing twentieth century sea disasters, including the sinking of the Titanic. Photographs included with clippings personalize salvation from modern maritime disasters.

The related shrine at Loreto, Italy, where a structure said to be the "Holy House" is encased in carved marble within the basilica, is particularly important for aviators, and by extension air travelers and people engaged in other forms of dangerous travel, including motorcyclists. This development of a twentieth century hazard cultus at a shrine dating from Medieval times is based on the old tradition that flying angels carried the Holy House from Nazareth to Loreto by way of Rijeka. The need of early twentieth century aviators for a special pilgrimage place combined with an appropriate traditional symbolism, and in 1920 Pope Benedict XIV proclaimed the Virgin of Loreto patroness of aviators. Images depicting the Loreto Madonna have been carried on numerous famous flights, including Charles Lindbergh's crossing of the Atlantic in the Spirit of St. Louis in 1927 and the Apollo 9 space mission (GRIMALDI 1984). Other shrines, mostly of minor importance, are so specialized that they are primarily noted for the relief they provide from such mundane problems as athlete's foot, pimples, and bad grades on school examinations.

II. The Altötting Example

The relationship between European pilgrimage traditions and peoples' efforts to cope with various hazards is evident at Altötting, Bavaria. This small town has been a Christian religious center since the eighth century, but the present pilgrimage dates to 1489 when the first miracle was recorded. The mystique of miraculous intervention in hazardous situations is focused on the veneration of a dark Madonna, richly encrusted with brocade and jewels donated by the faithful. The hearts of emperors and nobles lie mouldering in gold caskets within the small chapel that houses the image of the Virgin Mary. Special pilgrimages draw crowds of 35,000 to 50,000 pilgrims on a single day, and devotees come in groups and as individuals from all over southern Germany, most of Austria, and as far as Switzerland and Hungary. Throughout the year, the chapel is crowded with prayerful pilgrims while others carry wooden crosses around the arcade that surrounds the chapel.

The interior and exterior walls of the Altötting chapel are covered with *votive offerings*, or *ex-votos*, in the form of small paintings on tin, wood, glass, and paper framed under glass. These offerings record most of the hazards known to humankind, although those related to salvation from accidental death, the violence of war, and ill-health seem to predominate. At Altötting, as elsewhere, votive offerings may be placed as acts of *supplication* for a desired outcome in future activities perceived to be hazardous, as when a soldier goes off to war. More often, they are left at the shrine as offerings of *thanksgiving* for salvation from a hazard event. The highly specific hazard situations depicted in many of the paintings suggest that a large number are thanks offerings associated with *pilgrimage vows*.

The oldest ex-voto on display at Altötting dates to the early sixteenth century, but the tradition of leaving votive offerings at pilgrimage sites dates to pre-Christian times in Greco-Roman, Germanic, and Celtic traditions (BRENNEMAN 1985, GRIMM 1966, OGILVIE 1969, ROUSE 1975). Although many valuable old examples have been lost or destroyed, extensive collections of paintings depicting specific problems are still found at European shrines in Germanic regions, Italy, southern and eastern France, Spain, and Portugal. Descriptions and interpretations of this type of offering have been provided by numerous European scholars including CARRARA (1969), CIARROCHI AND MORI (1960), COUSIN (1981), KRISS-RETTENBECK (1973), TEMPERA (1977) and TOSCHI (1970).

B. Religious Responses to Hazard

I. The Pilgrimage Vow

The vow to make pilgrimage as a response to crisis is widespread in the folk and popular Roman Catholic traditions of Europe and Latin America. Although sometimes regarded as superstitious behavior, the pilgrimage vow is often a positive act from a psychological point of view, according to studies by anthropologists and cultural geographers (CHRISTIAN 1972, NOLAN 1973 a, 1973 b, TURNER AND TURNER 1978). Vows are frequently made under conditions of extreme duress when the supplicant, often correctly, perceives himself to be at the mercy of events beyond his direct control. By promising to make pilgrimage on the condition that he or his loved-ones be spared, the individual is relieved of a pressing need to take other actions and may, therefore, be able to deal more rationally with a developing situation. In other words, regardless of any theological interpretations, pilgrimage vows are often functional as *coping mechanism* that reduce excess stress in emergency situations.

Although more common in the past, mass pilgrimages and community vows of pilgrimage probably served similar adaptive functions. These *acts of communal devotion* may not have swayed the course of epidemic, drought, or earthquake in an objective sense, but they did serve as mass expressions of faith in deliverance, and thus served to consolidate social systems disrupted by catastrophe. In certain cases when the hazard was an invading army sharing a similar religious orientation, pronouncement of miracles and mass pilgrimage has sometimes directly alleviated the hazard condition. For example, enemy observations of weeping or bleeding images of Mary or Christ have been credited with decisions to spare the sack of towns in several shrine legends and at least three documented cases [NOLAN and NOLAN In Press].

II. Social-Psychological Effectiveness of Religious Responses

Even if most pilgrimages and pilgrimage vows do not, in any objectively measurable sense, make an impact on the geophysical or biological source of the hazard condition, they may change the outcome of events because of their importance as coping mechanisms. Students of hazard response have found that disaster must be measured not only in terms of the intensity of the impact event, but also in terms of ***human ability to withstand the impact and recover*** (BURTON, KATES and WHITE 1978, HASS, KATES, and BOWDEN, 1977). There has been a strong recent tendency, especially among English-language writers, to discredit religious behaviors as appropriate adjustments to hazard conditions. Some social scientists have interpreted such behavior as disfunctional because they view it as contributing to the scope of a disaster without adding any modifying benefits in its aftermath (KENDRICK 1957, SJOBERG 1962). There is, however, a growing body of evidence suggesting that religious responses combined with other adjustments may yield highly positive results (DAVIS 1970, NOLAN 1973, 1976, 1979). In addition, experimental studies have indicated that the perception of control increases viability (PERLUTER and MONTY 1977). The pilgrimage vow, for example, can function to control panic, reduce anxiety to tolerable levels, alleviate despair, and, when undertaken as a group action, unify a shocked and frightened people around symbols of community.

C. Categories of Hazard Cults

I. Types of Health Related Cults

The search for health for one's self or loved ones is a long standing motivation for a considerable amount of pilgrimage activity (BROWN 1981, CHRISTIAN 1972, FINUCANE 1977, SUMPTION 1975, WARD 1982). Pilgrims pray for health at most shrines, but only those pilgrim centers, such as Lourdes, which are specifically noted for cures, were included among the 823 categorized in Table 1 as having curative cults. Even with this conservative approach to classification, 49 percent of the 1,665 hazard cults considered were directly related to a search for human health and general viability. To the extent that numbers of pilgrimage cults provide insights into human perception of hazards, the hazards of illness and disease outrank all other threats by a wide margin. No region of any size within the study area is lacking in a shrine devoted primarily to healing, and there are no important differences between countries in the proportion of such cults relative to other hazard cults. Pilgrimage traditions specifically related to healing accounted for 53 percent of the identified hazard cults in Germany, 51 percent of the cases in Italy, 49 percent of the cases in Austria, and 48 percent of the French examples.

Because many curative shrines were established centuries ago, these data suggest that various forms of disease and handicap have been viewed as a paramount threat by many generations of Europeans. The importance of such cults remains strong in a modern world. Some of the most important pilgrimage centers founded in the nineteenth and twentieth centuries, such as Lourdes, France; Fátima, Portugal, and Beauraing, Belgium, are strongly associated with the search for health. Within the past two decades there has been an increasing emphasis on special pilgrimages for the sick, even at shrines with no previous reputation for special curative qualities. This, in turn, may be related to a growing conceptualization of pilgrimage as therapeutic for the patients and comforting to those who care for the sick. The idea of sudden miracle cures is de-emphasized, although not totally dismissed, in most European shrine literature.

It seems possible that the wide distribution and numbers of health related cults reflect a human response to the environmental hazard most effectively dealt with by pilgrimage rather than the hazard most pervasively feared. Dramatic cures do result from, or at least coincide with, pilgrimages and vows to make pilgrimage. Whether these cures are explained as the consequence of divine intervention or as examples of the complexity of interrelationships between body and mind, pilgrimage as part of the search for personal health produces tangible results. These results are, in some cases, scientifically documented, and their numbers apparently exceed what might be expected by chance alone (MARNHAM 1980). In the Eastern tradition, pilgrimage in old age to an especially holy place, particularly the shrines of the Holy Land, is not always thought of as a journey from which the pilgrim expects to return. Dying and being buried in the holy place can be viewed as a positive result (PASCAL 1958).

1. Disease and Handicap

Of the 823 healing cults considered, 36 percent are non-specialized, meaning that these shrines are not associated with a specific ailment. Forty percent are related to one or a few specific problems including childhood diseases, cancer, headaches, fevers, epilepsy, arthritis, lung diseases, blindness, leprosy, toothache, insanity, chronic-depression, and a host of other afflictions. The most commonly mentioned specific problems are eye disease or blindness, which account for 71 of the 328 shrines with specialized curative cults. Springs or well water is used in curative rituals at nearly 75 percent of the shrines related to eye problems, as compared to about 33 percent of all health-related shrines.

It might be argued that specific, personal ailments associated with this category of shrines do not fit the usual definitions of environmental hazards because the pilgrimages are made as individual attempts to alleviate problems affecting one person rather populations. In addition, handicaps such as blindness, deaf-

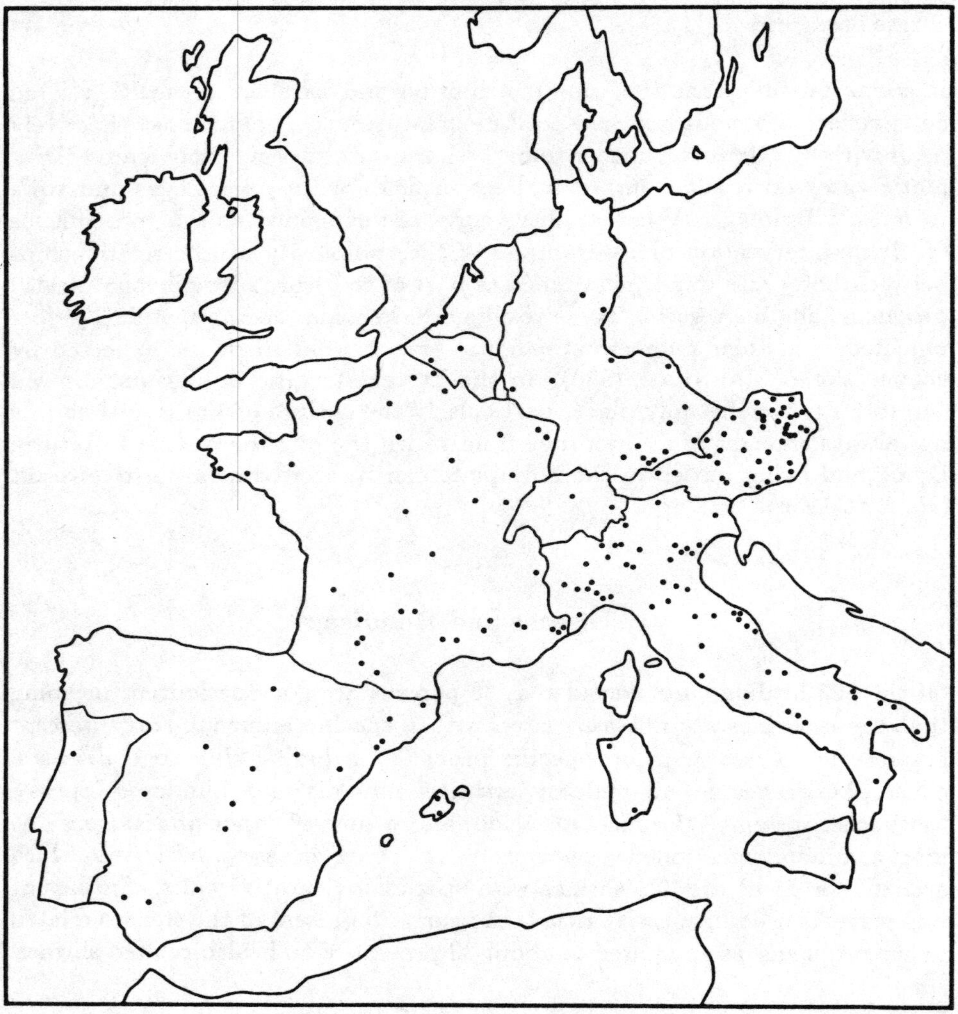

Fig. 1: Distribution of shrines created as votive offerings in the aftermath of plague and other epidemics
Source: Authors's survey data

ness, or lameness may not have significant environmental parameters. On the other hand, some concentrations of shrines associated with particular health hazards, such as a cluster of several shrines promising relief from lung disease in two adjacent Austrian provinces, suggests that medical geographers and hazard researchers might discover some interesting patterns in the spatial distribution of specific disease and handicap cults.

2. Epidemic Disease

Twenty-four percent of the health related cults are associated with epidemic diseases. Most references to cholera date from the past 250 years, and clearly refer to a specific disease. In the older shrine literature, however, plague may be a generic reference to any serious epidemic, including bubonic plague. Outbreaks of epidemic disease clearly constitute a biotic hazard affecting whole populations. BURTON, KATES and WHITE (1978, 21) list bubonic plague under Biological Hazards, subdivision Faunal. Other epidemic diseases have, also, had important demographic and environmental consequences (MCNEILL 1976).

Pilgrimage as an immediate response to plague has counter-productive results. Drawing large numbers of travelers together in often unsanitary conditions is likely to intensify an epidemic and encourage its spread to previously uninfected areas. For example, the region around the important Medieval English shrine at Walsingham was particularly hard-hit by the Black Death in 1348, probably as a result of an upsurge of pilgrimage during this time of stress (STEPHENSON 1972, 42). Why, then, does Europe contain so many active pilgrimage shrines that originated with vows made during epidemics, in some cases hundreds of years ago? (Figure 1). The most plausible explanation is that, although pilgrimages during epidemics are demonstrably disfunctional, vows to make pilgrimage when the epidemic ends have important positive implications. Epidemic tends to break down the social fabric to a greater extent than almost any other kind of catastrophe. Thus, communal unification in creation of a new pilgrimage tradition at the end of such a stressful period can make an important contribution toward restoration of normal social intercourse.

II. Problems Related to Human Reproduction

Five percent of the hazard cults deal with problems related to human reproduction. Twenty-four percent of these cults are perceived to provide aid in the search for a husband, and another 24 percent are thought to help women become pregnant. Thirty percent focus on problems related to pregnancy and

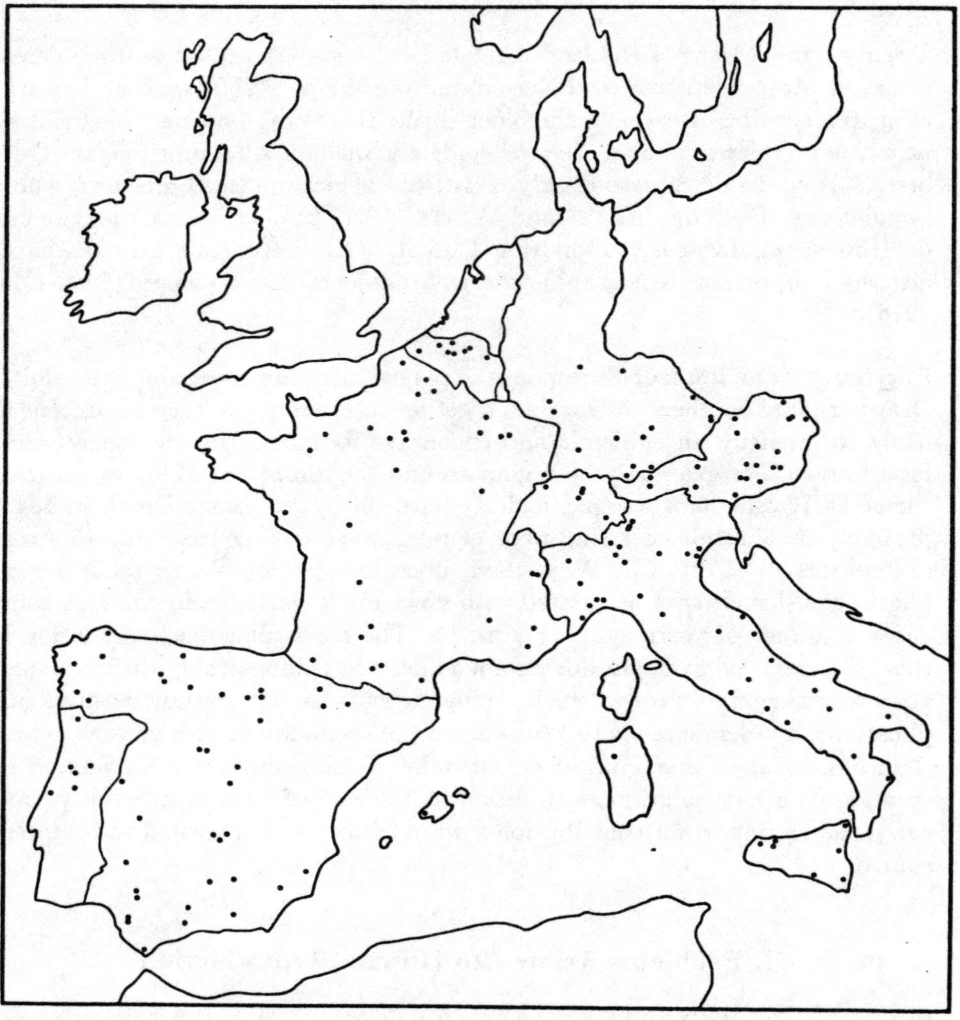

Fig. 2: Distribution of shrines created in thanks for victory
or for salvation from war
Source: Author's survey data

childbirth. The remaining 22 percent are either concerned with infant survival, or center around the "revival" of stillborn infants. The highest concentrations of shrines related to finding a husband and fertility are in Austria, France, and Portugal, in that order. Shrines promising safe pregnancy and childbirth are most frequently found in Switzerland, followed by Spain and Germany.

The idea of a hazard complex associated with human reproduction may seem unorthodox to most natural hazard researchers, but for women in European villages, inability to find a mate was long a threat to social viability. Problems of pregnancy and childbirth have, in the past, been among the most serious threats to life for women between the ages of about 15 and 50 and infant mortality rates were high.

Pilgrimages related to finding a mate may have highly practical functions. At a French shrine, for example, young women traditionally went together in small groups to pray for husbands. Young men from the district hid in the bushes along the route to inspect available brides. As the young women returned home, it was acceptable for a young man to strike up a conversation with a girl he admired. With 13 cases, Austria had more shrines where young people go to pray for mates than any other single country. As in Austria, most such shrines in other countries were located in hilly to mountainous rural areas such as Brittany, the Rhone Alpes, Trentino-Alto Adige, and the hills of northern Portugal. Further study might indicate that cults of this kind function to *reduce in-breeding* by keeping gene pools mixed on a district-wide basis in areas that might otherwise have largely endogamous mating systems.

There seems to be an interesting *"division of labor"* between the Virgin Mary and the saints in meeting needs associated with human reproduction. The task of providing a husband is more or less equally shared, but more than 66 percent of the shrines where women pray to become pregnant are dedicated to male saints. In contrast, the places where women seek easy childbirth are mostly devoted to the Virgin Mary, as are shrines where the health of newborn infants is sought.

A few shrines, mostly in eastern France and Austria are, or at least until recently, were associated with revival of still-born infants. Some of these cults may have become established when an apparently still-born baby showed signs of life. In most cases, infants dead at birth have been carried on long journeys to these shrines, symbolically restored to life to be baptized and buried there. The tradition no doubt had psychological benefit for the bereaved parents.

III. Threat of Human Violence

The predator humans most fear takes a human form. Pilgrimage cults related to the search for salvation from human violence make up 15 percent of the cases. Of these, nearly three-quarters were spawned by wars and revolutions. The remainder are related to salvation from attacks by pirates, robbers, bandits, murderers, rapists, and cruel husbands, along with a few cases stemming from unjust imprisonment and death sentences. Figure 2 indicates the distribution of active shrine-pilgrimage complexes that were founded specifically as votive offerings for salvation from and/or victory in war.

Although geographers concerned with response to environmental hazards have not usually focused on the violence and destruction that humans inflict on each other, these threats should be considered in studies that seek to unravel the complex threads of human response to hazard, an area in which sociologists have led the way. Much of the initial thrust for modern disaster response studies stemmed from an effort to predict which might happen in the event of nuclear war (Baker and Chapman 1962, Nolan 1973). Christian (1984) suggests a relationship between large numbers of apparition reports during the early 1950s and the social-psychological stresses of the Cold War.

Acts of human violence can be considered in a natural hazard context by subsuming them under the category of *faunal hazards*. This proves a reasonably good fit with human perception in many cases, especially when the attackers are viewed as cultural aliens, and therefore considered somewhat inhuman. At various times and in various places, the real and/or perceived threat presented by Moors, Saracens, Turks, Protestants, Jews, and revolutionary *iconoclasts* of various kinds has been described in Catholic shrine literature in much the same words as attacks by wolves, mad dogs, and wild boars.

In contrast, when combat between peoples with similar idea systems is described, the emphasis tends to be on the hazards of war in general. The antagonists are apparently viewed as fellow humans rather than two-legged fauna made especially dangerous by virtue of intelligence. In the former case, the threat is perceived as an environmental hazard as unpredictable as earthquakes and wild boars. In the latter, a certain element of predictability and control is apparently sensed, stemming from similarities in the cultural heritage.

In the cases of religious response to the hazards of warfare, the distinction has, on occasion, been appropriate. French soldiers in nineteenth century Italy might well stop rampaging to kneel before a weeping picture of the Virgin Mary, whereas no such behavior could be expected from Turkish troops in seventeenth century Austria. Ironically, however, some very powerful shrine formative stories are related to the conversion of religious aliens during times of war, and some of the worst acts of atrocity have been committed during revolutionary uprisings and civil wars when the combatants were fellow countrymen and sometimes even kinsmen.

Pilgrimages related to war and other acts of human violence are widely, but logically, distributed. For example, shrines established in response to past Moslem threats are found from Iberia across southern France and northern Italy into southern and eastern Austria, as well as in the southern Italian peninsula and on the islands of Sicily and Sardinia. These pilgrimages vary in time period of formation in expected ways with the most recent being the Austrian shrines deriving from the mid-seventeenth century period of Turkish expansion.

Proportions of hazard cults related to salvation from human violence show more variation from country to country than do cults related to maintenance of health. At the higher end of the scale, 25 percent of the Spanish cases and 23 percent of the Italian cases are associated with human violence. In France, Germany, and the Benelux countries, human violence accounts for 18 percent of the hazard cults. The proportion falls to 11 percent in Austria, eight percent in Portugal, and three percent in Switzerland and the British Isles. Substantial numbers of shrines said to have been founded in thanksgiving for ancient salvation from or victory over Moslem armies partly account for the higher than average numbers of this type of pilgrimage cultus in southern Europe. Other factors are involved, however. Italy, and to a lesser extent Spain, have higher than average proportions of shrines originating because of salvation from attacks by various types of outlaws. Pilgrimage cults related to salvation from cruel husbands or employers are mostly Italian and seem to have appeared during the fourteenth and fifteenth centuries, possibly as one of many manifestations of the pattern of socio-cultural change labeled the Renaissance.

IV. Physical Environmental Hazards

People experience technically unexplicable cures at shrines. Attacking armies, outlaw bands, and cruel individuals have, on occasion, dropped their weapons to kneel in prayer with their intended victims. These kinds of things have happened fairly often, and examples are a matter of historical record. In contrast, from an objective social-scientific viewpoint, it seems very unlikely that any *geomorphic* or *meteorological hazard event* has ever been stopped or redirected in its course by pilgrimages or vows to make pilgrimage. However, as in the case of epidemic disease, these religious coping devices often provide a useful means for dealing with crisis.

Fourteen percent of the hazard cults are associated with conditions created by meteorological, geomorphic, and non-human faunal hazards. These cults are less widely distributed than those related to threats to health and danger of human violence. Hazard researchers often ask, "Why do people live in places subject to physical environmental hazards?" Perhaps the answer lies in the suggestion that occasional floods, droughts, or earthquakes play minor perceptual roles in minds concerned with numerous hazards including disease and warfare. Evidence collected to date also suggests that traditional religious responses to regionally-specific environmental problems take numerous forms other than pilgrimage, and when a pilgrimage cultus is established, it tends to be highly localized (CHRISTIAN 1981, NOLAN and NOLAN In Press).

Of the 231 natural hazard cults surveyed, 30 percent are related to *storms* or extremely bad weather on land. Shrines with traditions related specifically to thunderstorms and hailstorms are most concentrated in Germany, Austria, Switzerland, and Spain, areas that experience these weather conditions fairly often. Twenty-two percent of the cases are associated with salvation for *perils of the sea* including fog, storm, and storm induced shipwreck. These shrines are, as should be expected, found mostly in coastal regions, often directly overlooking the sea.

Although *fog* was considered a hazard at sea, land fogs were usually viewed as positive. Stories collected from four Austrian shrines tell of people gathering around mountain chapels as Turkish armies approached. As these stories go, extermination by the Turks was imminent until fog closed in, thus disoriented the enemy and resulting in the salvation of the threatened population. These stories provide an interesting example of what BURTON, KATES and WHITE (1978, 36) have referred to as "*increasing the benefits of a hazard.*"

Nineteen percent of the natural hazard cults are associated with drought, and are found primarily in Spain, southern France, Austria and Switzerland. Salvation from floods or from too much rainfall at the wrong time of year for planting or harvest constituted 13 percent of the cases. Most examples of these cults are in Austria and southwestern France. Harvest and famine cults had a similar distribution suggesting a great persistence of pilgrimages related to agriculture in some areas than in others.

Faunal hazards made up nine percent of the cases and showed a scattered distribution with concentrations in Austria and Spain. Threats included venomous snakes, wolves, wild boars, mad dogs, and swarming locusts or other crop-destroying insects. Salvation from the latter problem was most frequently mentioned in Spain.

Pilgrimages related to geomorphic hazards such as earthquakes, volcanic eruptions, and landslides made up only seven percent of the religious responses to physical environmental hazards. Cults based on occurences of avalanches and landslides were found in Switzerland and adjacent parts of northern Italy. Shrines offering protection from volcanic eruption were, of course, confined to Italy, the only part of the region with active volcanoes. Pilgrimages related to earthquakes were found in geologically active areas of southern Europe; Italy, southern France, and Spain. Two cases celebrate the repeated salvation of a cult object from devastating earthquakes and may symbolize the on-going vitality of settlements along fault lines.

In contrast to a strong association between the Virgin Mary and cults related to salvation from illness and human violence, most natural hazard cults are focused on the power of the saints to intercede for human good. Perhaps this relates to the role of saints as "territorial demideities bound up ceremonially with the seasonal reproductive cycle, through feasts celebrated at critical points in the agricultural year." (TURNER and TURNER 1978, 207).

Salvation from perils of the sea is an exception in that all but one of the cults identified focused on the Virgin Mary. This reflects an ancient association between the Virgin, the sea, and the night sky's importance for maritime navigation (WARNER 1976, 265 – 266).

V. Harvest and Famine Cults

Forty pilgrimage traditions were described as important for the assurance of good harvests, as votives for the end of past famines, or as measures to stave off future bad harvests and famines. In most of these cases, drought, insect plague, flooding and other natural hazards are probably involved, but were not specified. Cults of this type seem to be most common in France and Austria, followed by Spain and Italy.

VI. Livestock Cults

Pilgrimages related to animal health and disease made up eight percent of all cases. These shrines are strongly concentrated in the southern parts of Germanic Europe (Figure 3). In Austria, pilgrimages to insure the well-being of livestock account for 14 percent of hazard cults surveyed in that country. The figure for Germany was 11 percent of the cases, followed by Switzerland, with seven percent. The German livestock shrines are predominantly in the south of the country. The Italian livestock cults are in the culturally Germanic South Tirol, and thus form part of the cluster centered on Austria. Shrines

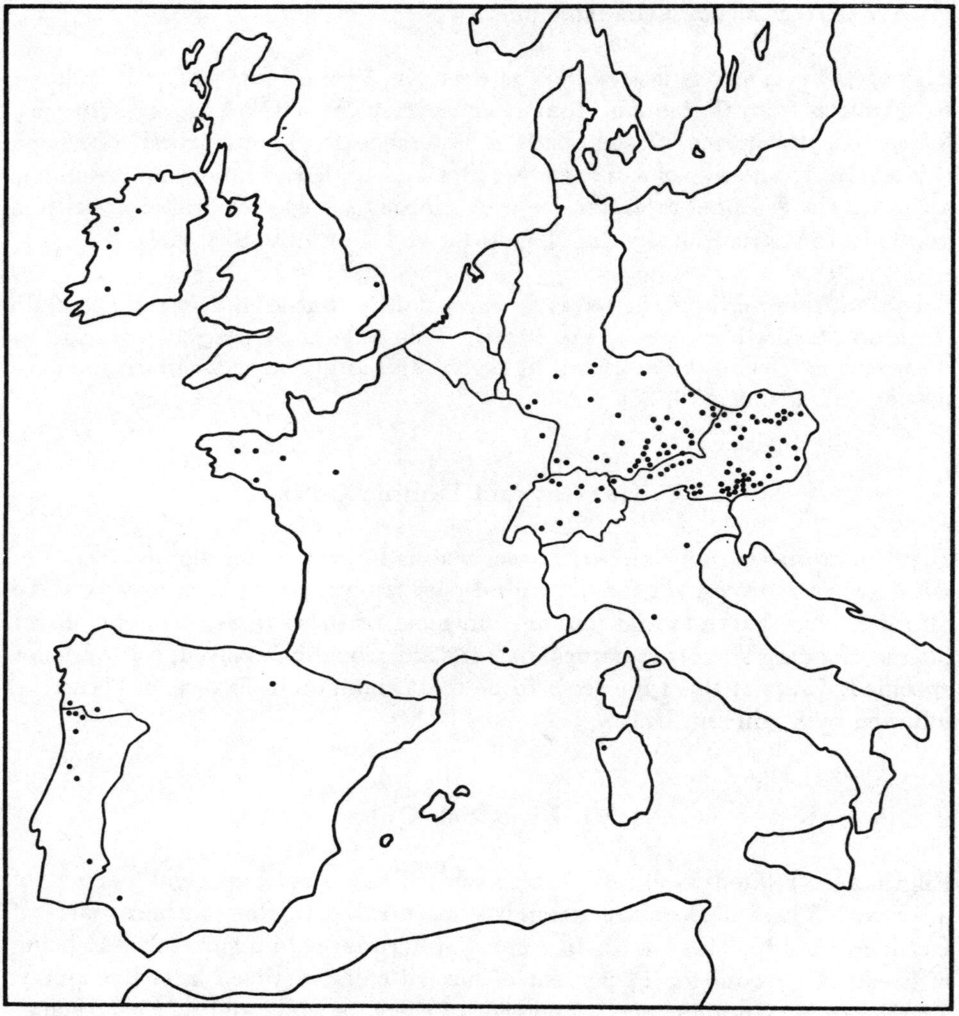

Fig. 3: Distribution of shrines devoted primarily to the health and well-being of livestock
Source: Author's survey data

dealing specifically with animal well-being make up six percent of the Spanish hazard cults, with a concentration in northern Portugal and adjacent Galicia, five percent of the British and Irish hazard cults, with most cases in Ireland, and two percent of the French hazard cults, mostly in Brittany.

An obvious explanation for the spatial concentration of the *veterinary cults* is the relatively great importance of livestock in Alpine farming systems. However, descriptions of horse-centered cults suggest survivals of ancient rites of horse worship and sacrifice translated into later Christian pilgrimage traditions. Cults related to the health of horses are predominant in southern Germany along with central through western Austria, the region where the *Umritt,* or horseback pilgrimages are most prevalent (ROTHKRUG 1979, 1980). Most of the livestock cults further east in Austria, westward in Switzerland, and beyond in Brittany, Ireland, and Iberia, focused on cattle. Interestingly, these cattle cults show very little distributional overlap with the Mediterranean area shrines where the behavior of bulls figures in tales of miraculous discoveries of Marian images. Distinctive traditions appear to be involved and invite more investigation by folklorists.

More than 90 percent of the cults related to animal health are found at shrines dedicated to saints. This supports the idea that Marian devotions have been slow to supplant the role of the saints as patrons of agriculture.

VII. Accidents

Pilgrimages related to accidents make up five percent of the cases, but these account for higher proportions of hazard cults in France and southern Germanic regions than elsewhere. A Germanic Alpine concentration of pilgrimages associated with fire probably reflects the use of wood as a building material for homes and churches long after stone, brick and other less flammable materials were in common use elsewhere in Europe.

Nearly half of the identified accident cults dealt with the *hazards of land travel.* The numerous cults providing protection from shipwreck were included under the natural hazard category of perils of the sea. Lines of cars at shrines dedicated to St. Christopher, and the proclamation of Our Lady of Loreto as the patroness of aviators, attest to the continued vigor of transportation-related cults.

A few shrines specialize in *occupational hazards*, particularly wood cutting and mining. Others, in a modern age, focus on *recreational activities*, including mountain-climbing, bicycle racing, and cave exploring. As a result of formation miracles, some shrines are strongly associated with salvation from drowning, getting lost, or falling from high places. Votive tablets and books of intentions at these shrines offer thanks for salvation from a variety of accidents and near-accident situations.

VIII. Supernatural Threats

A final category composed of 16 cases, or less than one percent of those examined, involves pilgrimage cults related historically to hazards once perceived to be imposed by ghosts, demons, devils, gnomes, dragons, and witches. In the past, these were thought of as serious environmental threats by many Christian Europeans, possibly because they symbolized forces of traditional pre-Christian religions or later heresies.

D. Conclusions

Very few modern Europeans worry about, or even believe in ghosts and dragons. If threatened with floods, they build dams, and if concerned with drought, they design irrigation networks. When they are sick, they go to doctors, and because travel for pleasure is easy and socially acceptable, they no longer need the excuse of making pilgrimage to see far-off lands.

But dams break, irrigation depends on a water supply, and there are sicknesses of body and soul that no doctor can cure. Travel purely for pleasure may come to grate on the spirit, and the threats of violence and war have not ended. Thus, the ancient combination of recreation and devotion, which underlay much Medieval pilgrimage, has its modern expressions. Pilgrims converge on these shrines by automobile and airplane, forms of transportation that are hazardous in themselves. And in the mountains of southern Austria, people still make the ancient rounds by foot to the crests of four mountains, traditionally to stave off, for one more year, the long-foretold end of the world (WIESER 1981).

An alternative to prayer and pilgrimage in finding the strength to meet potential catastrophe is belief in the power of science and technology. We are beginning to understand that this modern means of dealing with hazard does not provide all the answers, and probably never will. As planners turn toward societal, as opposed to technological, means for reducing the total costs of hazard impact, perhaps the significance of pilgrimage will come into focus and provide guidelines for ways of adjusting to ever-present threat in a modern world and of dealing with occasional disasters.

Annotation

[1] This article is a revision of a paper presented at the 74th Annual Meeting of the Association of American Geographers, New Orleans, April 9 – 12, 1978, and contains data on Western European pilgrimage collected since that data. The research was funded by grants from the Oregon State University Foundation, the OSU College of Liberal Arts Program, and the National Endowment for the Humanities. Contracts with Educational Filmstrips Company, Huntsville, Texas, for the production of audio-visual educational aids also helped offset some field expenses. Dr. Sidney D. Nolan, Jr. assisted with the field work and edited this article.

Summary

Prevention and alleviation of the meteorological and geomorphic hazards, which are the primary focus of natural hazard research, make up a relatively minor proportion of the hazard conditions for which pilgrimage offers one means of adjustment. It has been suggested that pilgrimage functions as a positive means of coping with hazard. It may or may not actually give people control over the hazards of life, but this religious behavior can provide a sense of control. The sense of, or belief in, control has been proved experimentally to increase the functional viability not only of men, but of animals. Perhaps the deep-rooted need not to feel totally helpless in the face of a hazardous environment partly explains the vitality of hazard cults in a secularly-oriented age.

Zusammenfassung:
Die Pilgerreise und Perzeption von Gefahren in Westeuropa

Meteorologische und geomorphologische Gefahren, deren Vermeidung und Abschwächung das wichtigste Ziel der Natural-Hazard-Forschung ist, bilden nur einen kleinen Teil der Gefahrenpotentiale, für die eine Pilgerreise Bewältigungsmöglichkeiten verspricht. Es wird ausgeführt, daß Pilgerreisen ein positives Mittel der Auseinandersetzung mit Gefahren darstellen. Unabhängig davon, ob sie tatsächlich Menschen zur Gefahrenkontrolle befähigen, können solche religiösen Verhaltensmuster ein Gefühl der Kontrollmöglichkeit vermitteln. Wie experimentell nachgewiesen wurde, verstärkt das Gefühl für oder der Glaube an Kontrollmöglichkeiten die Lebensfähigkeit nicht nur von Menschen, sondern auch von Tieren. Vielleicht verstärkt das tief verwurzelte Bedürfnis, sich einer gefahrvollen Umgebung nicht völlig hilflos gegenübergestellt zu fühlen, teilweise die Lebendigkeit von Kulthandlungen zur Gefahrenbewältigung in einem diesseitig ausgerichteten Zeitalter.

Bibliography

ADAIR, J. (1978): The Pilgrim's Way: Shrines and Saints in Britain and Ireland. — Thames and Hudson, Over Wallop, Hampshire.

ANTIER, J. (1979): Le Pèlerinage retrouvé. — Le Centurion, Paris.

BAKER, G. and CHAPMAN, D., eds. (1962): Man and Society in Disaster. — Basic Books, New York.

BROWN, P. (1981): The Cult of the Saints: Its Rise and Function in Latin Christianity. — University of Chicago Press, Chicago.

BRENNEMAN, W. (1985): The Circle and the Cross: Loric and Sacred Space in the Holy Wells of Ireland. — In: SEAMON, D. and MUGERAUER, R., eds.: Dwelling Place and Environment: Towards a Phenomenology of Person and World. — Martinus Nijhoff Publishers, Dordrecht, Boston, Lancaster. Pp. 137 – 158.

BURTON, I., KATES, R. and WHITE, G. (1978): The Environment as Hazard. — Oxford University Press, New York.

CARRARA, A. (1969): Bocche parlanti: gli ex voto di Montenero. — Collana Marilux, Montenero.

CHRISTIAN, W. (1972): Person and God in a Spanish Valley. — Seminar Press, New York and London.

CHRISTIAN, W. (1976): De los santos a Maria: panorama de las devociones a santuarios españoles desde el principio de Edad Media hasta nuestros dias. — In: TOLOSANA, C., ed.: Temas de antropologia española. — Akal, Madrid. Pp. 49 – 106.

CHRISTIAN, W. (1981): Local Religion in Sixteenth Century Spain. — Princeton University Press, Princeton.

CHRISTIAN, W. (1984): Religious Apparitions and the Cold War in South Europe. — In: WOLF, E., ed.: Religion, Power and Protest in Local Communities: the Northern Shore of the Mediterranean. — Mouton Publishers, Berlin, New York and Amsterdam. Pp. 239 – 266.

CIARROCHI, A. and MORI, E. (1960): Le tavolette votive italiane. — Edizioni Doretti, Udine.

CONSEJO SUPERIOR DE INVESTIGACIONES CIENTIFICAS (1978): Santuarios. — In: Diccionario de historia eclesiastica de España. — Instituto Enrique Florez, Madrid. Vol. 4, pp. 2207 – 2381.

COUSIN, B. (1981): Ex-voto de Provence: images de la religion populaire et de la vie d'autrefois. — Desclee de Brouwer, Paris.

COUTURIER DE CHEFDUBOIS, I. (1953): Mille pèlerinages de Notre-Dame. — Editions Spes, Paris. 3 vols.

DAVIS, N. (1970): The Role of the Russian Orthodox Church in Five Pacific Eskimo Villages as Revealed by the Earthquake. — In: National Research Council, comp.: The Great Alaska Earthquake of 1964: Human Ecology. — National Academy of Sciences, Washington, D. C. Pp. 125 - 146.

DORN, L. (1975): Die Wallfahrten des Bistums Augsburg. — Eos Verlag, Augsburg.

FINUCANE, R. (1977): Miracles and Pilgrims: Popular Beliefs in Medieval England. — Dent, London.

FISCHER, R. and STOLL, A. (1977 - 79): Kleines Handbuch österreichischer Marien-Wallfahrtskirchen. — Bergland Verlag, Wien. 3 vols.

GABRIELLI, A. (1949): Saints and Shrines of Italy. — Holy Year 1950 Publishing Company, Rome.

GILLETT, H. (1957): Famous Shrines of Our Lady in England and Wales. — Samuel Walker, London.

GRIMALDI, F. (1984): La Madonna di Loreto patrona degli aeronauti. — In: KRISS-RETTENBECK, L. and MOHLER, G., eds.: Wallfahrt kennt keine Grenzen. Verlag Schnell und Steiner, München und Zürich, pp. 300 - 305.

GRIMM, J. (1883 - 88): Deutsche Mythologie. — STALLYBRASS, J., trans. (1966): Teutonic Mythology. — Dover Publications, New York. 4 vols.

GUGITZ, G. (1956 - 58): Österreichs Gnadenstätten in Kult und Brauch. — Verlag Bruder Hollinek, Wien. 5 vols.

HAAS, E., KATES, R., and BOWDEN, M., eds. (1977): Reconstruction Following Disaster. — The MIT Press, Cambridge, Mass.

HENGGELER, P. (1968): Helvetia Sancta: Heilige Stätten des Schweizerlandes. — Buchdruckerei Franz Kälin, Einsiedeln.

KENDRICK, T. (1957): The Lisbon Earthquake. — Lippincott, Philadelphia.

KOLB, K. (1976): Marien-Gnadenbilder, Marienverehrung heute. — Echter Verlag, Würzburg.

KOLB, K. (1980): Vom Heiligen Blut: Eine Bilddokumentation der Wallfahrt und Verehrung. — Echter Verlag, Würzburg.

KRISS-RETTENBECK, L. (1973): Ex-voto, Zeichen, Bild und Abbild im christlichen Votivbrauchtum. — Atlantis-Verlag, Zürich.

LADAME, J. (1980): Notre-Dame de toute la France. — Editions France-Empire, Paris.

LÄPPLE, A. (1983): Deutschland, deine Wallfahrtsorte. — Paul Pattloch Verlag, Aschaffenburg.

LAURENTIN, R. (1983): Pèlerinages, sanctuaires, apparitions: Année sainte, redécouvir la religion populaire. — Office d'Edition, Paris.

LOGAN, P. (1980): The Holy Wells of Ireland. — Colin Smythe, Gerrards Cross.

LUSTENBERGER, O. (1978): Wallfahrtsorte in der Schweiz. — Benediktinerkloster, Einsiedeln.

MCNASPY, J. (1983): A Guide to Christian Europe. — Hawthorn, New York.

MADDEN, D. (1975): A Religious Guide to Europe. — Collier Books, New York.

MADER, F. (1984): Wallfahrten im Bistum Passau. — Verlag Schnell und Steiner, München und Zürich.

MANFREDI, D. (1954): Santuarios de la Virgin Maria en España y America. — Editorial Edisa, Madrid.

MARNHAM, P. (1980): Lourdes: A Modern Pilgrimage. — Coward, MacCann & Geoghegan, New York.

MCNEILL, W. (1976): Plagues and Peoples. — Anchor Press/Doubleday, Garden City, New York.

NOLAN, M. (1973 a): Research on Disaster and Environmental Hazard as Viewed from the Perspective of Response to the Eruption of the Volcano Parícutin in Michoacan, Mexico. — Texas A&M University Environmental Quality Program, College Station, Texas. Environmental Quality Note 14.

NOLAN, M. (1973 b): The Mexican Pilgrimage Tradition. — In: Pioneer America, vol. 5, no. 2, pp. 13 – 27.

NOLAN, M. (1979): Impact of Parícutin on Five Communities. — In: SHEETS, D. and GRAYSON, D. eds.: Volcanic Activity and Human Ecology. — Academic Press, New York. Pp. 293 – 338.

NOLAN, M. and NOLAN, S. (In Press): Religious Pilgrimage in Modern Western Europe. — The University of North Carolina Press, Chapel Hill.

OGILVIE, R. (1969): The Romans and Their Gods in the Age of Augustus. — W. W. Norton, New York.

PASCAL, P. (1958): Pilgrimages of the Orthodox Church. — In: Lumen Vitae, vol. 13, no. 2, pp. 248 – 236.

PERLUTER, L. and MONTY, R. (1977): The Importance of Perceived Control: Fact or Fantasy? — In: American Scientist, vol. 65, no. 26, pp. 759 – 765.

POCHIN MOULD, D. (1955): Irish Pilgrimage. — H. M. Gill & Son, Dublin.

ROTHKRUG, L. (1979): Popular Religion and Holy Shrines: Their Influence on the Origins of the German Reformation and their Role in German Cultural Development. — In: OBELKEVICH, J. ed.: Religion and the People, 800 – 1700. University of North Carolina Press, Chapel Hill. Pp. 20 – 86.

ROTHKRUG, L. (1980): Religious Practices and Collective Perceptions: Hidden Homologies in the Renaissance and Reformation. — In: Historical Reflections.

ROUSE, W. (1975): Greek Votive Offerings. — Arno Press, New York.

SALVINI, A. (1970): Cento santuari Mariani d'Italia. — Edizioni Paoline, Catania.

SANCHIS, P. (1983): The Portugese "Romarias." — HODGKIN, J. and WILSON, S. trans. — In: WILSON, S., ed.: Saints and their Cults, 261 – 89. — Cambridge University Press, Cambridge. Pp. 261 – 289.

SJOBERG, G. (1962): Disasters and Social Change. — In: BAKER, G. and CHAPMAN, D., eds.: Man and Society in Disaster. — Basic Books, New York. Pp. 356 – 384.

STAERCKE, A. (1954): Notre-Dame des Belges: traditions et folklore du culte Marial en Belgique. — Bruxelles.

STEPHENSON, C. (1970): Walsingham Way. — Longman & Todd, London.

SUMPTION, J. (1975): Pilgrimage: An Image of Medieval Religion. — Rowman and Littlefield, Totowa, New Jersey.

TEMPERA, A. (1977): Gli ex-voto: linguaggio di pietà Mariana: testimoniaze romane. — Edizioni Orizzonte Medico, Citta del Vaticano.

TOSCHI, P. (1970): Bibliografia degli ex-voto italiani. — Editions Leo Olschki, Firenze.

TURNER, V. (1973): The Center Out There: Pilgrim's Goal. — In: History of Religions, vol. 21, no. 3, pp. 191 – 230.

TURNER, V. and TURNER, E. (1978): Image and Pilgrimage in Christian Culture: Anthropological Perspectives. — Columbia University Press, New York.

WARD, B. (1982): Miracles and the Medieval Mind. Theory, Record and Event 1000 – 1215. — University of Pennsylvania Press, Philadelphia.

WARNER, M. (1976): Alone of All Her Sex: The Myth and the Cult of the Virgin Mary. — Wallaby Pocket Books, New York.

WIESER, A. (1981): Der Vierbergelauf. — Kärntner Druck- und Verlagsgesellschaft, Klagenfurt.

WHITE, G. ed. (1974): Natural Hazards: Local, National, Global. — Oxford University Press, New York.

UTZ, H. (1981): Wallfahrten im Bistum Regensburg. — Verlag Schnell und Steiner, München und Zürich.

VINCIOTTI, A. (1960): I mille santuari mariani d'Italia illustrati. — Associazione Santuari Mariani, Roma.

Gisbert Rinschede

THE PILGRIMAGE CENTER OF FÁTIMA/PORTUGAL

Introduction and Methodology

The pilgrimage center of Fátima, which celebrated the seventieth anniversary of the apparition of the Virgin Mary in 1987, has developed within a few decades from modest beginnings to an international place of pilgrimage. Surrounded by smaller hamlets (Aljustrel in the South, Moita Redonda in the North and Lomba de Égua in the East) and by the main center of Fátima to the South, a new center has developed in a round depression (Cova da Iria) in open country, solely due to the constantly growing stream of pilgrims, and is today known by the old field-name of Cova da Iria.

This study examines five major aspects of Fátima's development as a prominent pilgrimage center: (I) religious events which underlie the sanctity, (II) characteristics of the pilgrims — the driving force behind its popularity, (III) impact of pilgrim streams on the population and the development of this settlement (IV) the emergence and characteristics of the landuse components, and (V) predominantly touristic activities and activity space of the pilgrims, since secular and sacred components are intertwined in the pilgrimage process.

I. The Religious Events in Fátima's Rise

The emergence of the streams of visitors to Fátima and the development of its population, settlements and economy were due to the miraculous apparitions which occured there in 1916, and more importantly in 1917. These events took place at a time when numerous European states were involved in the first World War, when the communist revolution in Russia was being carried out and when the Portuguese nation was in a particularly difficult political, social

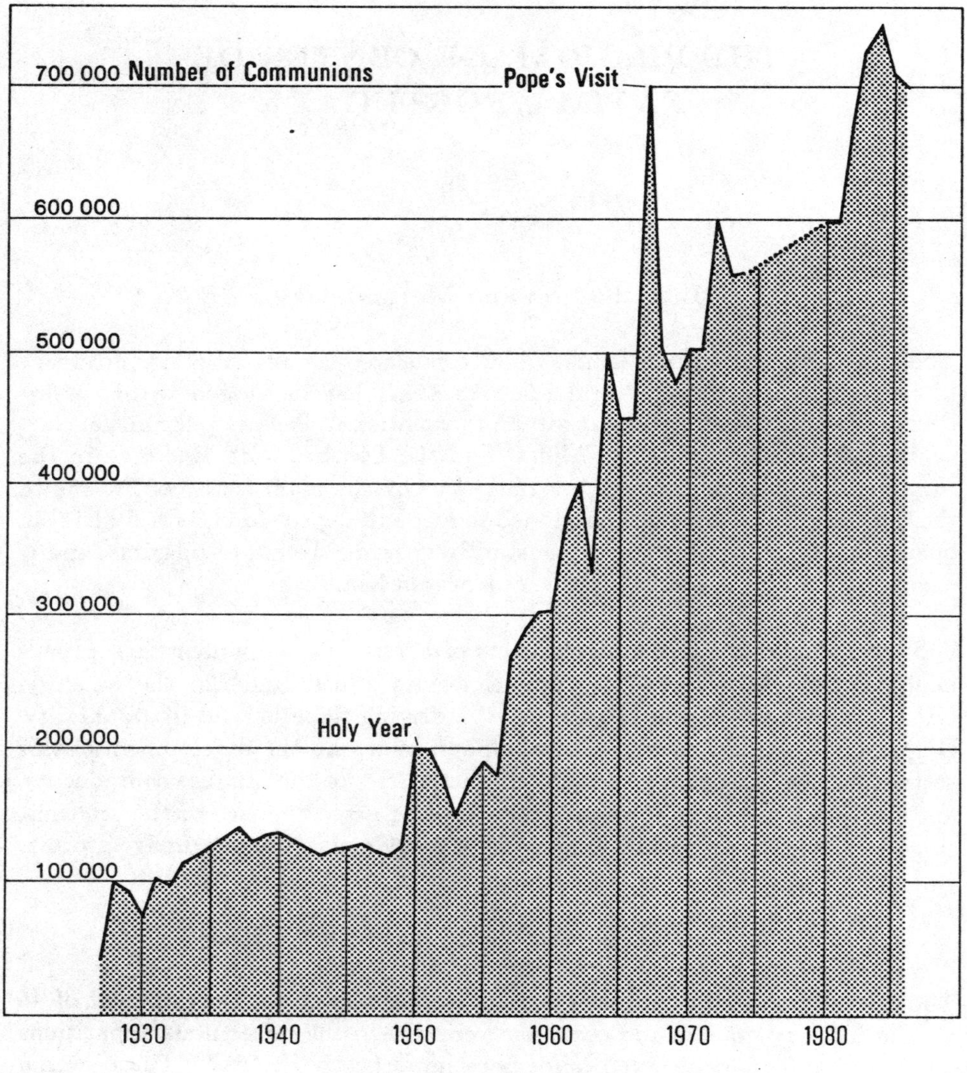

Fig. 1: Number of Communions in Fátima 1927 – 1986
Source: Information from the "Serviçio de Peregrinos" — SEPE, Fátima

and economic situation, in which, among other things, religious freedom was heavily restricted.

The three shepherd children, Lucia Santos and Francisco and Jacinta Marto saw their first three angel apparitions in spring, summer and autumn 1916 in their native village of Aljustrel and its immediate surrounding area. These angel apparitions were followed by six apparitions of the Virgin Mary in 1917, which occured on May 13, June 13, July 13, August 19, September 13 and October 13, as a rule in a semi-circular hollow (Cova da Iria, 2 km West of Aljustrel), in the vicinity of which the sanctuary is now situated. The 19th of August apparition alone took place in the Valhinos near Aljustrel. The second apparition of 1917 in Cova da Iria was witnessed by about 50 people, the third by as many as 4,000 and the fourth by 5,000 people. 25,000 people were present during the fifth apparition and at the last one in October 1917 there were actually 70,000 people present who experienced the so-called "Sun-miracle" at the same time.

II. The Pilgrims

1. Number and Types

During the seventy year history of Fátima the stream of visitors to this place of pilgrimage has constantly increased, if one does not take into account some yearly fluctuation. Altogether three main phases of development in the number of pilgrims can be distinguished: (RODRIGUES 1974, p. 119 ff.).
In the *first phase*, from 1917 to 1948, only a few hundred thousand pilgrims visited Fátima every year. This phase coincides with the first settlements around the sanctuary. In the *second phase*, from 1948 to 1965, the number of pilgrims per year rose to about a million. The *third phase*, from 1965 onwards, is characterized by a large increase in the stream of pilgrims to an average of 1.0 to 1.5 million in a normal year, with peaks of 3.0 million for the 50 year celebration (1967) when Pope Paul VI visited Fátima, and 2.0 million for the sixtieth anniversary in 1977. In 1984 the number of pilgrims was estimated at 3,890,000, in 1986 at 3,528,000 and in 1987 at 3,608,000 (Fig. 1).

Compared to other places of pilgrimage such as Lourdes, Assisi, Padua and above all Rome and Jerusalem, Fátima has a very high proportion of "genuine" pilgrims. This is due to Fátima's short history, and a consequent lack of special historico-cultural attractions, which would appeal to those who are purely tourists.
Most pilgrims arrive independently rather than as a part of organized groups. Compared to other places of pilgrimage the proportion of individual pilgrims, 90.2% in 1984, against 9.8% of pilgrims in organized groups, is particularly

high. The average group size in the last ten years varied considerably depending on the area of origin. The size of national groups varies between 800 – 1800 pilgrims per average year, because these days many parishes, dioceses and religious groups as well as national pilgrimages organize rather large groups and make the journey with 10 – 50 buses each in one day. In contrast, the size of groups from abroad during the same period of time remains quite constant at an average of 53 – 70 people, who usually travel in one or two buses (Tab. 1).

Tab. 1: Number of pilgrims in organized groups 1977 – 1984

	From Portugal			From abroad		
Year	Number of Groups	Number of People	Average Group-size	Number of Groups	Number of People	Average Group-size
1977	239	234,093	979	70	5,514	78
1978	232	374,581	1,614	94	6,100	64
1979	262	471,125	1,800	142	7,956	56
1980	298	302,795	1,016	219	15,498	70
1981	318	327,484	1,029	394	22,463	57
1982	291	256,653	882	466	24,800	53
1983	358	299,339	836	635	37,370	58
1984	389	343,681	883	697	39,324	56

Source: Information from the "Serviçio de Peregrinos" — SEPE, Fátima

2. Origin

At first only pilgrims from the immediate neighbourhood came to the place of the apparitions. Gradually however, the catchment area spread to all the provinces in Portugal. On the 13th of October 1927 the first national pilgrimage was organized and in 1929 the first foreign group of pilgrims, from Munich, reached this place of pilgrimage. After the 2nd World War, but especially since the mid-sixties, Fátima has increasingly become an international place of pilgrimage, so that already by 1965 pilgrims from 22 countries and in 1967 pilgrims from as many as 44 different countries visited Fátima (RODRIGUES 1974, p. 124 ff). Since the beginning of the eighties pilgrims from more than 100 different countries (1984: 109 countries) have been regularly registered at the information bureau.

Exact details can however only be given about the 383,005 *organized pilgrims* (1984), of which 343,681 pilgrims (89.7%) came from Portugal and 39,324 (10.3%) from abroad. A comparison with Lourdes, where the proportion of foreigners on organized pilgrimages is over 60%, shows that Fátima still appears to be in many respects a *national place of pilgrimage*, despite its high degree of fame. This fact will be brought out by a more precise analysis of the stream of pilgrims from France (see below).

The distribution of the 343,681 group-organized pilgrims from the various Portuguese districts (conselhos) in 1984 reveals a predominance of the northwesterly provinces, especially the densely populated and heavily industrialized coastal strip which stretches from Lisbon, through Coimbra to Porto and Braga. This area is also characterized by a heavy concentration of small farmers with holdings of less than a hectare in size (Fig. 2). In contrast, the more sparsely populated southwest emerges as particularly weak in generating pilgrims. The northwest and southwest of Portugal differ also with regard to their religious attitudes. Since religious activities are stronger in the northwest pilgrimages to Fátima are more frequent from that area.

The nearly 40,000 organized foreign pilgrims in 1984 came from a total of 40 countries (Fig. 3): 10,019 pilgrims came from the USA alone, 7,820 from Spain, 7,670 from Italy, 2,907 from West Germany, 2,890 from France, 1,823 from Belgium, 1,151 from Ireland, 1,098 from Great Britain and 683 from Brazil. The high proportion (almost 25 %) of pilgrims from the USA can, among other things, be traced back to the high level of activity of the Marian organization known as "Blue Army", which has its own house, or rather hotel in Fátima.

The high proportion of pilgrims from France is also surprising. The particular position of France, as well as Luxembourg, among the European pilgrim countries becomes even clearer when the individual pilgrims who travel primarily by car are included in the analysis (Fig. 4). The statistics are based on a total investigation of private cars and buses in Fátima on the 12th and 13th of August 1986, at the time of the yearly "National Pilgrimage of Portuguese Emigrants". This pilgrimage is usually combined with family reunions at the peak holiday time in August. Emigrant families drive from France, Luxembourg, West Germany, Italy, Holland, Belgium, Spain etc. and then travel with the extended family circle, and together with other local friends and acquaintances to the traditional large gathering in Fátima. This emigrant pilgrimage is connected with intense personal emotions as well as a strong national feeling,

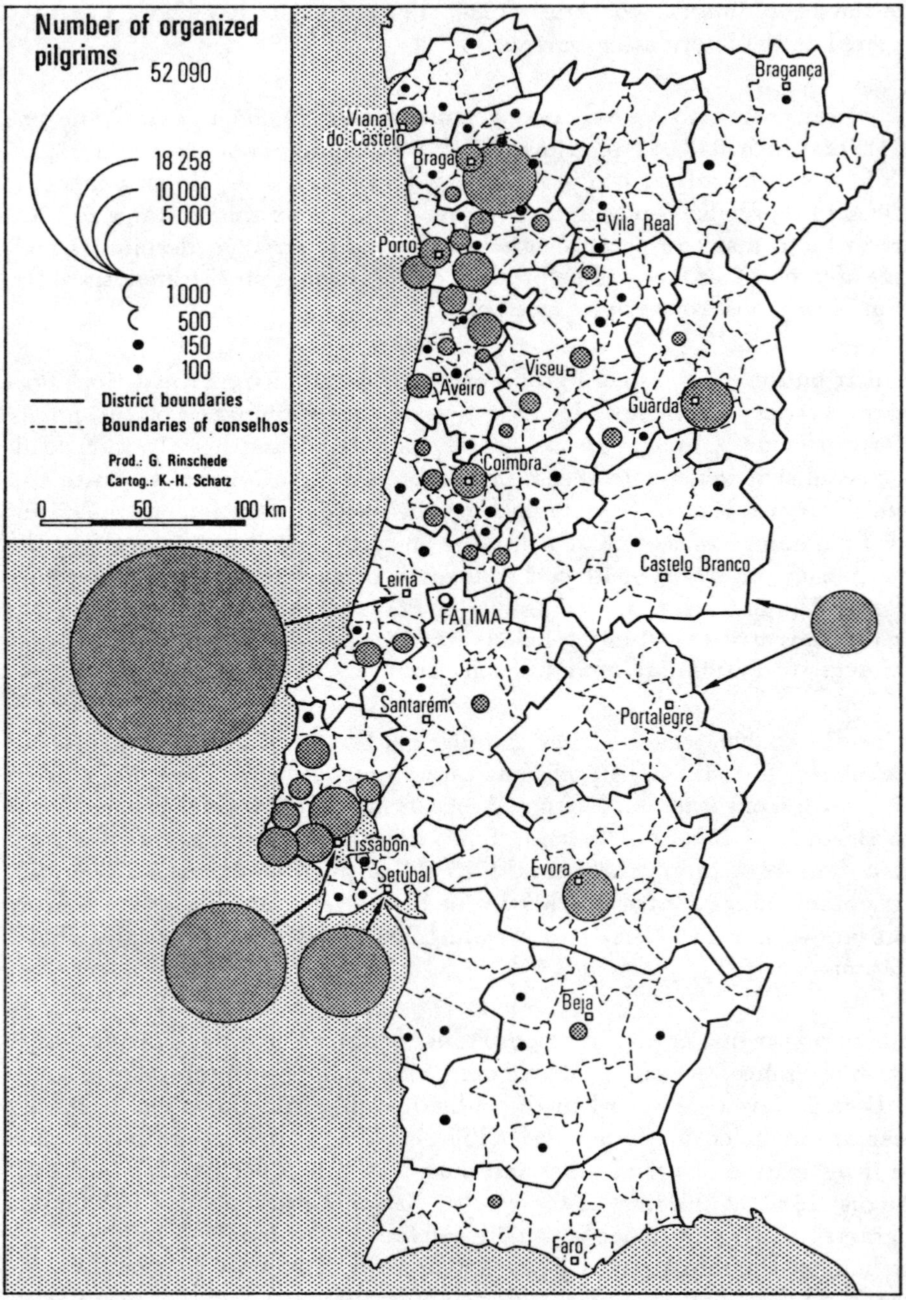

Fig. 2: Origins of pilgrims in organized groups from Portugal 1984
Source: According to information from the "Serviçio de Peregrinos" — SEPE, Fátima

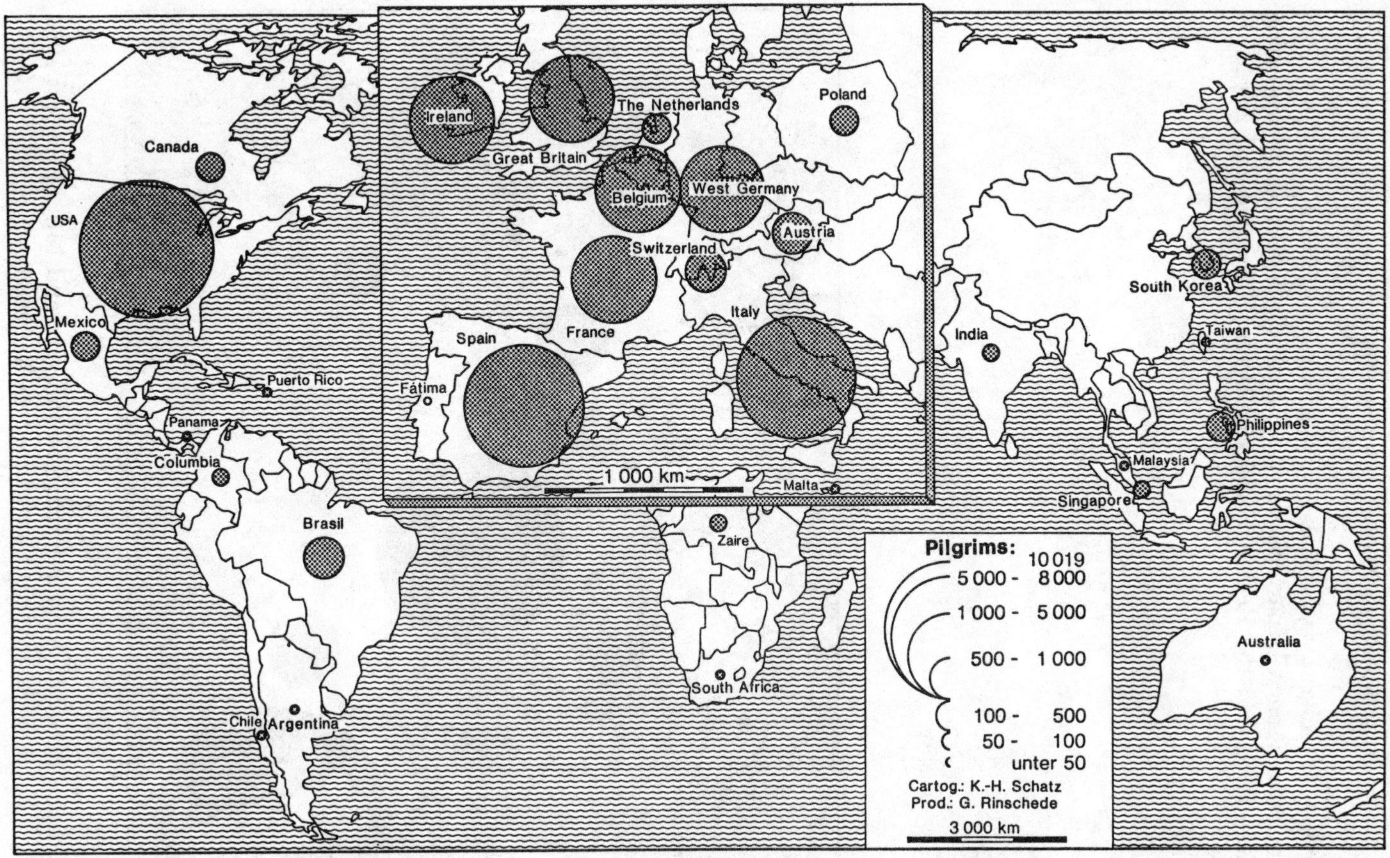

Fig. 3: Origin of pilgrims in organized groups to Fátima 1984
Source: According to information from the "Serviçio de Peregrinos" — SEPE, Fátima

as can be seen, among other things, at the farewell ceremony on the 13th of August in the great square in front of the Basilica.

The Portuguese emigrants who make the pilgrimage to Fátima come in particular from those French Départements which have the most metal- processing industries: Paris and the Région Parisienne, Lyon, Grenoble and Bordeaux (Fig. 5).

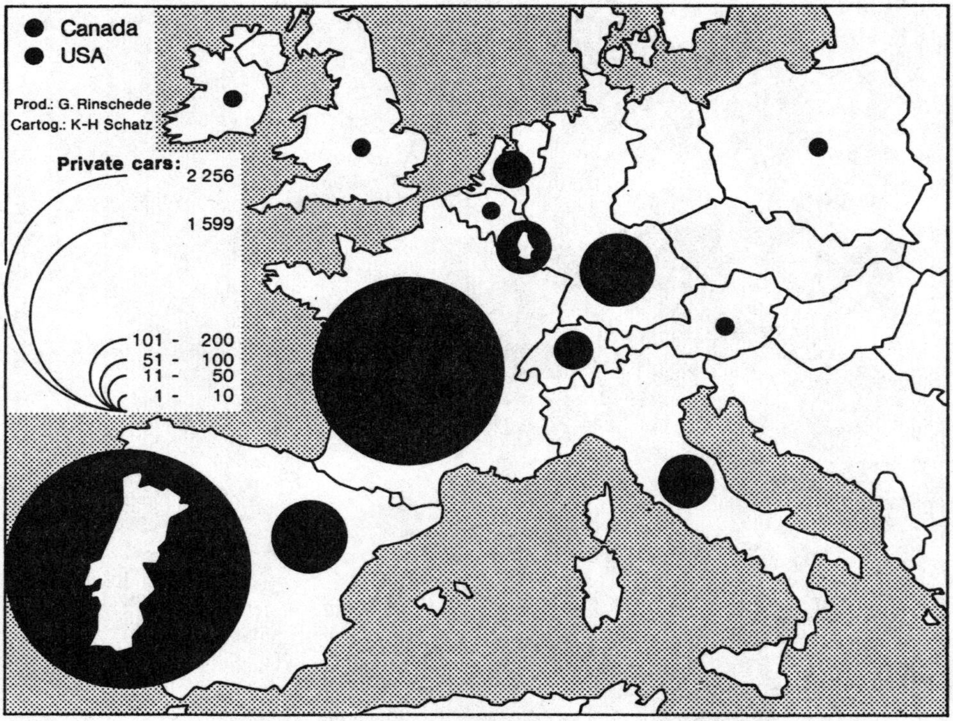

Fig. 4: Origins of private cars in Fátima on the 12th and 13th of August 1986
Source: Author's investigation 1986

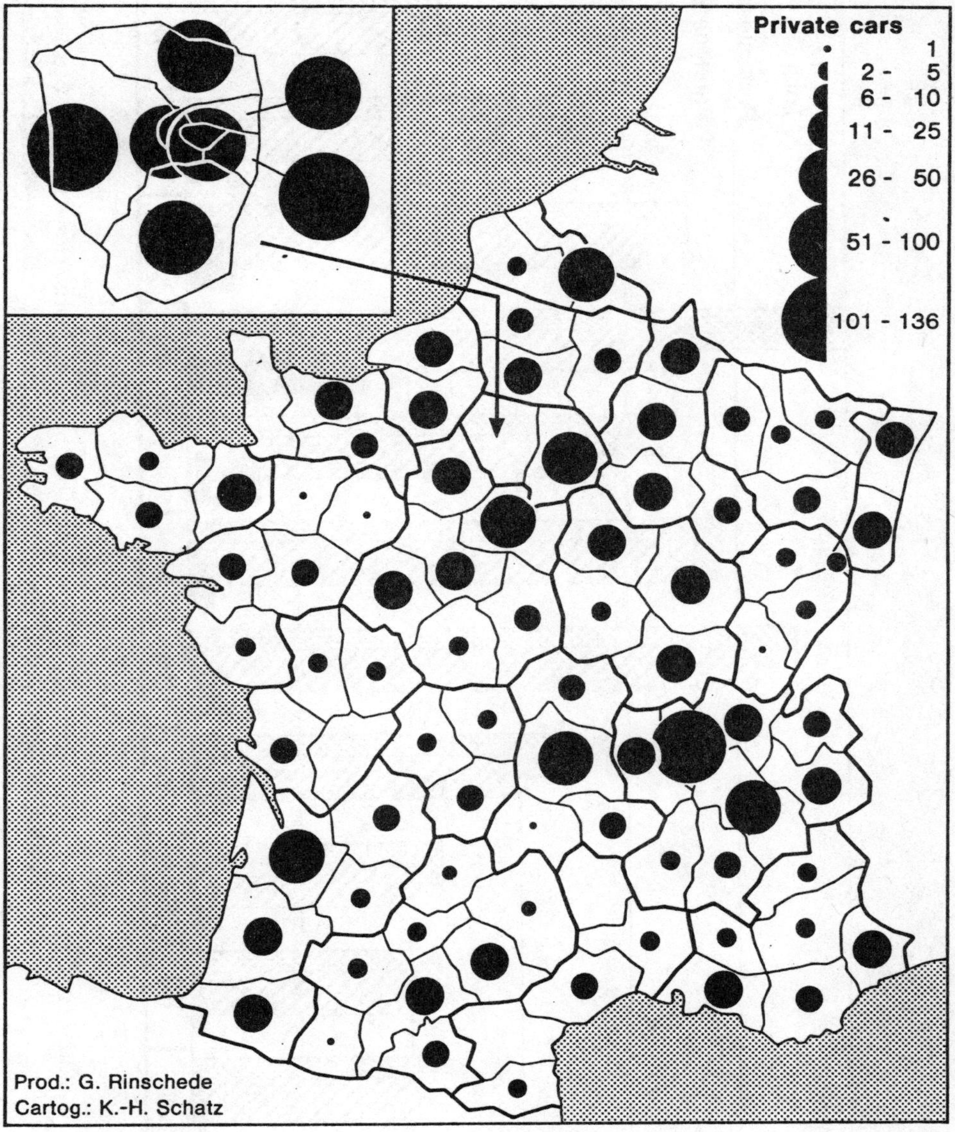

Fig. 5: Origins of private cars in Fátima from the French Départements, 12 and 13 Aug. 1986
Source: Author's investigation 1986

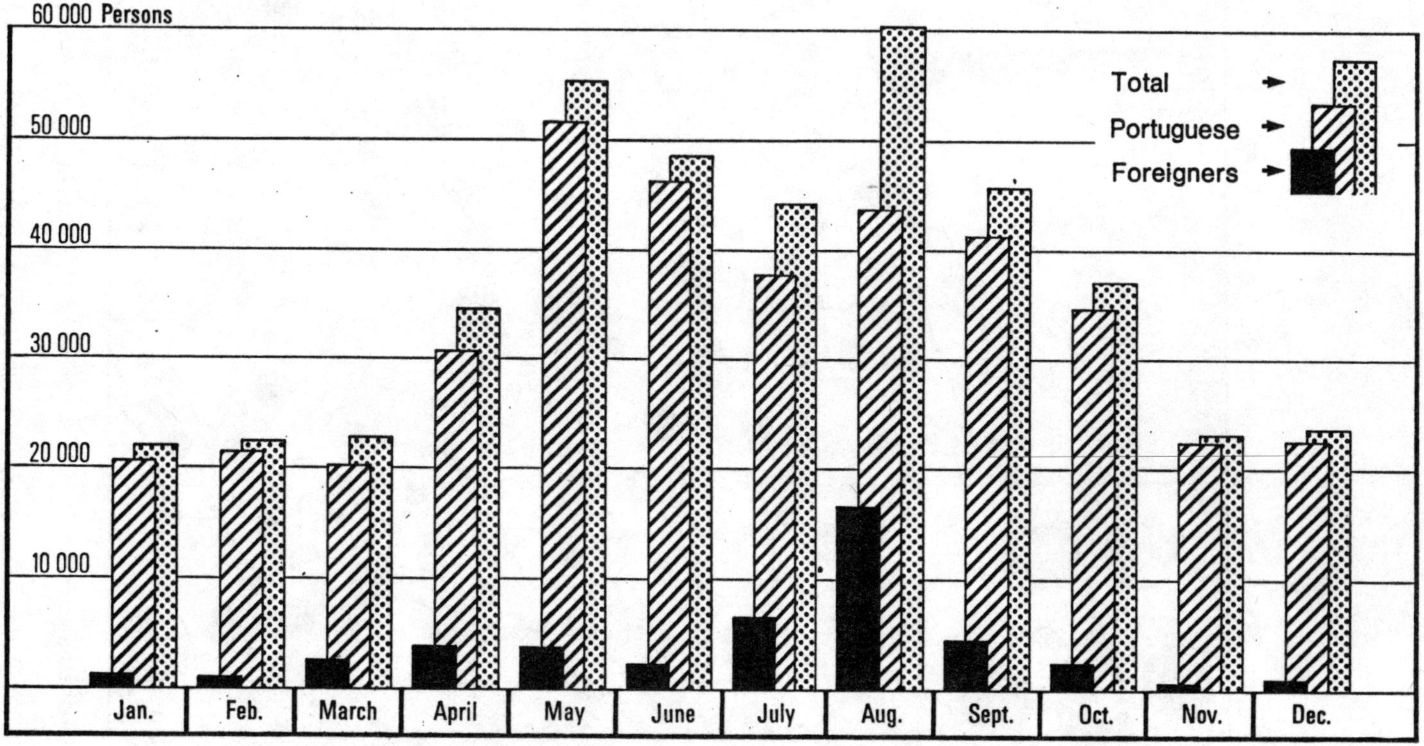

Fig. 6: Number of road users (Portuguese and Foreigners) in buses and private cars on the 3rd weekends in 1984
Source: According to information from the "Serviçio de Peregrinos" — SEPE, Fátima

3. Seasonality

As in many other places of pilgrimage, the stream of pilgrims to Fátima is characterized by a strong seasonality. There are not only seasonal variations, but also particular highpoints during the course of any one month, corresponding to the religious events of 1917.

The main pilgrim season during the course of a year is the period between May and October, those months in which the apparitions of the Virgin Mary took place. Until the fourties the pilgrim flow was concentrated mainly in the month of May, with only a few pilgrims in the other summer months and none in the winter months. Later, additional peaks developed in the mid- summer months and in October, the time of the last apparition.
During the last two decades two clear peaks have appeared in May and August separated by a little minimum point in June/July. The August- maximum has meanwhile revealed itself to be even higher than the traditionally important May-maximum of the first month of the apparitions. This development can be traced back to the increasing amount of holiday and free-time in Portugal and in most West-European countries, which is concentrated particularly in August. Traditional pilgrimages and modern tourism are increasingly becoming symbiotic. In this respect it seems, at least on examination of this development, more meaningful to talk of pilgrim-tourists (or rather pilgrim- tourism) than of pure pilgrims (Fig. 6).

With regard to seasonality there seem to be some differences between Portuguese and foreign pilgrims. The Portuguese still partly favour May, their special month of pilgrimage, whereas August is the general peak traveling time of foreign pilgrim-tourists.

To sum up, the pilgrim cyclicity of the eighties in Fátima consists of a marked high season from May to October, an early season in April, depending on the date on which Easter falls and a very weak off-season from November to March.

Since the apparitions between May and October occured as a rule on the 13th of each month, the emphasis of the religious celebrations and of the pilgrim flows lies on the 12th and 13th days of each month and partly also on the weekends immediately following (Fig. 7). Should the 12th and 13th days themselves fall on a weekend, a particularly large stream of pilgrims can be expected.

The 13th of May has a special meaning among the feast days (Fig. 8). Thus during the farewell service in May 1984 at 11am in the large forecourt of the Basilica there were an estimated 1 million visitors, compared with 180,000 in August and 100,000 in October.

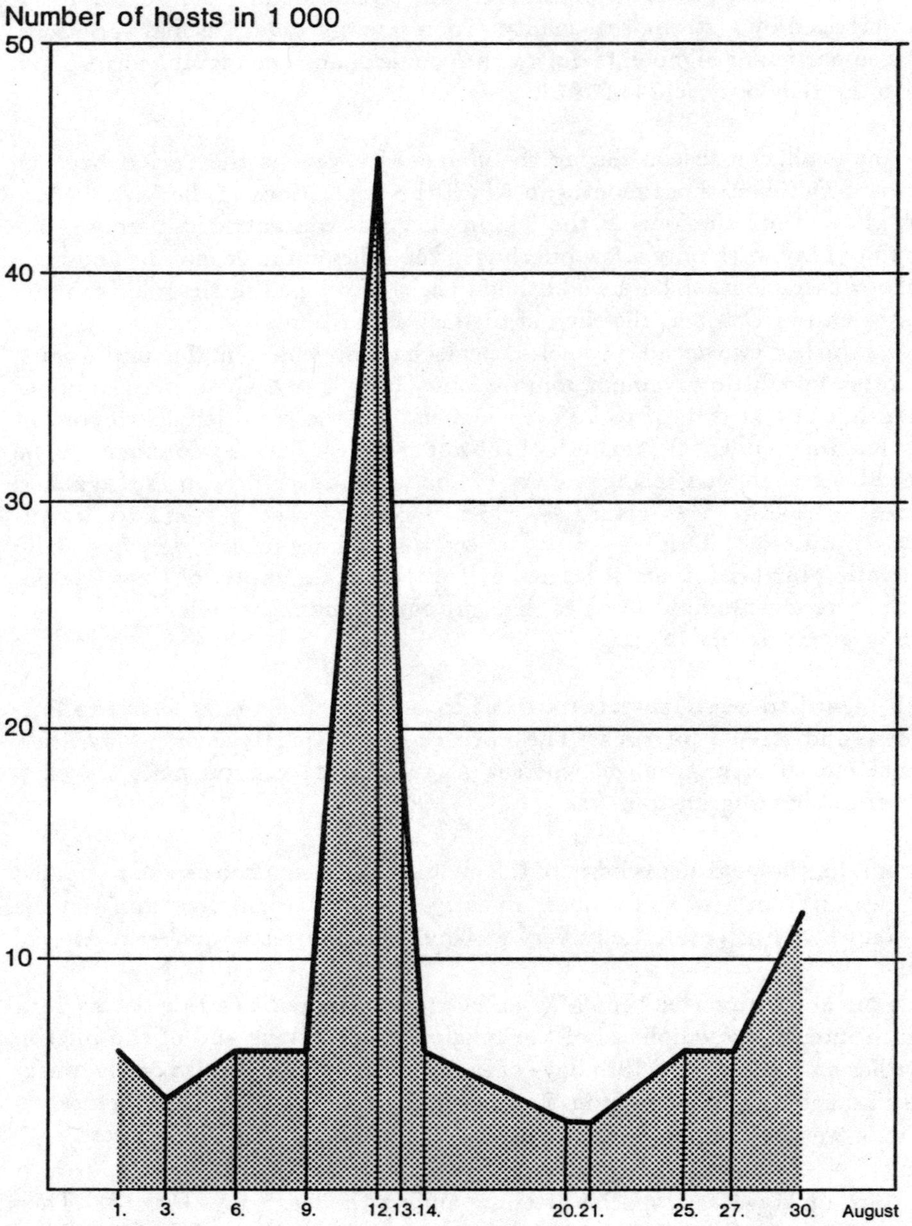

Fig. 7: Number of hosts given out in the basilica during the months of August 1983
Source: According to information from the "Serviçio de Peregrinos" — SEPE, Fátima

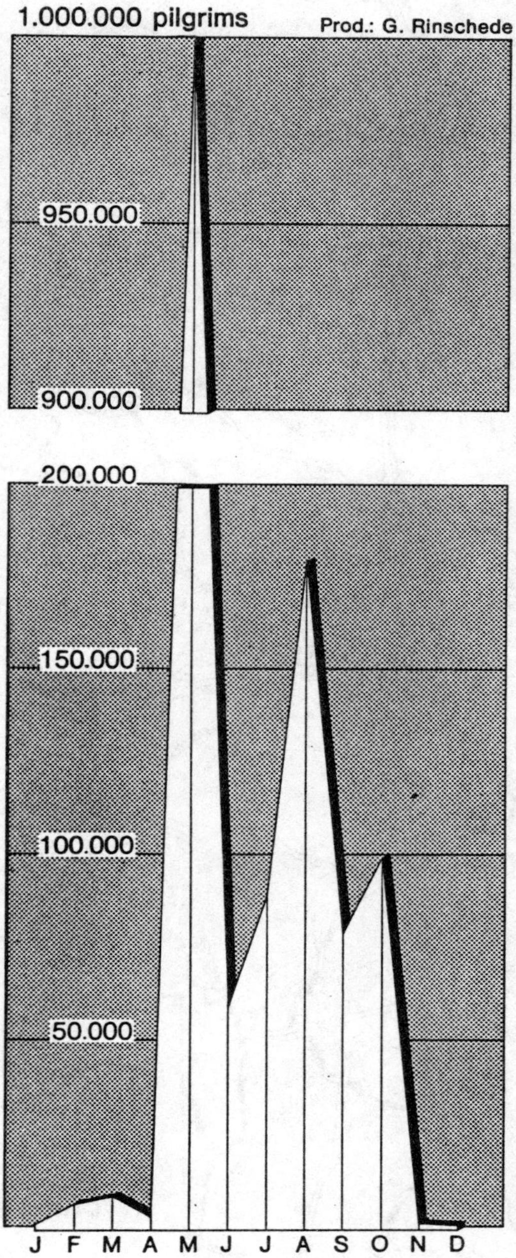

Fig. 8: Stream of pilgrims to Fátima on the 13th of each months (estimated), 11.00 mass, 1984
Source: According to information from the "Serviçio de Peregrinos" — SEPE, Fátima

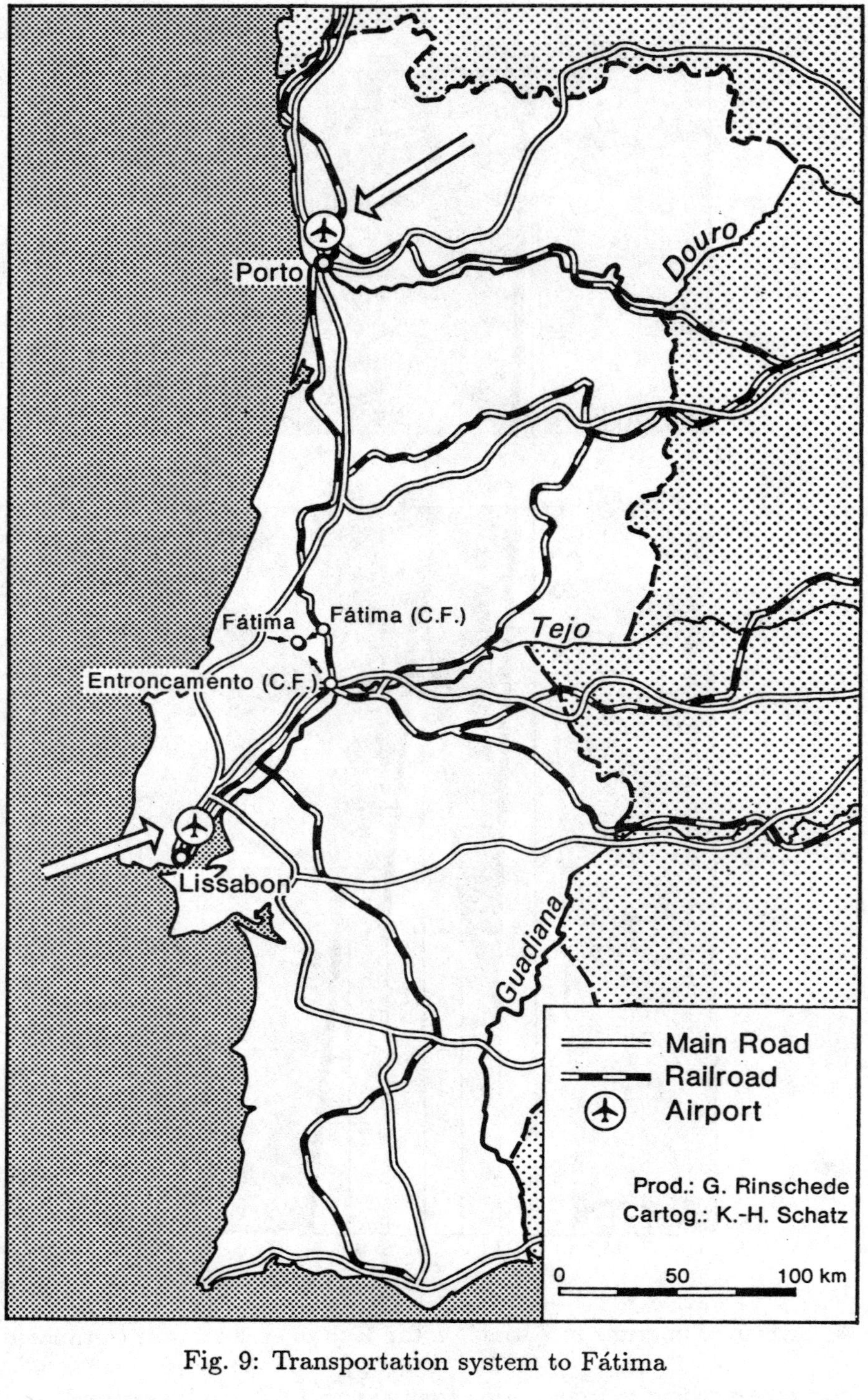

Fig. 9: Transportation system to Fátima

4. Means of Transportation

Modern places of pilgrimage with an international catchment area and several million pilgrims each year should have a good transportation system i.e. they should be accessible from all directions through a fully developed road network, a station with appropriate rail network and they should in addition have their own airport for international pilgrim-tourism. The 70 year old place of pilgrimage Fátima does not have these prerequisites (Fig. 9). Partly due to this reason *pilgrimages on foot* are still widespread. While in the early decades the journey to Fátima was made for the most part on foot or on a donkey, nowadays only a few thousand pilgrims still go on foot every year. They come mainly from the rural area surrounding Leiria and the adjoining coastal strip and reach the sanctuary from the north via the Rotunda de N.a Sr.a da Encarnação and the hamlet Moita Redonda. For this reason a mobile station is set up at the Rotunda on the 13th of each month, which can supply the foot-pilgrims with food and drink, when required, and can also give them medical assistance.

The foot-pilgrims are also looked after in the precincts of the sanctuary itself. Thus, in 1984 alone 8,066 pilgrims were given overnight accommodation and 21,276 warm meals were served. A distribution of these data in the months of 1984 confirms the absolute peak of foot- pilgrimages in May, followed by far by the months of August and October (Fig. 10).

The single-track *railraod line* from Porto to Lisbon carries the pilgrims traveling from the north and south to the stations of Fátima and Entroncamento, situated at a distance of approximately 20 or 40 km. The remaining distance has to be covered in a day's march or by bus. A special charter-bus system also looks after the pilgrims who have arrived as passengers at the international *airports* in Porto and Lisbon.

By far the largest number of pilgrims from home and abroad in Europe reach Fátima nowadays in buses and in their own cars. According to censuses and estimates carried out, more than a third of all motorized pilgrims make the journey in buses and nearly two thirds in private cars. Private cars are used by a particularly large number of home pilgrims in August and September, and foreign pilgrims in the holiday month of August (Fig. 11 + 12). Whereas the Portuguese pilgrims emphasize the use of buses during May and June, foreign bus groups reach Fátima more or less regularly between May and October.

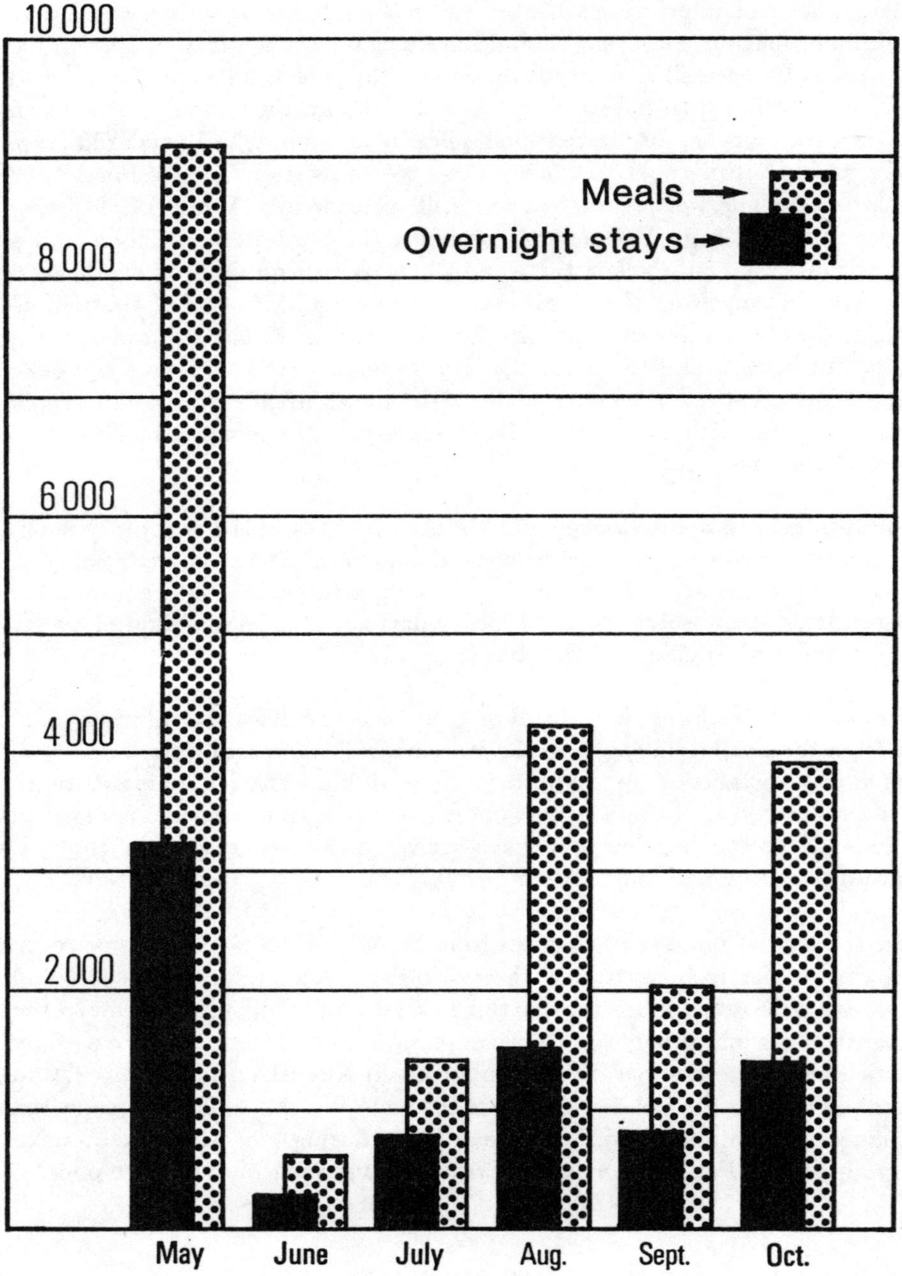

Fig. 10: Number of foot pilgrims who were given overnight accommodation and meals 1984
Source: According to information from the "Serviçio de Peregrinos" — SEPE, Fátima

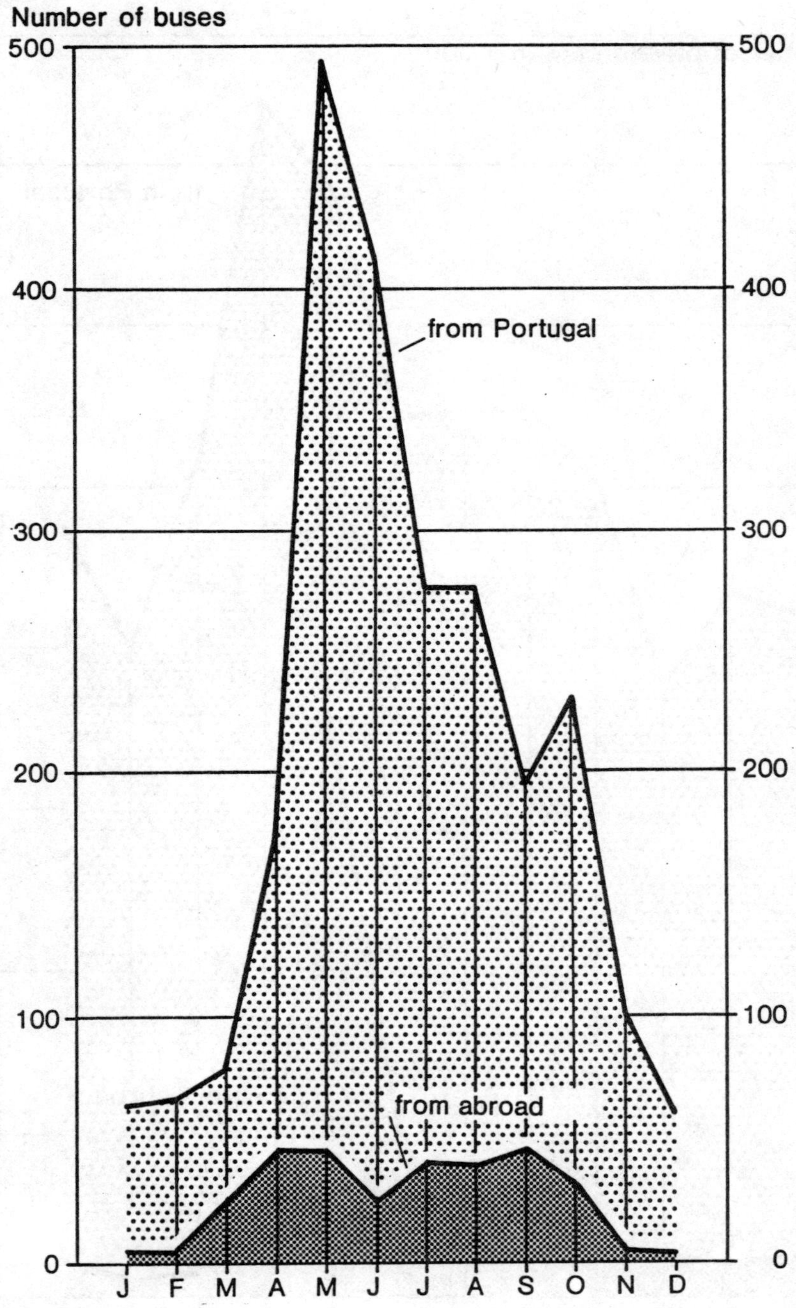

Fig. 11: Number of buses from Portugal and abroad 1984
Source: According to information from the "Serviçio de Peregrinos" — SEPE, Fátima

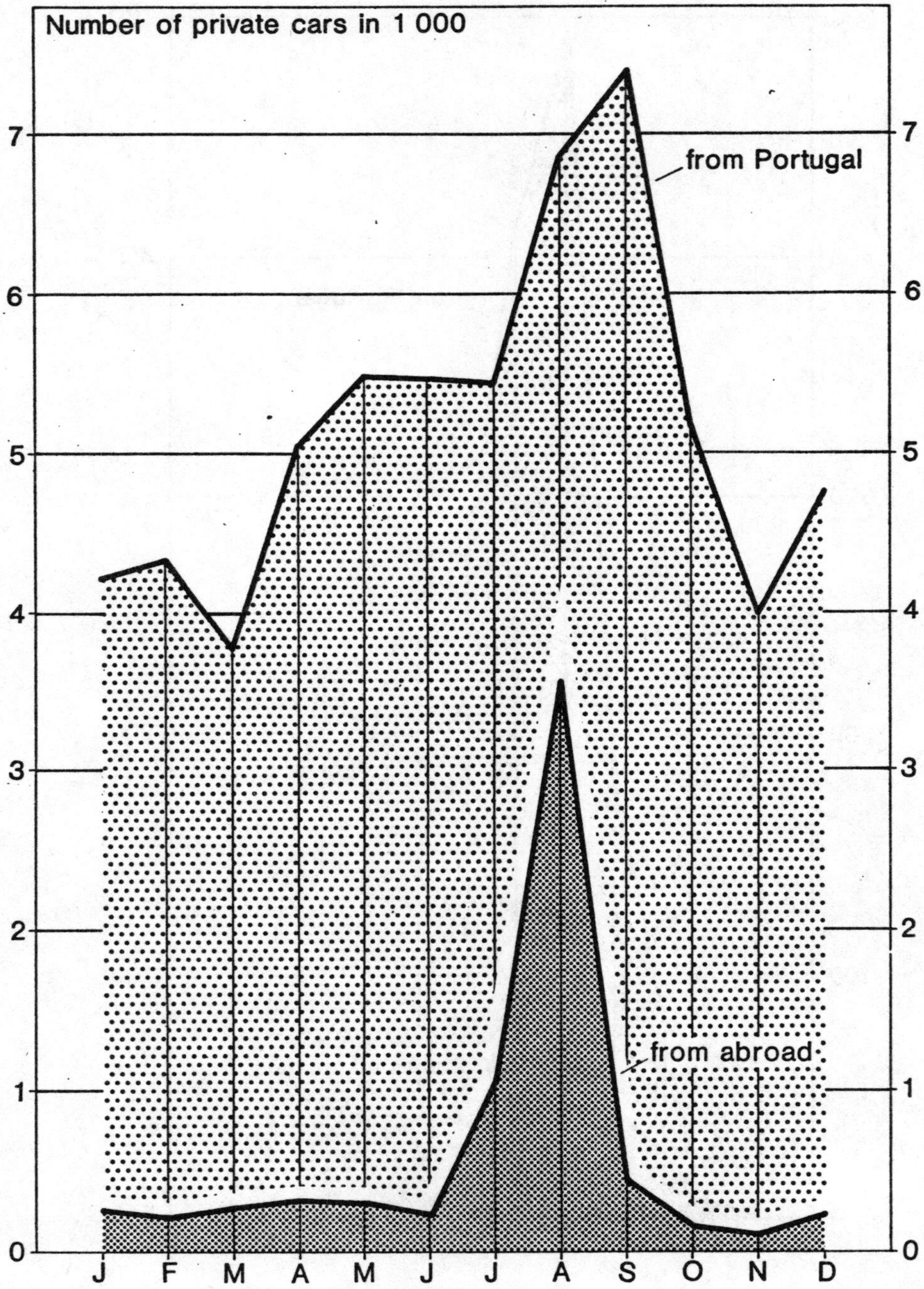

Fig. 12: Number of private cars from Portugal and abroad 1984
Source: According to information from "Serviçio de Peregrinos" — SEPE, Fátima

III. Influence of the Pilgrims on Population and Settlement Development

The spatial activity of the pilgrims' social groups becomes above all apparent in the population and settlement development of a pilgrimage place. These effects are, in Fátima's case, even more evident because the present place Cova da Iria, at the time of the apparitions in 1917, was merely a round depression on a dry karst-plateau, which only offered scarce possibilities for human settlement and intensive land-use.

1. Population Development

After several hundred thousand pilgrims had already visited the place of the apparitions in Cova da Iria during the first few years, the first settlers (7) established there in 1923 (RODRIGUES 1974). In 1987 Cova da Iria had about 3,000 permanent inhabitants, including the members of the religious institutions and seminaries.

Four different phases of population development at Fátima may be identified (Fig. 13): (RODRIGUES 1974, p. 78 ff).
The *first phase* lasted from 1923 till 1928, during which time only seven families with a total of 32 people settled in Cova da Iria.
The *second phase* from 1928 to 1935 is characterized by a discernible population increase. During this time from the laying of the foundation stone in 1928 through the building work of the Basilica, many workers settled in the immediate vicinity of their place of work.
In the *third phase* from 1936 to 1949 the rise in population was only very slight, because only few pilgrims could come to Fátima due to the Spanish civil war and the second World War.
The *fourth phase* since 1950 records the highest rise in population in the history of Cova da Iria. Constantly increasing streams of pilgrims, from home and abroad, and particularly large numbers of visitors for the Holy Year (1951) and the 50 year anniversary (1967) were the bases of a strong momentum, which caused more and more inhabitants of the surrounding area to move to Fátima to find work.

2. Settlement Development

The general settlement development in Cova da Iria followed the same chronological pattern as the population development.

The first building in Cova da Iria was an apparition chapel with a picture of the Virgin Mary, completed in 1919 and severely damaged by a bomb attack in 1922. In the same year the first family home was also built. A few years later more homes were built on the road from Batalha to Vila Nova de Ourém, which passes through the Cova da Iria settlement (OLIVIERA 1968 – 1970; RODRIGUES 1974).

In 1926/27 a chapel, in which services could be held, a hospital/sanatorium, two shops selling devotional articles, a guest-house and a hotel were built among other things in the area around the sanctuary. Work on the present Basilica was begun in 1928, and completed in 1953. In the period between 1926 and 1947 numerous huts, mostly made out of wood, grew up in the immediate vicinity of the sanctuary giving the surroundings a very temporary appearance for decades (GIRÃO 1958; OLIVIERA 1968 – 1970, RODRIGUES 1974).

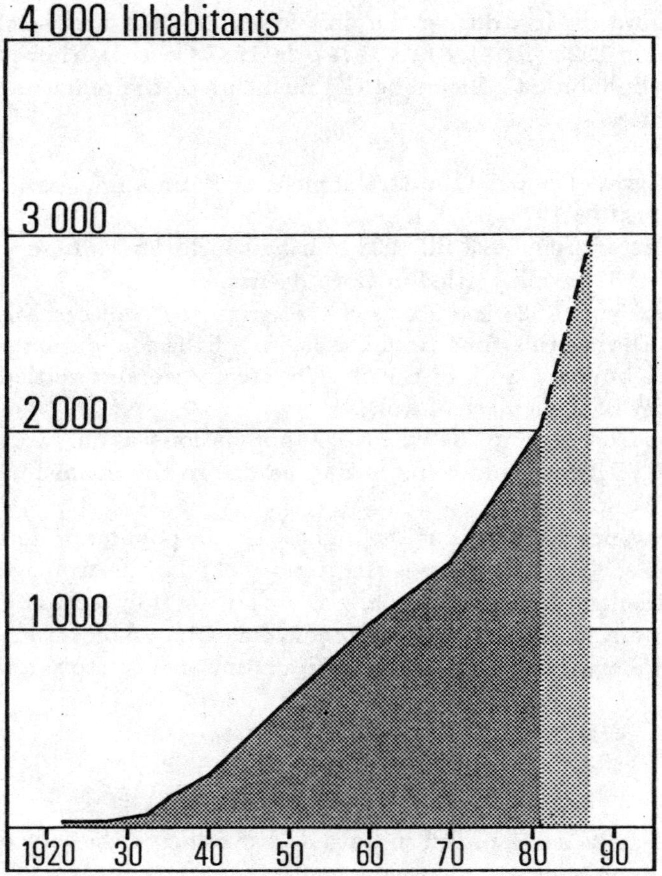

Fig. 13: Population development in Cova da Iria 1917 – 1987
Source: RODRIGUES 1974; information from the "SEPE", Fátima 1987

Thus in 1948 Cova da Iria still consisted of a small collection of buildings on both sides of the sanctuary. Although the temporary buildings predominated, there were already 52 permanent residential buildings, which served at the same time as home and business premises, and also for the overnight stay of pilgrims (Fig. 14).

For this reason, during the course of the initial decades various blue prints (1929/30, 1944, 1948) were drawn up for the planned building-up of the sanctuary, the immediate surrounding area and the whole of Cova da Iria (OLIVIERA 1968 – 1970; RODRIGUES 1974). The present Cova da Iria is basically organized according to the last plan of 1948. The details of this plan provide for a 800 m x 400 m precinct of the sanctuary (Recinto de Santuário) within which private buildings are forbidden. There is also an extended protected area, within which authorization from the local authority, Vila Nova de Ourém, must be obtained for private building projects, and the possible expropriation of private properties if necessary for the construction of roads. In addition to the older direct accesses to the sanctuary — the Rua Jacinta Marto in the west and the Rua Francisco Marto in the east — two new spacious by-passes were built — the Avenida Beato Nuño in the north and the Avenida Papa João XXIII in the south, as well as the main access via the Avenida Dom José Alves Correia da Silva, which borders directly south onto the sanctuary. In the west and east these roads meet in the two round squares known as the "Rotundas"; which give the Cova da Iria road network its striking character.

Cova da Iria has until now developed in westerly and easterly directions beyond the two rotundas, but especially in a northerly direction to the villages of Moita Redonda and Lomba de Égua. While within the protected area — apart from the main shopping streets — mostly religious and public buildings have emerged, construction for private settlement has been directed to the outskirts. So both villages Moita Redonda and Lomba de Égua are now to be regarded as part of the urban area of Cova da Iria, due to their proximity and settlement development.

Meanwhile, on the 19th of August 1977, due to the influx of pilgrims, Fátima was elevated to a town, consisting of the villages of Fátima, Cova da Iria, Aljustrel, Lomba de Égua, Moita Redonda and Lagoa da Carreira.

IV. Influence of the Pilgrims on Land-use Patterns

The various activities of the pilgrims have many different spatial effects on the place of pilgrimage. Religious activities cluster at specific religious sites, overnight accommodation and catering needs give rise to restaurant and accommodation facilities and purchasing activities result in a dense network of shops selling devotional articles.

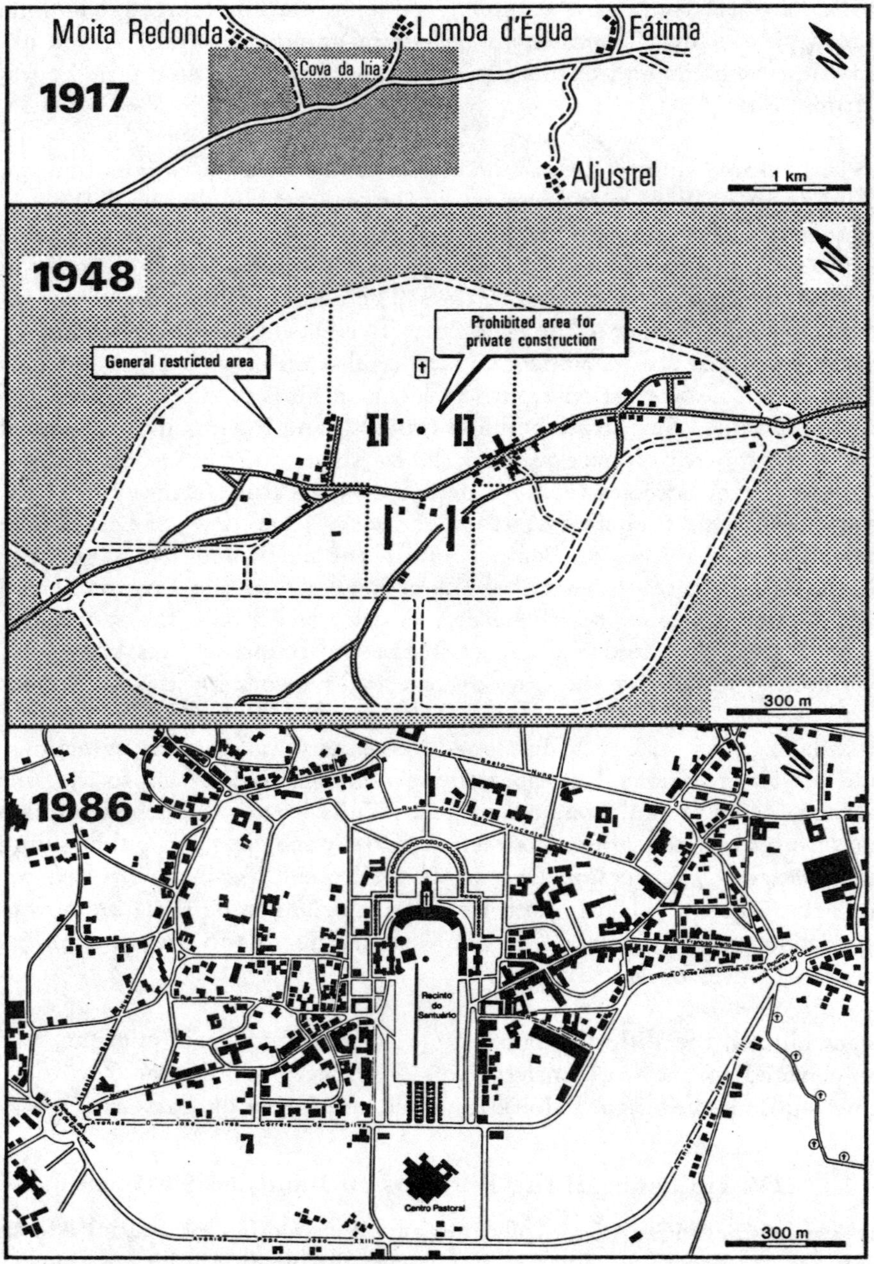

Fig. 14: Settlement development in Cova da Iria 1917, 1948 and 1986
Source: OLIVIERA 1986, p. 27; RODRIGUES 1974, p. 57;
author's mapping 1985/86

1. Religious Sites

The religious activities of the pilgrims have been concentrated from the beginning on those sites where the three shepherd children witnessed the apparitions of the Virgin Mary between May and October. These places are: the present religious center in Cova da Iria and the area around Valinhos in their home village of Aljustrel. The sites of the angel apparitions (Loca do Cabeco or Loca do Anjo and the well behind Lucia's house, Poço do Anjo) and both the parental homes of Jacinta and Francisco Marto and of Lucia Santo in Aljustrel are however also visited by pilgrims.

The *Religious Center* is the area of the shrine (Recinto do Santuário) in Cova da Iria with the rosary-basilica, the stations of the cross under the columns, the apparition chapel, the holm oak and the fountain in the middle of the forecourt. In addition to these holy places there are on both sides of the big forecourt a hospital building, a building for the spiritual exercises of two religious orders and a few administration buildings. On the other side of the main access road to the south there is also the "Pastoral Centre of Paul VI" which was officially opened by Pope John Paul II in 1982 (Fig. 15).

Ajustrel, 2 km east of the sanctuary, constitutes a nearby religious center of secondary importance. Here can be found: the parental homes of the three shepherd children, the angel's well Poço do Anjo, a group of statues on a hill known as "Loco do Anjo", where the first angel apparition occured and most importantly, Valhinos with a monument to the Virgin Mary, where the fourth apparition of the Virgin Mary occured. In the immediate vicinity of Valhinos is a Hungarian Way of the Cross with St Stephen's chapel, which was erected in 1964 by Hungarian refugees in memory of Cardinal Mindszenty. In the main village of Fátima the parish church in which the three shepherd children were christened can also be visited.

The cloisters and seminaries of 52 different religious institutions are also to be counted among the religious places: 37 female orders and 15 male orders. The first religious communities settled directly on the land on both sides of the fourecourt (Irmãs Reparadoras de N.a Senhora das Dores/1934 and Irmãs Servas de Nossa Senhora de Fátima/1937). After them followed the Dominicans (1937), the Carmelites (1939), the Conceptionists (1942) and the Irmãs Doroteias (1945). Most of the religious communities from abroad settled in Fátima after the Second World War, but particularly after the Holy Year (1951). They established houses for novices, homes for old people, schools, kindergartens and above all different accommodation facilities, such as their own guest-houses and hotels (OLIVIERA 1969, p. 24; RODRIGUES 1974, p. 58 ff).

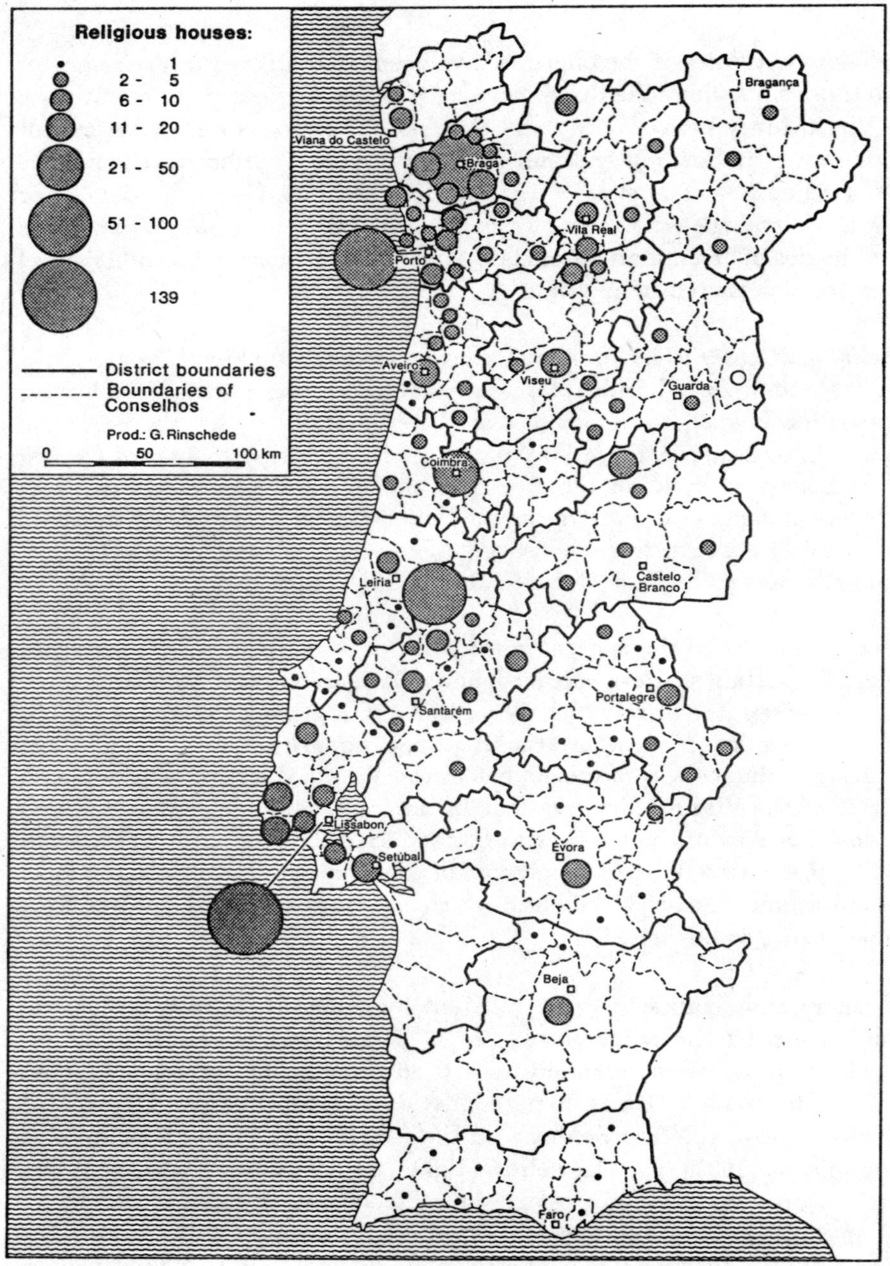

Fig. 16: Religious houses (Institutos Religiosos) in the Conselhos/Portugal 1986
Source: According to statistics in "Anuário Catolico de Portugal 1986 e 1987", Braga 1986

The religious institutions take up an area in Fátima which, apart from a few exceptions, stretches in a 300 to 500 m wide semi-circular band westwards, northwards and eastwards from the "Recinto do Santuário" and extends to the edge of the village centers of Moita Redonda and Lomba de Égua. The area of private development begins only outside this semi-circle.

Fifty years after the settling of the first order in Portugal, Fátima occupies a leading position, with a concentration of 52 religious institutions. After the old episcopal towns of Lisbon (139), Porto (87) and Braga (54), which constitute a particular attraction for religious cloister communities, Fátima now occupies an important fourth position before Coimbra (30) (Fig. 16).

2. Restaurants and Accommodation Facilities

In places of pilgrimage which receive visitors for more than a day, various kinds of accommodations, eating facilities and related amenities must be provided. Particularly when the stream of visitors is concentrated on specified jubilee days — such as is the case in Fátima on the 12th/13th of each month from May to October — several hundred thousand to a million people have to be supplied with food and accommodation.

a) Camping and Picnic Sites (Fig. 17)

Overnight stays in the open and self-catering represent traditionally the most important possibilities of accommodation and supplies for pilgrims in Fátima. This is because hotel and restaurant trade developed only during the course of the last decades, and during peak times can accommodate only a small percentage of the pilgrims.

Today as before the pilgrims spend the night as near as possible to the sanctuary, among specifically set-up car parks in the northern vicinity of the sanctuary and near the south-bordering "Centro Pastoral Paulo VI", under trees, on the side of the road, even under the columns and the entrance gates of various buildings of the sanctuary. Wrapped up in blankets and sleeping bags, people try to get through the night under canvas, in tents, cars or buses, in order to reach the first service next morning as quickly as possible. As a result of this, the sanctuary and its surrounding area give the impression of a Bedouin encampment on the major feast days of the year (12/13 May and 12/13 August).

b) Hotels, Guest-houses and Restaurants

In early years, the pilgrims had the option of spending the night either in the open, or in wooden huts, on easy terms. In 1929 the first hotel was built, called "Hotel de Madeira" because it was made totally of wood. Soon there after overnight accommodation facilities began to be offered to the pilgrims not only by further hotels and guest-houses, but also by some cafés and restaurants (RODRIGUES 1974, p. 135 ff). Today about 3,300 beds are available in Cova da Iria in 37 different hotels, guest-houses and restaurants (casas de pasto), as well as in some private houses (Fig. 17).

The densest concentration of hotels, restaurants and cafés is to be found in the southerly surroundings of the sanctuary, on the main access roads Rua Jacinta Marto and Rua Francisco Marto and on their south-bordering side-streets.

3. Religious Article Shops

In many places of pilgrimage, the selling of devotional objects and other souvenirs constitutes an important commercial activity and often determines the appearance of the streets leading to the shrine. In Fátima, the devotional objects were at first offered in temporary wooden huts, where food, drink and other articles could be bought at the same time. In addition about 300 itinerant traders came, mostly on feast days, until 1948, and plied their trade in the immediate vicinity of the sanctuary (RODRIGUES 1974, p. 59, 149 ff).

But when after 1948 the sanctuary and its surroundings began to be developed according to the plans of that time, these huts were forbidden and street trading declined. Instead, 90 small shops in the size of kiosks were put on sanctuary land for the selling of devotional articles. The first U-shaped building complex with 45 shops was built in 1950 in the Praceta de S. José and the second of the same building style in the Praceta de Santo Antonio. In addition to these simple shops, the sanctuary operates a religious article shop, on its own land in which religious literature is also sold.

The remaining shops selling devotional articles, mostly private are much bigger than the kiosk-shops of only a few square metres in size. They are concentrated on the main access roads Rua Jacinta Marto and Rua Francisco Marto, with increasing density near the sanctuary. Most hotels, guest- houses and some restaurants also have special trade stands at the entrance or in a separate annexe (Fig. 18).

The spatial influence of the pilgrims is more and more visible in the still rural surroundings of Aljustrel itself, the secondary religious center of Fátima.

This is because the pilgrims nowadays do not only reach the holy places on foot over the cross roads, but also by private car since the construction of car-parks, mostly over the Aljustrel country road. Meanwhile in the narrow activity space between the parental homes of the three shepherd children and the various places of the apparitions numerous religious article shops have sprung up, some of which sell food and drink as in the beginning at Cova da Iria. During the high season from May to October garages and other ground-floor rooms of houses here are emptied, temporary huts of corrugated iron and foliage are put up and courtyards are roofed over with canopies, so that here also in the less developed Aljustrel one can profit from the stream of pilgrims drifting through (Fig. 19).

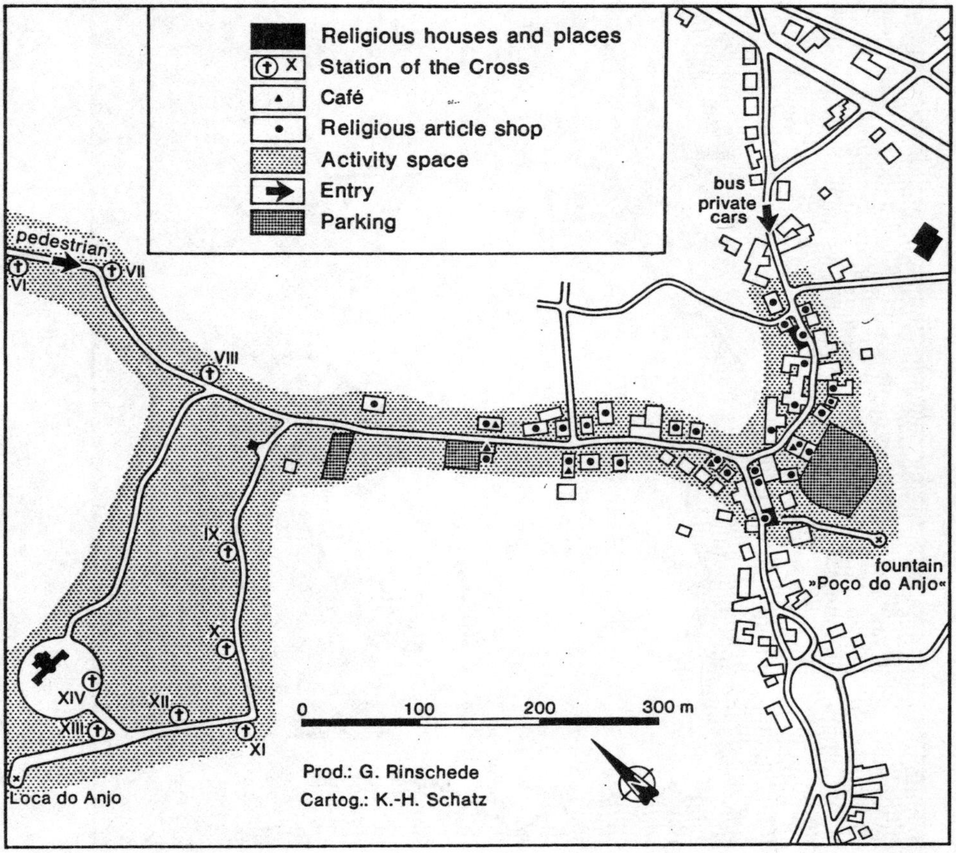

Fig. 19: Functions in Aljustrel/Fátima 1986
Source: Author's mapping Aug. 1986

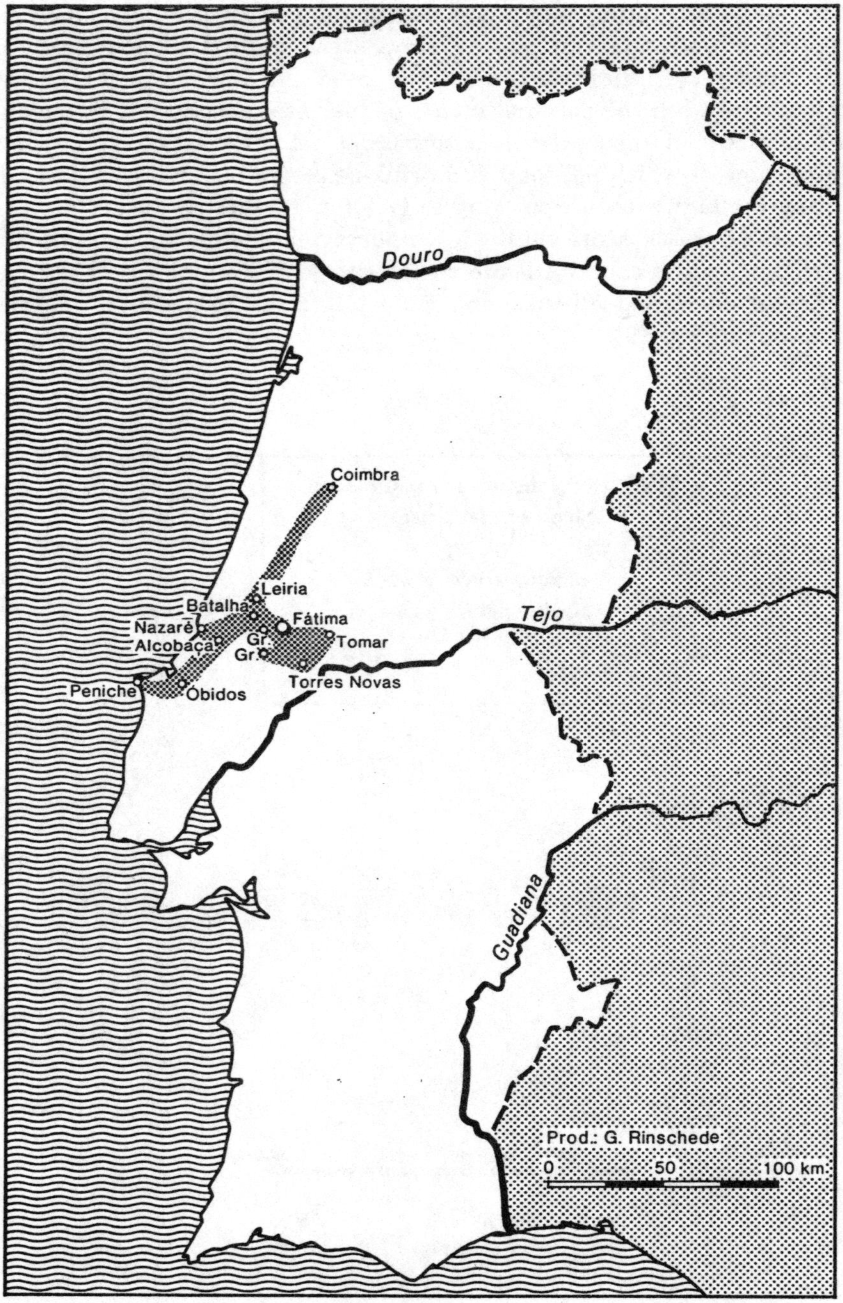

Fig. 20: Activity spaces of the pilgrim-tourists in the area surrounding Fátima 1986
Source: Author's investigation 1986

V. Tourist Activities and Activity Space of the Pilgrim-tourists

Visitors come to Fátima as pilgrims, pilgrim-tourists and tourists. Since it is not easy to differentiate between these types of visitors according to motivation and activities, it is even more difficult to give their exact proportion of the total number of visitors. Generally, however, it can be established in Fátima that the proportion of "pure" pilgrims is by far the largest, while the proportion of pilgrim-tourists is quite high and the proportion of "pure" tourists is very low.

Each of these types of visitors has not only a motivation particular to himself, but also his own activity space. Therefore, the activities of the pure *pilgrims* are limited to the holy places. This is usually because they have already often visited Fátima, maybe they make such a pilgrimage every year or even several times a year.

The *pilgrim-tourists* look for sights of different types on their way to Fátima, the actual destination of their journey, and on day trips in the surroundings of Fátima.
The proportionally small number of *tourists* can mostly be determined by their clothes. They visit Fatima as a rule on the way home from the beaches of Portugal. In the following I would like to examine the activities and activity spaces of the pilgrim-tourists in more detail.

First of all the holy places in Fátima are visited by these pilgrim- tourists, especially the religious center, the stations of the cross and the waxworks museum in Cova da Iria itself, as well as the native houses of the shepherd children, Valhinos and other places of apparitions in Aljustrel.

In addition, the pilgrim-tourists visit numerous sights starting from Fátima on half-day or day trips within an area of about 100 km (Fig. 20). Popular destinations are the caves of Moeda, Alvados, Mira de Aire and San Antonio, which were only discovered in the last forty years. Of nearly equal importance for the pilgrim-tourists are the visits to castles and castle ruins, as well as chapels, churches and cloisters, which constitute in part local and regional places of pilgrimage. Many of these pilgrimage places (Santuários) are situated in the northern part of Portugal where most of the religious houses (Fig. 16) are to be found, too (Fig. 21). Noteworthy among these are places like the episcopal town of Leiria, the episcopal and university town of Coimbra, Batalha, Porto de Mos, Milagres, Ourém and Vila Nova de Ourém. Finally, various fishing places with popular beaches are visited, such as Nazaré, São Pedro de Muel, Peniche, Pedrogão, Viera etc., as well as thermal baths in the coastal area, such as in Monte Real.

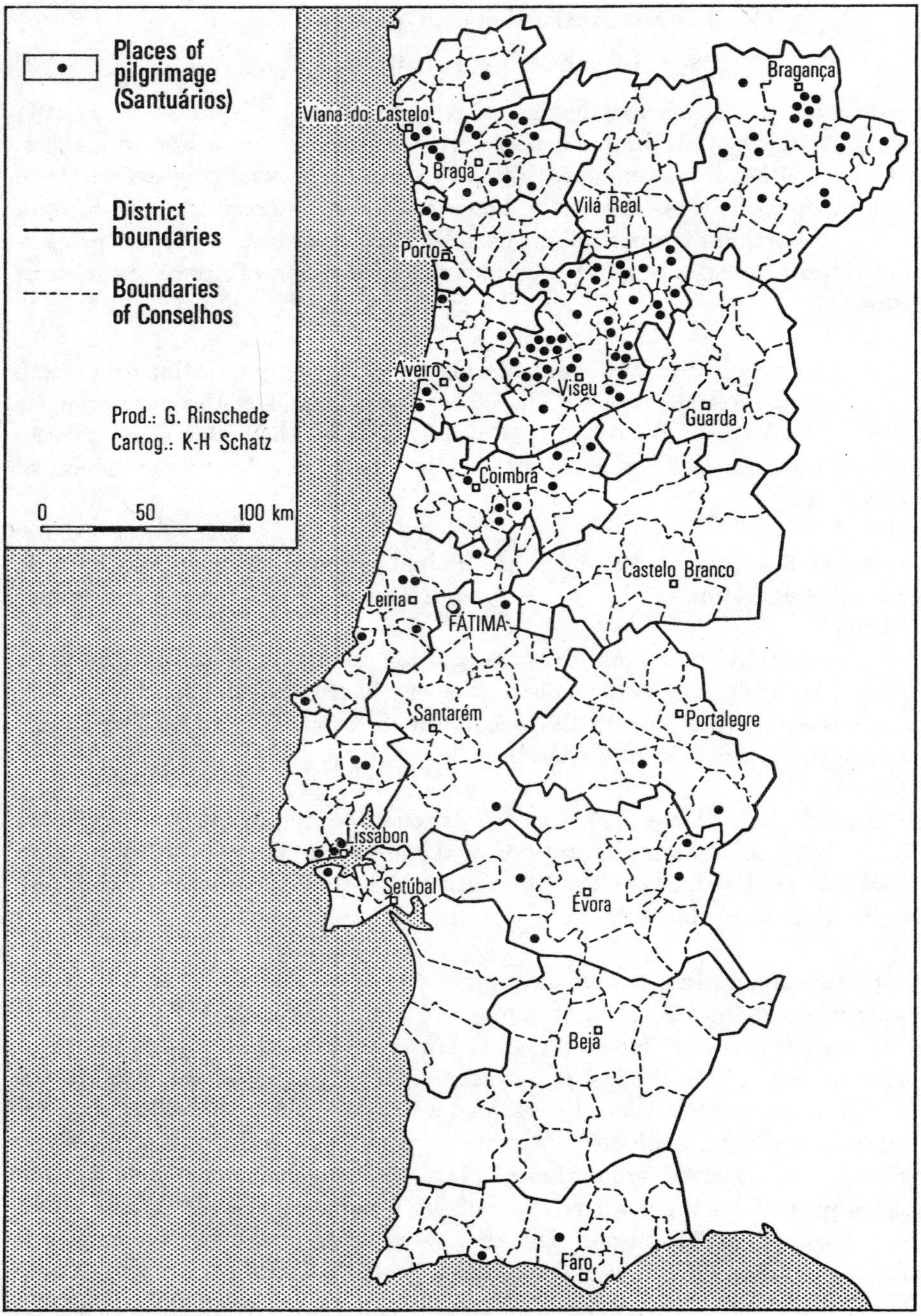

Fig. 21: Distribution of places of pilgrimage (Santuários) in Portugal 1986
Source: According to statistics in "Anuário Catolico de Portugal 1986 e 1987", Braga 1986

Pilgrim-tourists from abroad, some on their weeklong bus journeys, visit not only the capital Lisbon, Porto and some places in the Algarve, but also include in a sort of cultural sightseeing tour other towns in Spain, France and Italy. Places of pilgrimage are preferred, such as Santiago de Compostela, Guadalupe, Zaragoza, Montserrat and Torreciudad in Spain. Lourdes, La Salette and Lisieux in France, Rome, Assisi, Padua and Loreto in Italy, Maria Einsiedeln in Switzerland and for the last few years Medugorje in Yugoslavia, too.

Conclusion

Fátima is an example of those new Marian places of pilgrimage, which have developed in the most recent past after apparitions of the Virgin Mary and miracles. It therefore belongs to a series of places, together with the approximately 70 year older place of pilgrimage La Salette and the 60 year older Lourdes, both in France, as well as the most recent place of pilgrimage Medugorje in Yugoslavia, which was not visited before the first apparition in 1982. In La Salette two shepherd children experienced the apparitions of the Virgin Mary in 1846, in Lourdes a shepherd girl in 1858, in Fátima three shepherd children in 1917, and in Medugorje all together six children from 1982 to 1985.

All these places of pilgrimage have, like Fátima, developed into international places of pilgrimage. Although it took about 12 to 15 years until international groups of pilgrims first reached La Salette, Lourdes and Fátima, in Medugorje however, thanks to modern means of communication and transportation, hardly a year went by before the first group of pilgrims from abroad arrived.

The influence of the streams of pilgrims on population and settlement development are clearly recognizable in the above-mentioned places. In Fátima, as well as for example in La Salette, new settlements on open land developed at the places of the apparitions; they have religious sites of the most varied kind, hotels, restaurants and religious article shops. New places of pilgrimage such as Medugorje show the first signs of this development, which is favoured among other things by a tour of accessible religious sites and touristic sights, as well as through a convenient infra-structure and travel network. In Fátima these favourable factors are only present in part and are slowly being developed.

Summary

Apparitions of angels and the Virgin Mary in 1916/17 in Fátima/Portugal were the cause of a constantly swelling stream of pilgrims, which in 1987 comprised 3.6 million pilgrims from inland and from over 100 different countries in the world. According to the times of the apparitions, the pilgrim flow is characterized by a strong seasonality with largest numbers in the months of May to October, and particularly on the 13th of these months.

Several thousand pilgrims from the surrounding area even today reach Fátima on foot, and also by rail; however, by far the greatest number travel by car or bus.

The influence of the pilgrims is first of all visible in the population and settlement development of the present place Cova da Iria, which emerged from open fields and now has over 3,000 permanent inhabitants. Included among the religious places in the precincts of the sanctuary are the rosary-basilica, the stations of the cross under the columns, the apparition chapel, the holm oak, the great forecourt surrounded by administration buildings and a hospital, and the "Pastoral Center of Paul VI".

A secondary religious center is to be found in Aljustrel, 2 km east of the sanctuary. 52 different religious institutions added to the holy places by establishing among other things numerous cloisters, houses for novices, old peoples' homes, schools, kindergartens and accomodation of the most varied kind.

Because of the marked seasonality of the stream of pilgrims, the greatest part of the pilgrims spend the night in camping or picnic sites in the immediate vicinity of the sanctuary; some however stay in the numerous hotels and guesthouses. The religious article shops are concentrated on the main access roads, with increasing density near the sanctuary.

The activities of the pilgrims are not only restricted to the religious places in Fátima, but rather extend to the touristic sights in its vicinity. Pilgrims from abroad often visit Fátima as part of a tour of pilgrimage places in Portugal, Spain, France and Italy.

Zusammenfassung: Das Pilgerzentrum Fátima/Portugal

Engels- und Marienerscheinungen der Jahre 1916/17 in Fátima/Portugal waren der Anlaß für einen ständig ansteigenden Pilgerstrom, der im Jahr 1987 3.6 Mio. Pilger aus dem Inland und aus über 100 verschiedenen Staaten der Erde umfaßte. Den Erscheinungszeiten entsprechend ist der Pilgerstrom durch eine starke Saisonalität in den Monaten Mai — Oktober und besonders zum 13. eines jeden Monats gekennzeichnet.

Mehrere Tausend Pilger aus der Umgebung erreichen Fátima auch heute noch zu Fuß, aber auch mit der Eisenbahn, der weitaus größte Teil aber mit dem Pkw und Bus.

Der Einfluß der Pilger ist zunächst in der Bevölkerungs- und Siedlungsentwicklung des heutigen Ortes Cova da Iria sichtbar, der auf freier Feldflur entstanden ist und heute über 3000 ständige Einwohner verfügt. Zu den religiösen Stätten im Bereich des Santuários zählen die Rosenkranzbasilika, der Kreuzweg unter den Kolonnaden, die Erscheinungskapelle, die Steineiche, der von Verwaltungsgebäuden und einem Hospital umgebene große Vorplatz und das "Pastorale Zentrum Pauls VI.". Ein religiöses Nebenzentrum befindet sich in Aljustrel, 2 km östlich des Santuários. Zu den heiligen Stätten zählen 52 verschiedene religiöse Institutionen, die u. a. zahlreiche Klöster, Novizenhäuser, Altenheime, Schulen, Kindergärten und Unterkunftsmöglichkeiten verschiedenster Art errichtet haben.

Wegen der starken Saisonalität des Pilgerstroms nächtigt der größte Teil der Pilger auf Park- und Picknickplätzen in unmittelbarer Umgebung des Santuários, aber auch in zahlreichen Hotels und Pensionen. Die Devotionalienläden konzentrieren sich an den Hauptzugangsstraßen mit zunehmender Dichte in Nähe des Santuários.

Die Aktivitäten der Pilger beziehen sich nicht nur auf die religiösen Stätten in Fátima, sondern auch auf touristische Sehenswürdigkeiten in seiner Umgebung. Pilger aus dem Ausland besuchen Fátima häufig auf einer Rundreise zu anderen Pilgerstätten in Portugal, Spanien, Frankreich und Italien.

Bibliography

GIRÃO, Aristides de Amorim (1958): Fátima, Terra de Milagre (Ensaio de Geografia Religiosa). — Universidade de Coimbra, Faculdade de Lettras. — Coimbra.

JUNTA de Freguesia de Fátima (1978): Vila de Fátima. Fátima.

OLIVIERA, Francisco Pereira de (1968 – 1970): Para a História da Urbanização da Cova da Iria. — In: Fátima 50, no. 16 – 19, 21, 24, 28, 36. — Santuário de Fátima.

OLIVIERA, Francisco Pereira de (1970): A Urbanização da Fátima 50, No. 38 a. 39. Santuário de Fátima.

PEIRONE, Frederico (1970): Fátima: Nótulas de Geografia Humana. — In: Fátima 50, No. 33 a. 35. Santuário de Fátima.

REIS, Sebastião Martins dos (1967): Síntese Crítica de Fátima — Incidências e Repercussões. — In: Boletim Cultural da Junta Distrital de Lisboa. Série III, N.os 67 - 68, Lisboa pp. 5 - 187.

RINSCHEDE, Gisbert (1986): The Pilgrimage Town of Lourdes. — In: Journal of Cultural Geography, Vol. 7:1, Bowling Green, Ohio. pp. 21 - 34.

RINSCHEDE, Gisbert and Angelika SIEVERS (1987): The Pilgrimage Phenomenon in Socio-geographical Research. — In: The National Geographical Journal of India, Vol. 33, pt. 3, Sept., pp. 213 - 217.

RODRIGUES, Maria de Fátima Serafim (1974): Fátima — Problemas Geográficos de um Centro de Peregrinação. — Chorographia — Colecção de Estudos de Geografia Humana e Regional. — Lisboa.

RODRIGUES MAGALHÃES, Maria de Fátima Serafim (in press): População e desenvolvimento urbanístico. — In: Exposição Urbanística de Fátima.

ROSSI, Severo and Aventino de OLIVIERA (1982): Fátima — Missões Consolata. — Fátima.

Robert H. Stoddard

CHARACTERISTICS OF BUDDHIST PILGRIMAGES IN SRI LANKA

Although pilgrimages have been studied by geographers for many decades, we still are uncertain about the universality of certain basic geographic characteristics of this religious activity. It is true that NOLAN (1983; 1984; forthcoming) has provided a wealth of data on Christian pilgrimages, especially in Western Europe, and several geographers have analyzed aspects of the hajj.[1] But, there have been relatively few studies about groups in many other settings, such as the Muslems in the Philippines, the Christians in India, and the Hindus in Africa. We need to expand our collective knowledge about pilgrimages by studying them in a wide variety of cultural settings if we are to develop geographic generalizations about this distinctive form of religious behavior.

The goal of this paper is to provide more information about pilgrimages by examining three basic geographic questions as they pertain to Buddhist pilgrimages in Sri Lanka. Because answers to those questions are affected by inhering cultural conditions, this discussion commences with background information about the religious setting of Sri Lankan pilgrimages.

I. The Religious Setting

Almost 70 percent of the Sri Lankan population is Buddhist, according to the 1981 census (Table 1). Of the remainder, half is Hindu and a quarter each is Muslim and Christian. Generally the three religious groups are distinct ethnically and locationally.

Table 1: Religious Populations, Sri Lanka, 1981
Percentages

	Buddhist	Hindu	Muslim	Christian	Other
SRI LANKA	69.30	15.48	7.56	7.61	0.06
District					
Colombo	70.4	7.7	9.9	11.8	0.2
Gampala	71.1	1.9	3.5	23.4	0
Kalutara	84.3	4.5	7.6	3.6	0
Kandy	73.6	12.7	11.1	2.6	0
Matale	78.6	11.6	7.3	2.4	0
Nuwara Eliya	41.6	50.3	2.5	5.6	0
Galle	94.2	1.9	3.2	0.6	0.1
Matara	94.6	2.4	2.6	0.4	0
Hambantota	97.1*	0.5#	2.2	0.2#	0
Jaffna	0.6#	85.0*	1.8#	12.6	0
Mannar	3.2	27.2	27.4	42.1*	0.1
Vavuniya	16.5	68.7	7.1	7.7	0
Mullaitivu	1.4	77.9	4.9	15.8	0
Batticaloa	2.8	66.2	23.9	7.1	0
Amparai	37.5	18.7	41.7*	2.1	0.1
Trincomalee	32.3	31.6	29.9	6.1	0.2
Kurunegala	90.1	1.2	5.3	3.3	0
Puttalam	48.0	3.9	10.2	38.9	0.1
Anuradhapura	90.1	1.2	7.3	1.3	0
Polonnaruwa	90.1	1.8	6.5	1.5	0
Badulla	68.8	24.3	4.6	2.3	0
Moneragala	92.7	4.7	2.0	0.6	0
Ratnapura	84.8	11.6	2.0	1.7	0
Kegalle	85.2	7.9	5.2	1.7	0

* = District with highest percentage per column
\# = District with lowest percentage per column

Source: Sri Lankan Department of Census and Statistics, 1981

1. Distributions of Religious Groups

Not only are Buddhists the religious majority, but they are mostly members of the dominant ethnic group: the Sinhalese. Similarly, according to 1946 census data, the Sinhalese are generally Buddhists (Table 2, A). Consequently, it is not surprising that these two characteristics display a high degree of areal correlation, as measured by a rank correlation at the district scale (Table 2, B). Likewise, the distributions of ethnicity and religious affiliation by districts display a high degree of similarity (Fig. 1 and 2).

Table 2: Religious Affiliations by Ethnic Group

A. Percentages per Ethnic Group, 1946

Ethnic Group	Buddhist	Hindu	Muslim	Christian
Sinhalese, Low Country	88			11.9
Sinhalese, Kandyan	99			
Tamils, Sri Lankan		80.6		16.5
Tamils, Indian		89.3		
Moors, Sri Lankan			99	
Moors, Indian			95	
Malays			92	
Burghers				96

B. Rank Correlation for 24 Districts, 1981

Ethnic Group	Buddhist	Hindu	Muslim	Christian
Sinhalese	.96			-.67
Tamils		.99		.62
Moors			.99	.40

Sources: Sri Lankan Department of Census and Statistics, 1981, and author

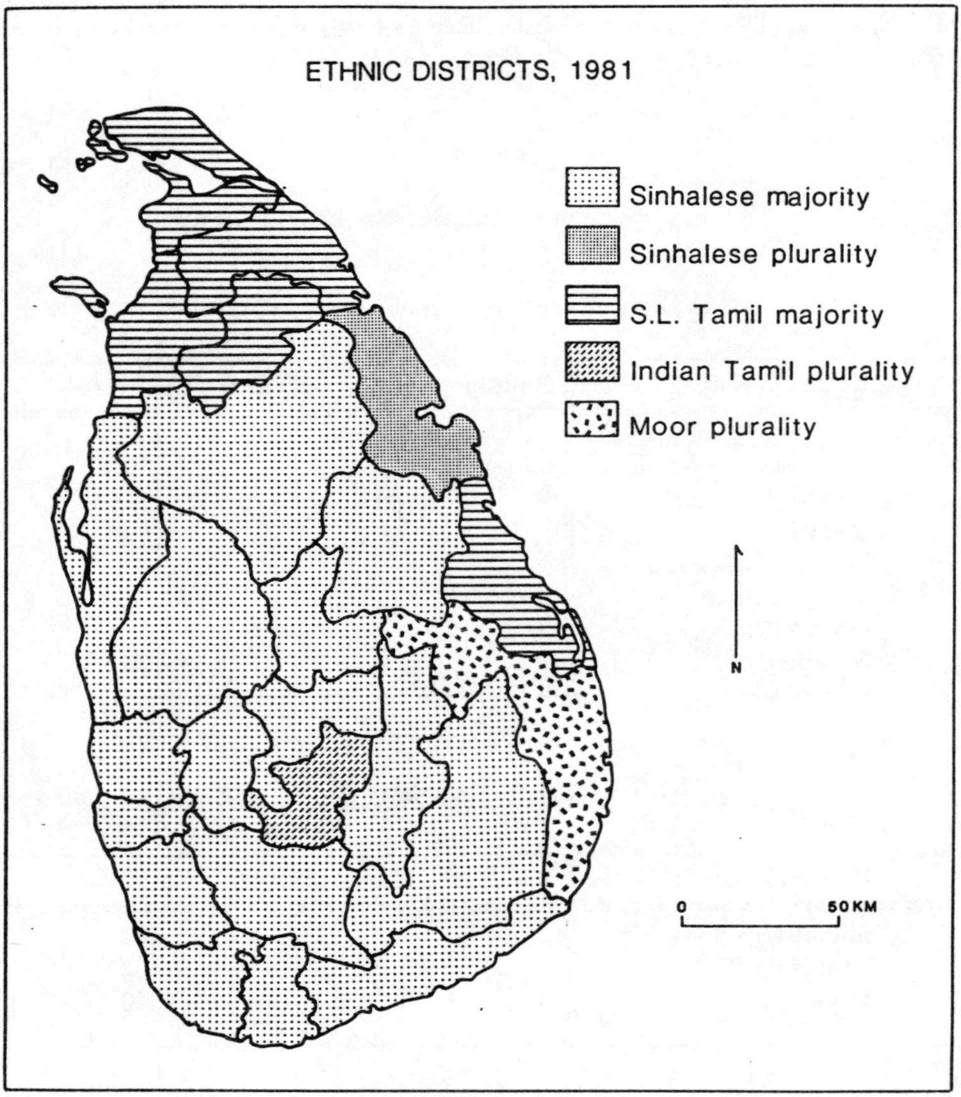

Fig. 1: Ethnic Districts, 1981
Source: Sri Lankan Department of Census and Statistics, 1981.

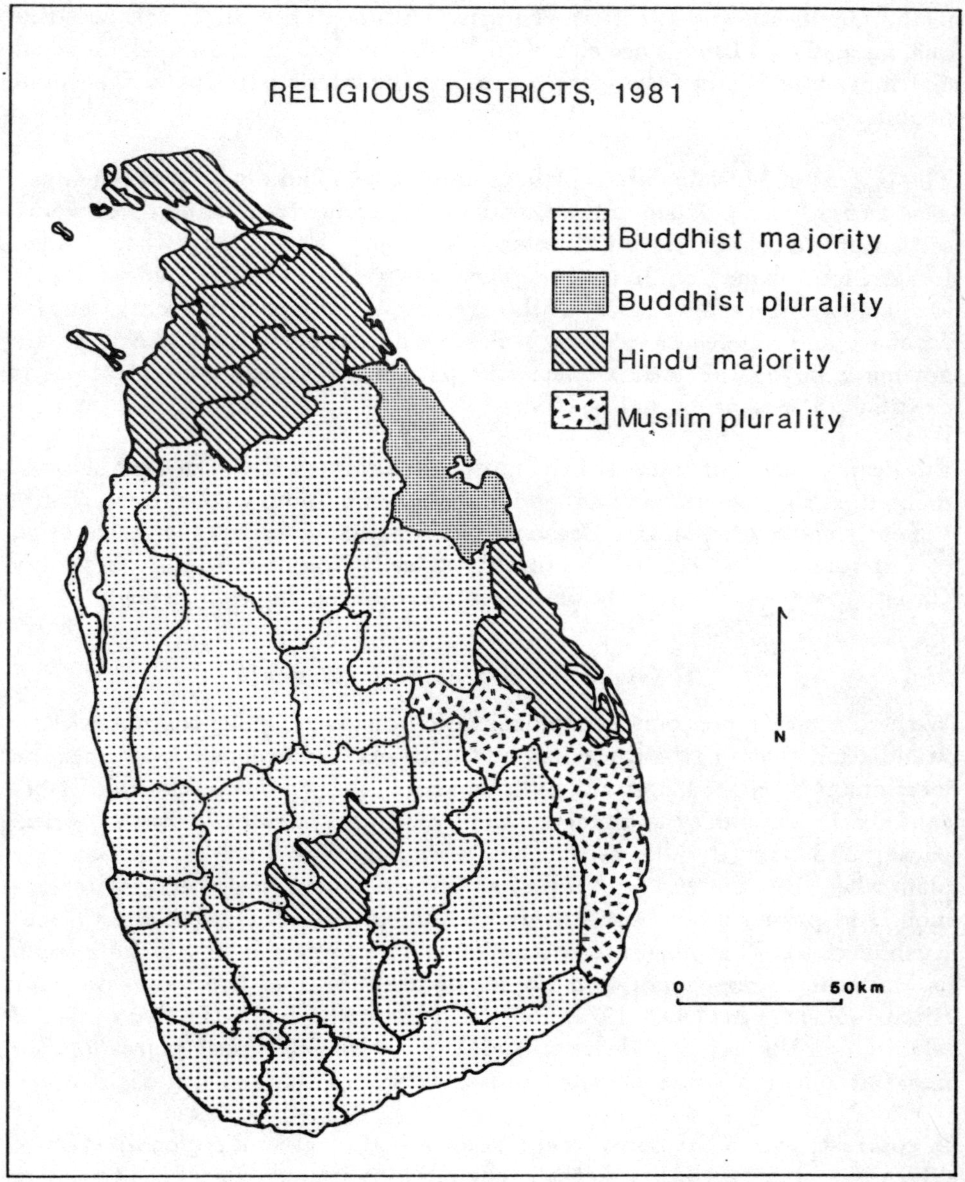

Fig. 2: Religious Districts, 1981
Source: Sri Lankan Department of Census and Statistics, 1981.

Hindus are primarily Tamils, which includes the two groups classified as Sri Lankan Tamils and Indian Tamils (Table 2, A). The ancestors of the first group probably came to the island in the second century B. C., while those of the second category were brought into the country to work in colonial plantations in the nineteenth and twentieth centuries. Although not all Tamils are Hindus, virtually all Hindus are either Sri Lankan or Indian Tamils. The spatial distribution of Hindus, therefore, resembles the ethnic patterns of the Tamil population.

The origins of Muslems are a little more diverse. Those who were classified once as Sri Lankan Moors are descendants of Arabic traders, many of whom settled in the country during the eleventh century. Even though the so-called Indian Moors came from India, their ancestors were also Arabic traders. Other Muslems are the ethnic Malays, who are descendants of seventeenth century Javanese and nineteenth century Malayans. However, these distinctions are not made in the 1981 census; thus, the pattern of Muslem concentrations is essentially the same as that of Moors.

Ethnically, the Christians in Sri Lanka are Burghers (the Eurasian descendants from the colonial periods) and Sinhalese and Tamil who converted since the early sixteenth century. Because of this ethnic diversity, the distribution of Christians is less related to ethnicity than the other religions. Generally Christian populations tend to be concentrated along the western coast.

2. General Pilgrimage Patterns

With this rather pronounced regionalization of the religious communities, it would seem that pilgrimage places and patterns of movement would also be locationally separated. Certainly pilgrimages to foreign destinations differ because each community is attracted to places important to its own historical background. For Buddhists, the four most holy places are in the Gangetic plain where Buddha was born, attained Enlightenment, preached his first sermon, and passed away (respectively at Lumbini, Bodh Gaya, Sarnath, and Kushinagara). Pilgrimages to the major Saivite centers in south India (such as Madurai, Rameswaram, and Chidambaram) are considered obligatory for Hindus (PATHMANATHAN 1979, 150). Muslems who fulfill the five duties of Islam go on the hajj (to Mecca). And, the foreign pilgrimage places for Roman Catholics are Rome, Lourdes, and other famous Marian shrines in Europe.

In contrast, within Sri Lanka there is not a high degree of regionalization of pilgrimage places according to their religious associations. There is a tendency for Buddhist pilgrimage places to be in the central portion of the island, for Hindu sacred sites to be along the northern and eastern coasts, and for Christian holy places to be along the west coast; but there are numerous exceptions to these generalities.[2] Furthermore, some sacred places are actually the common destination for pilgrims of different religions. For example, pilgrims from all four faiths go to the mountain top called Sri Pada or Adam's Peak. Likewise, Muslems and a few Christians, as well as the predominant Buddhists and Hindus, journey to Kataragama. Also, some Hindus, Muslems, and Buddhists join the multitude of Christian pilgrims at Kocchikade.

Obviously generalizations about the distributions of pilgrimage places lack precision because it is difficult to specify which sites properly belong in the defined set. Lacking data on pilgrimage travel and lacking an objective definition of what constitutes a "pilgrimage," it is impossible to specify exactly which places constitute "the set" of pilgrimage places in Sri Lanka. Nevertheless, because this paper deals with aspects of Buddhist pilgrimages, an attempt is made to identify the major destinations for pilgrims who are Buddhists.

3. Buddhist Pilgrimage Places (Fig. 3)

One procedure for identifying major pilgrimage places is to look for agreement among previous enumerations. For this paper, five sources were consulted. One list, prepared by the Sri Lankan Department of Buddhist Affairs (1986), contains all the places offficially designated as "sacred areas and sites" (Table 3). The other lists were obtained from the writings of De Silva (1980, 240 – 242), Gombrich (1971, 108 – 110), Kekulawala (1979, 54 – 63), and Sievers (1985, 265). As indicated by Table 3, all of the places listed by De Silva were also identified as important by two or more other sources; therefore, in this paper these ten places are regarded as the major pilgrimage destinations (Fig. 3). It should be noted that several sites are considered especially sacred within the Anuradhapura area; but at this map scale they are not displayed individually so the total number of pilgrimage places does not appear to sum to the "sixteen great places" or *solos mahasthana* (De Silva 1980; Gombrich 1971, 109; Kekuawala 1979, 61).

It is within this religious context that three questions about the geographic characteristics of Buddhist pilgrimages are posed: (1) Is the relationship between number of pilgrims to a site and the distances they travel similar to the distance decay associated with other types of nodal places? (2) Do patterns of pilgrimage movement change with time? (3) Does the nature of pilgrimage create greater social interaction among participants than assemblages at other nodal centers?

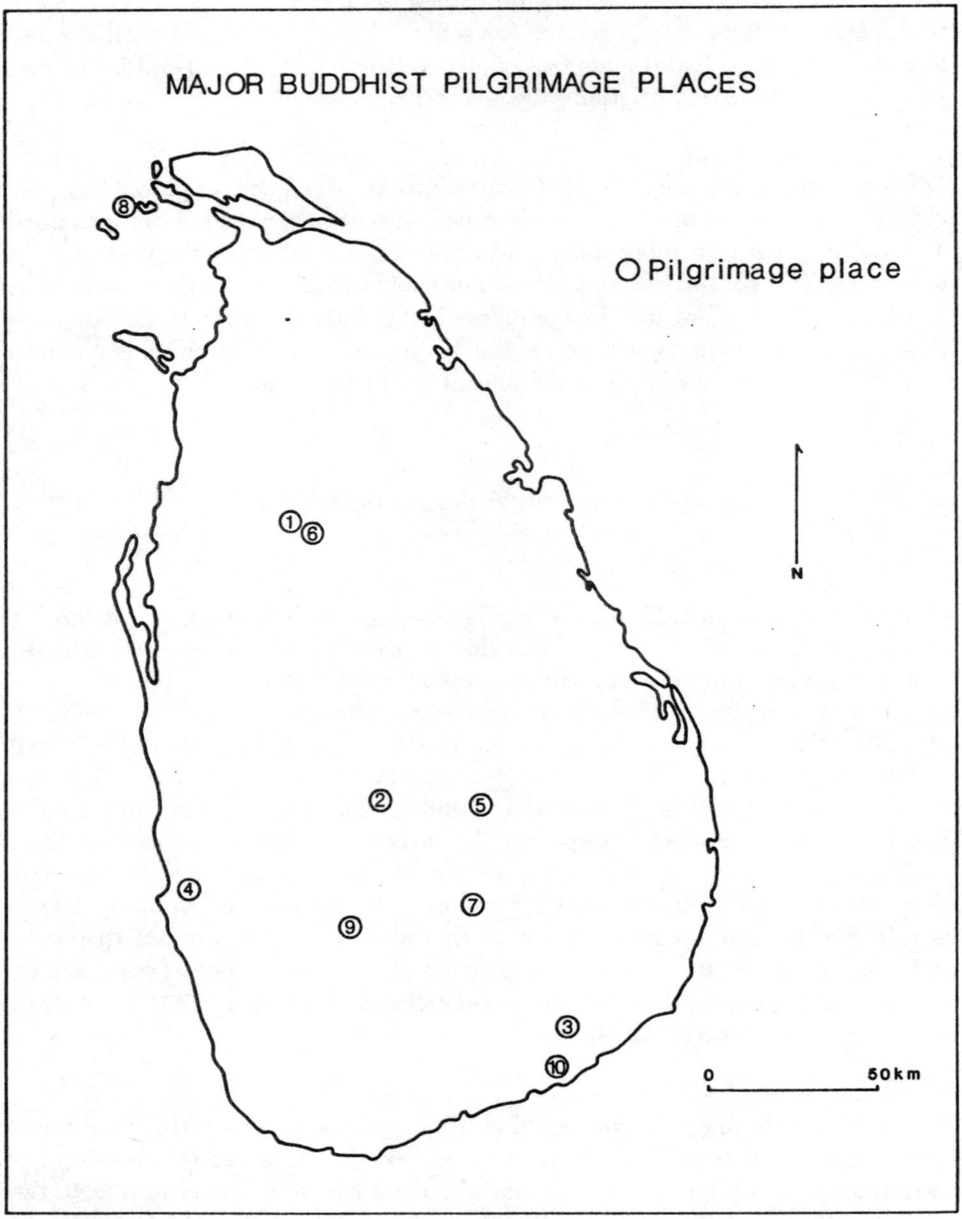

Fig. 3: Major Buddhist Pilgrimage Places
Source: See Table 3.

Table 3: Buddhist Pilgrimage Place Listed (X) by Indicated Author

Name and Location	B. A.	dS.	G	K.	S.	No. on Fig. 3
Alu Vihara	X					
Anuradhapura	X	X	X	X	XX*	1
Aukana					X	
Dambulla	X					
Dantadhata, Kandy	X	X		X	X	2
Devanagala	X					
Devinuwara	X				X	
Dighavapi			X		XX	
Dimbulagala	X					
Embekke					X	
Ethkanda, Kurunegala	X					
Kalutara bodhi	X					
Kataragama	X	X	X		XX	3
Kelaniya	X	X	X	X	XX	4
Mahiyangana	X	X	X	X	XX	5
Mangalama, Seruwawila				X		
Mihintale	X	X	X	X	XX	6
Muthiyangana	X	X	X		XX	7
Nagadipa		X	X	X	XX	8
Polonnaruwa	X				X	
Rajamaha, Kotte	X					
Saman Devale, Ratnapura	X					
Shankhapala, Pallebedda	X					
Sri Pada		X	X	X	XX	9
Tissamaharamaya	X	X	X		X	10
Vijayasunderamaya, Dambadeniya	X					

*XX = Top category (by SIEVERS)

Sources:
B.A. = Department of Buddhist Affairs, 1986
dS. = DE SILVA, 1980
G. = GOMBRICH, 1971
K. = KEKULAWALA, 1979
S. = SIEVERS, 1985

II. The Role of Distance in Pilgrimages

The first question concerns the number of pilgrims that travel various distances. If pilgrimage behavior is similar to movement to other types of nodal places, then the relationship between the number of travelers and length of trip should display a distance decay. There are indications, however, that in certain circumstances the aggregate behavior of pilgrims may not match this fundamental geographic relationship. This is because, for some pilgrims, the purpose of travel is not merely to arrive at the sacred destination; the journey itself is an act of worship. The merits of pilgrimage are increased by enduring the sacrifices encountered over long distances, especially when accomplished on foot.[3] Unfortunately, the extent to which such a sacrificial element affects pilgrimages in general is not known.

Does pilgrimage behavior of Buddhists in Sri Lanka contrast with that of travelers to other kinds of centers? An easy answer is unattainable because of the lack of quantitative data. Nevertheless, an answer is partly provided by examining the purpose for going on a Buddhist pilgrimage.

Basically, a Theravada Buddhist undertakes a pilgrimage as a part of what can be termed "going to worship" (*vandanave yama*). Worshipping involves making an offering to the Buddha at a dagoba, at a bodhi tree, and/or in a room containing a statue of the Buddha. Because a dagoba (or stupa) contains a physical relic of the Buddha, worship at such a place is felt to be equivalent to honoring the living Buddha and, therefore, especially meritorious (KEKULAWALA 1979, 44). From the Buddhist perspective, several of the holiest places in the country are the sites of ancient dagobas.

The bodhi tree also has a high level of sanctity because it is associated with the Buddha's attaining Enlightenment. Since it is believed that the Maha Bodhi at Anuradhapura is a branch brought from the original tree at Bodh Gaya, it is especially sacred.

No temple is without a statue or image of Buddha; therefore, a temple per se tends to be less distinct and have less attraction than a dagoba or bodhi tree. Nevertheless, the famous unenclosed Samadhi in Anuradhapura and, to a lesser degree, the large Avukana statue are highly revered.

For many Buddhists, worshipping at these sacred places may require their traveling a considerable distance because major sites may not be located near their homes. The reason for making such a trip, therefore, is merely to move from the place of residence to the site where one or more sacred objects are located. Nevertheless, as stated above, such travel is called a pilgrimage because the term is equated with "going to worship."

It is important to note that the trip itself is usually not considered part of an act of worship. And normally the route constitutes the most direct connection — in other words, not necessarily along a path regarded as a sacred way (STODDARD 1979/80; TANAKA 1977). One exception to this generalization might be the trail and flights of stairs leading to Sri Pada. Likewise, although increasing the distance or hardship of travel is not a major objective for most pilgrims to Kataragama, some regard walking the final kilometers as more meritorious than driving the entire way (CARTMAN 1957, 114). Also, when devout travelers pass the Kalutara bodhi tree, they will stop a few minutes to honor the Buddha and leave a donation; but, in contrast, local residents do not necessarily stop each time they go by the sacred site during their routine activities. This contrast implies that distance (and infrequency) does, indeed, make the occasion more special.

In spite of these situations implying some merit in sacrificial travel, generally the purpose of Buddhist pilgrimages in Sri Lanka is not to engage in a type of worship involving movement per se. Instead, the reason for travel is to arrive at the sacred destination in much the same manner as trips to other nodal places. Consequently, the aggregate flow of pilgrims undoubtedly displays the distance decay function. In fact, such a relationship has been reported for Theravada Buddhist pilgrimages elsewhere (as cited by PREUSS 1974, 166, for Thailand).

III. Changes in the Nodal Regions of Pilgrimages

If pilgrimages are regarded as similar to trips taken to other kinds of nodal centers, then another question arises: Do patterns of pilgrimage movement change with time? We know that, with changes in communication and transportation, the size and relative importance of many kinds of nodal regions and centers have undergone modifications. For example, in many regions of the world, the relative economic importance of small trade centers has declined as big cities have become more attractive. This, in turn, has altered the hierarchical relationships among trade centers and their associated nodal regions. Is the same kind of change occurring among pilgrimage sites and their holy hinterlands?

On the one hand, it can be argued that, because the sanctity of many sites is based on their historic association with the Buddha, their importance would remain constant through time. Although the total number of pilgrims attracted to various sites might increase through time (because of a larger Buddhist population and a more accessible transportation system), the relative sizes of pilgrimages to various centers would not necessarily change.

On the other hand, some places, such as Kataragama, have become increasingly popular in recent decades (WIRTZ 1966). Such changes may result partly from the reinforcing nature of attractiveness. As certain places attract more pilgrims than others, the more popular ones then may be regarded as more important and, hence, attract even greater numbers of worshippers. More extensive communication networks, as well as improved transportation facilities, would facilitate the growing popularity of special places. In other words, a differential growth of pilgrimages to various sacred places would be very similar to the uneven attractiveness of nodal centers in economic, political, and other non-religious systems.

There are indications, however, that sometimes popularity may diminish the sanctity of a place and hence its religious attractiveness. This relationship between popularity and attractiveness seems to be illustrated by the decrease in the number of pilgrims to a suddenly popular rural (mainly Christian) shrine. In the early 1970s, a Catholic shrine in the small village of Devagama began attracting increasing numbers of pilgrims; but after 1975, the sizes of pilgrimages diminished. Although he speculates about several contributing factors for this decline, STIRRAT (1979, 100) reports that the commercialization associated with the masses of pilgrims had a negative effect on some "devoted" pilgrims. They felt the popularization of the place diminished its sanctity, so they were less inclined to visit the place than previously.

To definitively answer this question about changes in pilgrimage regions would require a tremendous amount of information about origins and destinations of pilgrims for both contemporary and historical times. Such data are not available; and, therefore, conclusions based on objective measurements are also impossible.

Furthermore, even if origin-destination data were collected, the lack of a standard definition of "pilgrimage" would complicate analyses. As an illustration, consider all the persons who travel along the coastal highway southwards from Colombo and who break their journey briefly to worship at the Kalutara bodhi tree. If each such worshipping traveler is defined as a pilgrim, then undoubtedly this site has a larger religious hinterland now than 50 years ago, both in absolute numbers and in comparison with local temples. In contrast, if a definition of a pilgrim excludes persons who merely "visit" a sacred site while on a multiple-purpose trip, then the number of "true" pilgrims to the Kalutara bodhi tree may not have changed much.

In spite of an imprecise definition and the lack of quantitative data, there is a general sense that the major sacred sites in Sri Lanka now attract more pilgrims from longer distances than they did previously. This shift in flow patterns results primarily from the diminished friction of distance, but it probably relates also to other factors. The increase in mass communication has popularized events that were little known in remote villages several decades ago. In addition, people now think in terms of larger units of areal organization for economic, social, and political institutions. WINSLOW (1982, 199), in her regional analysis of Buddhism in Sri Lanka, summarized the changes by declaring that the shift from local organizations to extra-village centers did not necessarily mean the decline of village activities; but their characteristics were altered as regional and national centers became the foci for economic and political organizations. It appears that the same kind of modifications are occurring among the nodal regions of pilgrimages.

IV. Pilgrimages as a Unifying Force

The third question raised here is this: Does the nature of pilgrimage create greater social interaction among participants than assemblages at other nodal centers? According to TURNER (1973, 194), pilgrims leave the hierarchical social relationships of their structured society and enter into a normative communitas that encourages social interaction among participants. Enroute and at a sacred site, pilgrims enjoy an unstructured and undifferentiated community of equal persons.

In his study of Theravada Buddhist pilgrimages in Thailand, however, PREUSS (1974) did not find such a transformation in social relations. He states (204 & 205):

In spite of the spirit of 'brotherhood' recognized and encouraged by shrine monks and custodians, the residues of social structure still remain ... These aspects of structure refer to status differences in the secular realm which are symbolically validated within the religious context of an assembly of Buddhist devotees ... While these groups of devotees may be temporarily united spatially (and perhaps emotionally) during the mass veneration of the sacred object, in general there is no social mixing between groups or between pilgrims of different regional and economic backgrounds.

In Sri Lanka, WINSLOW (1982, 193 – 199) came to a similar conclusion. She noted that participants who travel as a group may gain internal unity, but this does not apply to interaction between groups. In fact, when members of different religions go to the same site, they may experience more divisiveness — partly because of the conflict in use of the site.

One of the geographic implications of these observations is that pilgrimages may not generate any more feelings of unity and equality among participants than, for example, hikers at a scenic spot, music-lovers at an operatic performance, or academicians at a national meeting. In other words, the social interactions of pilgrims may not be much different from those of other travelers assembled at a center because of a common interest.

It should be noted that these results come from the impressions of two Western scholars and are not based on detailed data concerning the amount and type of social relationships among pilgrims in Sri Lanka. This conclusion about the lack of greater social interaction among pilgrims than travelers to other nodal centers, therefore, should be regarded as only tentative.

V. Conclusions

The topic of pilgrimage is fascinating for geographic study because the spatial behavior of some participants does differ from many other kinds of human activities. One difference is that pilgrims in certain circumstances do not attempt to minimize distance, as assumed by the least-effort principle. Some pilgrims prefer longer and more arduous journeys rather than shorter and faster routes. Likewise, pilgrimages that resemble long circumambulations around sacred areas involve movement as a form of worship rather than merely a necessity for getting from one location to another. Thus, it is known that under certain conditions pilgrimage behavior differs from other types of movement to nodal places; and it is important that scholars of pilgrimages stress these contrasting behavioral patterns.

Nevertheless, geographers must be careful that they do not overstate differences that may not apply to all types of pilgrimages. Pilgrimage activity observed within one cultural setting may not be typical of that in other settings. Consequently, it is essential that generalizations about pilgrimages be based on numerous studies which involve a diversity of conditions.

It seems that pilgrimages by Buddhists in Sri Lanka do not differ greatly from the patterns of movement associated with other types of nodal centers. Unfortunatly this conclusion is only tentative because it is not substantiated by empirical data. Nevertheless, it does suggest information that needs to be incorporated into the growing body of knowledge about pilgrimages.

Notes

[1] Some who have studied aspects of the hajj are ABDUL 1982, BIRKS 1977, DIN & HADI forthcoming, ISAAC 1973, MAKKY 1981, ROWLEY & EL-HAMDAN 1977, RUTTER 1929, and SHAIR & KARAN 1979.

[2] See Map 2 in SIEVERS (1985, 264).

[3] See, for example, the comments by THOMAS (n. d., 39) about pilgrims travel on foot from Varanasi to Rameswaram and by TURNER (1973, 227) about acquiring more merit by ignoring modern means of transportation.

Summary

Although pilgrimages have been studied by geographers for many decades, we still are uncertain about the universality of some basic geographic characteristics of this religious activity. We need to expand our collective knowledge about pilgrimages if we are to develop geographic generalizations about this distinctive form of religious behavior. This paper adds to our pool of information by examining Buddhist pilgrimages in Sri Lanka.

Almost 70 percent of the Sri Lanka population is Buddhist, according to the 1981 census. Not only are Buddhists the religious majority, but they are mostly members of the dominant ethnic group: the Sinhalese. Thus, the distributions of ethnicity and religious affiliations display a high degree of similarity (as measured at the district level).

The ethnic and regional patterns of Hindus and Muslems are also distinct. It would seem that, with this rather pronounced regionalization of the religious communities, pilgrimage places and patterns of movement would also be locationally separated; but such is not the case. In fact, some places, such as Sri Pada (Adam's Peak) and Kataragama, are the destinations of pilgrims from more than one religious group. The major pilgrimage places for Buddhists are shown on Fig. 3.

Within this religious context, three questions are posed: (1) Is the relationship between number of pilgrims to a site and the distances they travel similar to the distance decay associated with other types of nodal places? (2) Do patterns of pilgrimage movement change with time? (3) Does the nature of pilgrimage create greater social interaction among participants than assemblages at other nodal centers?

The lack of empirical data prevents analyses that would provide precise conclusions. Tentative answers to the first two questions are "yes" and to the last one "no". In other words, it seems that pilgrimages by Buddhists in Sri Lanka do not differ greatly from the patterns of movement associated with other types of nodal centers.

Zusammenfassung: Eigenarten Buddhistischer Pilgerfahrten in Sri Lanka

Obwohl Pilgerfahrten schon seit vielen Jahrzehnten von Geographen erforscht wurden, weiß man noch sehr wenig über grundlegende geographische Besonderheiten dieser religiösen Aktivität. Wir müssen unser Wissen über Pilgerfahrten erweitern, wenn wir geographische Schlußfolgerungen über diese besondere Form religiösen Verhaltens entwickeln wollen.

Nach der Volkszählung von 1981 sind fast 70 % der Bevölkerung von Sri Lanka Buddhisten. Diese bilden nicht nur die religiöse Mehrheit, sondern gehören auch meistens zu der vorherrschenden Bevölkerungsgruppe: den Singhalesen. Die Verteilung der ethnischen und religiösen Zugehörigkeit zeigt daher weitgehende Ähnlichkeit (zumindest auf der Distriktebene).

Auch bei Hindus und Mohammedanern zeigen sich ethnische und regionale Besonderheiten. In Anbetracht einer ziemlich ausgeprägten regionalen Konzentration der Religionsgemeinschaften könnte man annehmen, daß ihre Pilgerorte und Pilgerfahrten auch räumlich voneinander getrennt sind; dies ist jedoch nicht der Fall. Tatsächlich sind manche Orte, wie Sri Pada (Adam's Peak) und Kataragama, Ziele von Pilgern aus mehr als einer Religionsgruppe. Die wichtigsten Pilgerorte sind auf Abb. 3 ersichtlich.

In diesem Zusammenhang werden drei Fragen gestellt: (1) Nimmt bei Pilgerfahrten ähnlich wie bei nichtreligiösen Reisen die Anzahl der Besucher mit zunehmender Entfernung ab? (2) Ändert sich das Muster der Pilgerfahrt im Laufe der Zeit? (3) Ruft die Fahrt zu einer Pilgerstätte stärkere soziale Kontakte zwischen den Teilnehmern hervor als dies beim Zusammentreffen von Menschen an anderen Zielorten der Fall ist?

Der Mangel an empirischen Daten erlaubt keine Analysen mit genauen Schlußfolgerungen. Die ersten beiden Fragen sind vorerst zu bejahen, die letzte Frage muß verneint werden. Mit anderen Worten, es scheint, daß sich buddhistische Pilgerfahrten im Stil nicht wesentlich von Bewegungsmustern unterscheiden, die mit Fahrten zu anderen Zielorten verbunden sind.

Bibliography

ABDUL, K. H. D. (1982): Economic Implications of Moslem Pilgrimage from Malaysia. — In: Contemporary Southeast Asia, 4, pp. 56 – 75.

BHARDWAJ, S. M. (1973): Hindu Places of Pilgrimage in India: A Study in Cultural Geography. Berkeley: University of California Press.

BIRKS, J. S. (1977): Overland Pilgrimage from West Africa to Mecca: Anachronism or Fashion. — In: Geography, 62, pp. 47 – 58.

CARTMAN, J. (1957): Hinduism in Ceylon. Colombo: M. D. Gunasena & Co., Ltd.

DEPARTMENT OF BUDDHIST AFFAIRS (1986): Sacred Areas and Sites in Sri Lanka. Colombo: Department of Buddhist Affairs, unpublished list.

DE SILVA, L. (1980): Buddhism: Beliefs and Practices in Sri Lanka, 2nd ed. Colombo: Ecumenical Institute.

DIN, A. K., and A. S. HADI (forthcoming): Moslem Pilgrimage from Malaysia. — In: Morinis, E. A., and R. H. Stoddard (Eds.): Sacred Places, Sacred Spaces: The Geography of Pilgrimages.

GOMBRICH, R. F. (1971): Precept and Practice: Traditional Buddhism in the Rural Highlands of Ceylon. Oxford: Clarendon Press.

ISAAC, E. (1973): The Pilgrimage to Mecca. — In: Geographical Review, 63, pp. 405 – 409.

KEKULAWALA, S. L. (1979): The Religious Journey into *Dharma Dharmavatra*: Pilgrimage as an Expression of Buddhist Religiousness. — In: Carter, J. R. (Ed.): Religiousness in Sri Lanka. Colombo: Marga Institute, pp. 35 – 65.

MAKKY, G. A. W. (1981): Mecca the Pilgrimage City: A Study of Pilgrim Accommodation. East Lansing: Department of Geography, Michigan State University, unpublished Ph. D. dissertation.

NOLAN, M. L. (1983): Irish Pilgrimage: The Different Tradition. — In: Annals of the Association of American Geographers, 73, pp. 421 – 458.

NOLAN, M. L. (1984): Apparitions in Western Europe. — In: Geography of Religion and Belief Systems, 7, pp. 4 – 7.

NOLAN, M. L. (forthcoming): Christian Pilgrimage in Modern Western Europe. Chapel Hill: The University of North Carolina Press.

PATHAMANATHAN, S. (1979): The Hindu Society in Sri Lanka: Changed and Changing. — In: Carter, J. R. (Ed.): Religiousness in Sri Lanka. Colombo: Marga Institute, pp. 149 – 159.

PRUESS, J. B. (1974): Veneration and Merit-Seeking at Sacred Places: Buddhist Pilgrimages in Contemporary Thailand. University of Washington, unpublished Ph. D. dissertation.

ROWLEY, G., and EL-HAMDAN, S. A. S. (1977): Once a Year in Mecca. — In: The Geographical Magazine, 63, pp. 403 – 409.

ROWLEY, G., and EL-HAMDAN, S. A. S. (1978): The Pilgrimage to Mecca: An Explanatory and Predictive Model. — In: Environment and Planning, 10, pp. 1053 – 1071.

RUTTER, E. (1929): The Muslim Pilgrimage. — In: Geographical Journal, 74, pp. 271 – 273.

SHAIR, I., and KARAN, P. P. (1979): Geography of Islam Pilgrimage. — In: Geo-Journal, 3, pp. 599 – 608.

SIEVERS, A. (1985): Zur Bedeutung des Pilgertourismus in Sri Lanka (Ceylon). — In: Geographia Religionum: Interdisziplinäre Schriftenreihe zur Religionsgeographie, 1, Berlin: Dietrich Reimer, pp. 257 – 286.

SRI LANKAN DEPARTMENT OF CENSUS AND STATISTICS (1981): Census of Housing and Population, 1981. Colombo: Government of Sri Lanka, unpublished tables.

STIRRAT, R. L. (1979): A Catholic Shrine in Its Social Context. — In: Sri Lanka Journal of Social Sciences, 2, pp. 77 – 108.

STODDARD, R. H. (1968): An Analysis of the Distribution of Major Hindu Holy Sites. — In: The National Geographical Journal of India, 14, pp. 148 – 155.

STODDARD, R. H. (1979/80): Perceptions About the Geography of Religious Sites in the Kathmandu Valley. — In: Contributions to Nepalese Studies, 7, pp. 97 – 118.

TANAKA, H. (1977): Geographic Expression of Buddhist Pilgrim Places on Shikoku Island, Japan. — In: The Canadian Geographer, 21, pp. 116 – 124.

THOMAS, P., n. d.: Hindu Religion, Customs and Manners, 2nd Indian ed. revised. Bombay: D. B. Taraporevala Sons.

TURNER, V. (1973): The Center Out There: Pilgrim's Goal — In: History of Religions, 12, pp. 191 – 230.

WINSLOW, D. (1982): Pantheon Politics: A Regional Analysis of Buddhism in Sri Lanka. Stanford: Department of Anthropology, Stanford University, unpublished Ph. D. dissertation.

WIRTZ, P. (1966): Kataragama: The Holiest Place in Ceylon. Colombo: Lakehouse.

Ulrich Oberdiek

SĀDHUS IN GAṄGOTRĪ

I. Introduction

Gaṅgotrī has developed into an important pilgrimage site and is of similar importance as the other three holy places of the Kumaon Himālayas, Yamunotrī, Kedarnāth, and Badrīnāth. The sacred specialists of Gaṅgotrī may be divided into four groups: (1) wandering sādhus visiting the area only for a short time; (2) heads, and monks/nuns of the āśramas; (3) sādhus living here solitarily for a long term; (4) priests of the temple. This study deals with the third group. The data on the sādhus were collected during a field trip in 1986 and represent a very preliminary attempt at the topic only. The questions were designed to generate a very basic picture, ascertaining only broad categories as a starting point, that show the sādhus in their religious affiliation, their sādhana, religious motivation (i.e. data pertaining to "history of religion"), and a few general ethnographic data. Eleven sādhus, representing the whole population of this type, have been interviewed. So the present study, as a first step, aims at determining the religious-ethnographic structure of the sādhu-population of this pilgrimage site which is next to the source of India's holiest river, its environment being the classical 'ambiente' for sādhus living in retreat. It is also intended to find out possible relationships between the sādhus' affiliation, their motivation to come here, and whether it correlates with the meaning and type of this pilgrimage place, which makes it necessary to add some information on Gaṅgotrī itself.

As far as I know this is the first study dealing with this pilgrimage site and a group of its sacred specialists. In the past usually only a few sentences, or paragraphs, were dedicated to Gaṅgotrī, mostly in studies on pilgrimage. For this reason, and in order to provide the background for the setting in which the sādhus live (which is necessary if the two are to be compared), sections on Gaṅgotrī's present appearance, its historical dimension, and its meaning as a pilgrimage place precede the survey. Also, a few specific points will be discussed and interpreted that came up during the interviews which are characteristic of the sādhus' way of life, or self-image etc. The outcome of

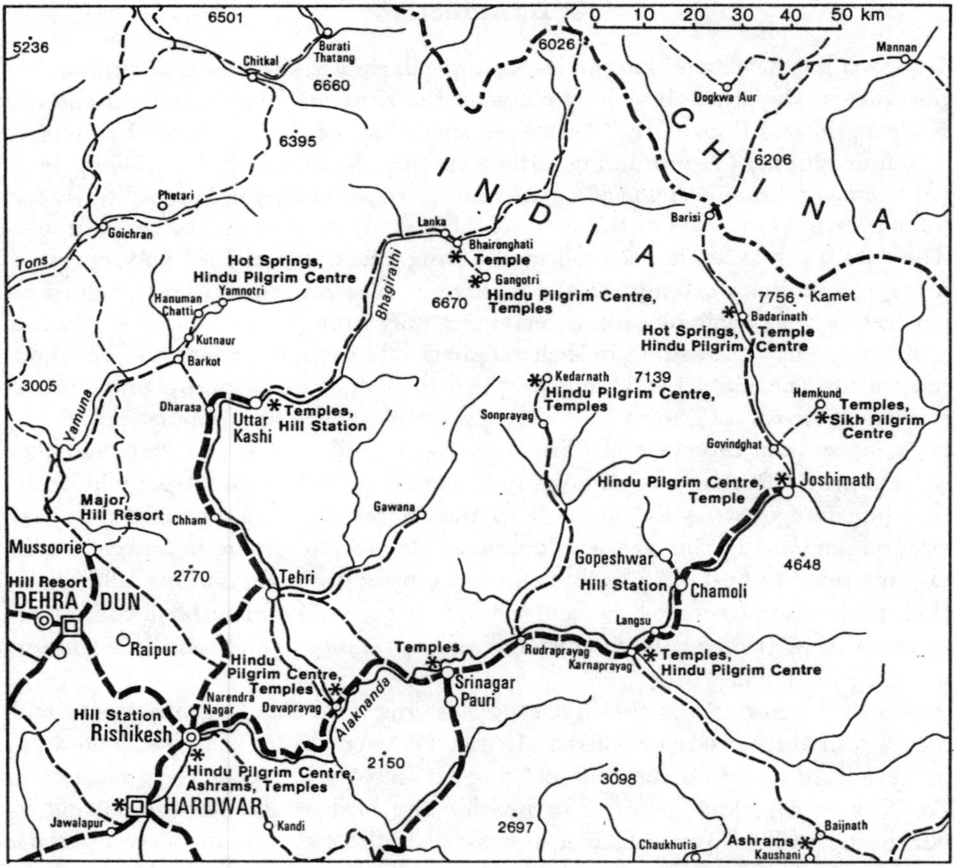

Fig. 1: The Hardwār-Gaṅgotrī area
Source: Himalaya 1 : 1,500,000, Nelles Verlag München

the interviews (a table in the appendix shows most of the data) represents a structure that may help to show this possible relationship with the general religious structure of the village (e.g. whether this Śaivic place attracts mostly Śaiva sādhus, whether their relationship with other groups of sacred specialists is different here from the general Indian situation, what their function is in regard to the general public etc.), or it may be compared with data of other pilgrimage sites or sādhu populations elsewhere — tasks that have not been accomplished yet.

Further studies on this basis might be done by comparing the categories (e.g. in comparison with other pilgrimage sites), or concentrate on values, behavior — i.e. work with the 'contents' of categories. For valid analysis and interpretation both need to be utilized within a system.

For the present, only some of these questions can be answered on the basis of the data of this preliminary study, but this line of thought may be fruitful for future work. Since renouncers, especially solitary sādhus, can be viewed as the real 'creators of values', and as being creative in 'religion and speculation' (see note 56), anthropological and sociological work on this topic, combined with indological knowledge, can be considered an important field of study, e.g. to find out whether they still function thus today. Except for three, I visited the sādhus with my informant, Ravindra Prasad Semwal, who lives in the village, and without whose introduction the contact would have been much more difficult, for socio-cultural and language reasons. Seven of the sādhus spoke Hindi; here Ravindra functioned as an interpreter.

The Indian words have been defined/translated in the glossary: the writing of Indian words follows indological transliteration, but the commonly used (mostly Hindi) form of places and names was kept, if known.

The appendix contains a table with ethnographic data (Table 1). Finally I would like to express my thanks to Ravindra for his help, and to the sādhus who submitted to these non-monastic activities.

II. Gaṅgotrī and Surroundings (Fig. 1)

Gaṅgotrī[1] (30° 59' N., 78° 56' E.) is situated in the District of Uttarkāśi of the Kumaon Himālayas, in Uttar Pradesh, India, at an altitude of 3048 m, on both banks of the Bhāgīrathī river. This river and the Alaknadā unite at Deoprayāg (about 70 kilometers East of Rishikesh) to become the Ganges river (Sanskrit Gaṅgā). The distance between Rishikesh and Gaṅgotrī is 248 kilometers. The road ends here and is open from May to October.[2]

Fig. 2: Gaṅgotrī's center from the Northern side with the Bhagīrathī river in the middle, the temple on the right side.
Source: Author's drawing

The Kedar-Gaṅgā-River divides the Southern section of the village and merges with the Bhāgīrathī. Gaṅgotrī consists of about one hundred buildings, which are dominated on the Northern banks by the Gaṅgā temple with its dharmaśālā and administrative buildings. There are about ten āśramas in the village[3], the dwellings of almost ten sādhus (the rest are outside the village boundaries), a Government Rest House (Forest Rest House), a Post Office, a doctor's office, a police post, and private houses. Between temple and river, at the lower part close to the river is the "shopping street", consisting of approximately ten make-shift souvenir- and devotional article shops along with as many street "restaurants" upstream, temporary shacks with tent cloth and plastic covering for roofs. They feed the pilgrims, serving tea and the usual vegetarian meals common in India: rice, capaties, sabžī, dāl. One can also buy some food here: a few vegetables, cookies, sugar, tea, ready made noodle soup and a few more articles. Meat, alcohol, onions and garlic are not permitted here because of Gaṅgotrī's sanctity, a rule that is found in other pilgrimage places and āśramas as well, and which is observed in many Brahmin families; it is based on the concept of pure and impure substances, actions, and castes and is still an important factor in Hindu society.[4]

The activities of the people other than sacred specialists are more or less related to Gaṅgotrī as a pilgrimage place; the occupations of the people are mostly dependent on the pilgrimage traffic and include its trade, and services (such as firewood provision, porter services, rental of blankets etc.). In the sacred domain income consists of donations of pilgrims to āśramas and sādhus, and temple income. As mentioned before, the road is open from May to October. Most inhabitants leave the place from November to April for their lower home villages in this area; mahantas, monks, and nuns of āśramas return to their home āśramas, which are mostly in Rishikesh, Haridvār, or Uttarkāśi. According to my informant there are only about ten persons in Gaṅgotrī during the winter, mostly sādhus living in solitude, and a few government officials.

Vegetation in and around Gaṅgotrī consists mainly of conifers, often cedar trees; somewhat higher (starting around 3300 m) the birch tree becomes more prevalent. The surface is rocky and stony, mostly granite. About fifty meters below the confluence of the Bhāgīrathī and Kedar-Gaṅgā rivers the Gauri Kuṇd cataract offers a picturesque sight. Then the river passes through a deep and narrow canyon for about half a kilometer.[5]

III. Gaṅgotrī as a Pilgrimage Place (Fig. 2)

The importance of Gaṅgotrī as a place of pilgrimage is based, in the first place, on the myth (in Purāṇas and other Sanskrit sources) in which the king and sage Bhagīratha[6], with the collaboration of Śiva, induced goddess Gaṅgā, daughter of the mountain king Himavat, to incarnate as a river to purify the ashes of his ancestors. In her descent from heaven Gaṅgā became entangled in Śiva's hair, from where she finally emerged to become visible on earth. This place, Gomukh (Hindi: cow's mouth), is located nineteen kilometers upstream from Gaṅgotrī. It can be reached on foot or by horse. Here the Gaṅgotrī Glacier (about 40 km long and 5 km wide) gives birth to the Bhāgīrathī river.[7] For the devout Hindu the importance of this place cannot be overestimated and is probably best understood through the above-mentioned myth (Bhāgīrathī, the river's name down to Deoprayāg, is the feminine form of Bhagīratha and points to the king as the initiator of Gaṅgā's incarnation). BHARDWAJ speaks of the symbolic meaning of different physical places in Hinduism: to reach the source of the Gaṅgā means to reach the abode of Śiva[8], and the glacier's icicles have been compared to locks of Śiva's hair.[9] Although several buses full of pilgrims reach Gaṅgotrī every day only about twenty walk up to Gomukh. The reason is not necessarily the difficult walk but the fact that Gaṅgotrī is often regarded as synonymous with the source of the river.[10]

Apart from Gomukh's mythical importance Gaṅgotrī is frequented for it's Gaṅgā temple and the water of the river; a ritual bath frees the pilgrim from sin. Additionally, a small quantity of holy water is taken home by the pilgrims. After arriving in the village, the pilgrims perform their bath in the river and then proceed to the temple to perform their pūjā. The temple contains idols of Gaṅgā and Bhagīratha[11]. Dedicated to Gaṅgā is the Gaṅgā Daśaharā[12], the most important festival of the village. It culminates in a ritual in which the idol of Gaṅgā is carried to the river in a procession of villagers and pilgrims accompanied by a brass band. At the river, recitations and other ritual acts are performed, after which the deity is carried back to the temple.

The river water, considered holy and purificatory, is collected in small vessels (obtained in the shops) which are then sealed in front of the temple grounds. This activity is traditionally either done, or supervised by Brahmins.[13] The water is said to heal diseases and is also used for ritual purification, e.g. in pūjās at home. Both usages may go back to the original meaning that a bath in the river frees from sin, i.e. eliminates negative karma, which is the reason for the pilgrimage journey after all.

A further and indirect reason to visit Gaṅgotrī as a pilgrim is its location in that part of the Kumaon Himālaya that is not far from two other eminent pilgrimage sites: Kedarnāth and Badrīnāth. A fourth is the source of the Yamunā river, which, according to Salomon, is the fifthholiest river of the Hindus.[14] Yamunotrī and Gaṅgotrī are visited for their sanctity as the sources of holy rivers, Badrīnāth for its Śrī Badarīnātha temple where Viṣṇu in his manifestation as "Lord of the jujube tree" is venerated.[15] This site (Badarīkāśrama of the Sanskrit texts)[16] is an old place of worship for Vaiṣṇavas. It is considered to be one of their three holiest places. About thirty kilometers south of Badrīnāth, Śaṃkara's (788 – 820) Northern māṭha (Jyotirmāth or Joshimāth) is situated.

Kedarnāth is a major Śaiva pilgrimage site for it has the fifth of the twelve most famous Śivaliṅgas (jyotirliṅga)[17], and due to the Śaṃkarācārya temple. The philosopher Śaṃkara, venerated as an incarnation of Śiva[18], is said to have died here. In Salomon's medieval texts[19] Badrīnāth and Kedarnāth belong to the group of "fields of liberation" (muktikśetrāni) — pilgrimage to them is equated with a bath in the Gaṅgā.[20] Thus, these four places are considered the most important for pilgrimage in the area of Garhwal and are offered, as a package tour or separately, from Haridvār or Rishikesh[21] — the succession, for geographical reasons being: Yamunotrī-Gaṅgotrī-Kedarnāth-Badrīnāth. Besides charter buses several regular buses go daily; the number of private vehicles or taxis is negligible, but a number of renouncers walk up to the site. According to my informant more than half of the pilgrims come from Rājasthān which corroborates my own observation. AMADO states the number of pilgrims per season of Badrīnāth, Kedarnāth, and Gaṅgotrī for 1974 — 230,000, 96,000, and 48,000 respectively.[22]

The guide books by Indian authors[23] for pilgrimage sites in Garhwal (which are toured by the average pilgrim within a couple of days — more than 1000 kilometers of mountain roads) mostly list distances, lodging, and very limited sightseeing information only. There are exact directions for the pilgrim as to which bus or train he should take, the temple he should visit and the pūjā he should perform. These instructions are often rather technical and patronizing.[24] The latter is certainly not intended (or experienced by the reader) this way because patronizing behavior of this kind is common in India; it emerges from the country's traditional social/cultural base of hierarchy and, therefore, authority. This tradition-preserving attitude can be observed widely within religion, which by definition strives for security of its clients, i.e. is of a basically 'conservative' character. The significance or meaning of a pilgrimage site is usually not dealt with in guide booklets because in Hindu socialization the meaning is usually internalized rather early, and explanations are not necessary. They are found in the mythological literature (see notes 6, 20) and are encultured with local variations. So the lack of information[25] in guide booklets is quite understandable and it is even consequent not to have detailed descriptions of content matter.

IV. Gaṅgotrī in Early Descriptions

The early phases in the exploration of the source of the Gaṅgā have been depicted by COLEBROOKE[26] and describe the first attempts to provide a reliable map of the area, starting from China, because it was then believed that the source was north of the Himālayas and that the river was several hundred kilometers longer than it actually is. One of the early maps was published in TIEFFENTHALER's three volume set of a description of Hindustan.[27]

In the same volume of the "Asiatick Researches" where COLEBROOKE gave his account, RAPER reported of his unsuccessful expedition to reach Gaṅgotrī and the source of the Gaṅgā in 1808 (see below).

Gaṅgotrī is mentioned first by British colonial officers since FRASER[28] visited the place as the first European in 1815. His and other reports are rather brief; HODGSON's[29] account is somewhat longer but for the most part only geographical. The following data can be extracted from these reports:

RAPER, trying to reach Gaṅgotrī, in 1808 had to give up at Bat'hérì (now Bhatwari) about seventy kilometers from Gaṅgotrī due to difficult road conditions.[30] According to Hamilton,[31] Gaṅgotrī was first visited by Captain RAPER's Munshi (a secretary; Raper himself writes it was Captain Hearsay's Munshi) who was in RAPER's travel group.[32] He is believed to have gone two miles beyond Gaṅgotrī.[33] Therefore, the data on breadth and depth of the river on May 26 and 31, 1808, given by HAMILTON in his publication of 1828 should be ascribed to Raper's Munshi. Since the data refer to Gomukh also[34], it contradicts HODGSON's statement that the Munshi had been in Gaṅgotrī only, and two miles beyond. But according to HAMILTON's description of the source[35] this place should be Gomukh — or a different location of similar physique. The latter assumption is supported by the then following obscurities of his text, especially erroneous altitude readings (see note 46). It probably results from the compilation of several reports in HAMILTON's account.

After FRASER in 1815[36], HODGSON (and HERBERT)[37] followed in 1817 to visit Gaṅgotrī.[38] The geographical 'knowledge' of the natives at that time was apparently accentuated by mythical 'data'. Thus SKINNER reports[39] that, according to a statement of an inhabitant, the spot of confluence of Bhāgīrathī and Jāhnavī near Bhaironghati, ten kilometers below Gaṅgotrī, was considered narrow enough to leap over (whereas SKINNER measured sixty yards). The first European travellers did not get farther than a few hundred meters beyond the village and they report the natives' opinion that it is impossible to venture higher.[40]

Gaṅgotrī is described as a small mountain temple of twenty feet in height[41], which was built by the chief commander of the Gurkha troops in Garhwal, Amar Singh Thappa, "in the early 18th century"[42] (perhaps because of the confluence of the Bhāgīrathī with the Kedar-Gaṅgā). Early in the nineteenth century there was only a simple wooden building for travellers near the temple[43].

According to others Gaṅgotrī was composed of several huts for pilgrims and Brahmins of the temple.[44] FRASER's statement, too, implies that before the temple there was nothing in Gaṅgotrī.[45] HODGSON mentions that the two Brahmins of the temple were not able to tell the distance to the source, and that they themselves had never gone beyond the village and thought no one except the Munshi had ventured farther.[46] He goes on to observe that on his way to Gomukh he passed a place called Bhojpatra, which reminds of the present Bhojbāsā, now consisting of a government Rest House and the āśrama of Lāl Bihari Bābā, about four kilometers before reaching Gomukh.[47] HODGSON apparently was the first European to visit and describe Gomukh.[48] His group climbed the glacier but gave up after about one kilometer, facing the danger of avalanches and crevasses. FRASER reports of the natives' attitude towards the "conquest" of Gomukh[49] — a religious and devotional one that would forbid direct approach. Apart from that, the physical inaccessibility prevents the ascent. This does not necessarily mean though, that nobody was able, or dared to visit Gomukh. Even the name, "mouth of the cow", denoting the opening in the ice where the water emerges, suggests that this was physically observed, and not imagined.

The first pilgrims in all probability were sādhus who sociologically, as members of the "nucleus" of religious specialists, and connected with their quality as creative innovators (see note 56), were in a position to go there. Although this was a kind of 'deviating' behavior from the orthodox Hindu standpoint (of reverential distance) it nevertheless invigorates the system at a meta-level.

FRASER calls the Gaṅgotrī temple the most holy in this area but also mentions Badrīnāth, Kedarnāth, and Yamunotrī as being more accessible or wealthier.[50] So Gaṅgotrī did not become an important pilgrimage place only due to the present traffic facilities, although the number of pilgrims was low in the eighteenth and nineteenth centuries.

Customs and myths of this area are rarely mentioned in the reports. SKINNER speaks of fakirs[51] (he probably means sādhus, or specifically Nāga saṃnyāsins) who came to Gaṅgotrī in order to die here, as it is customary to do in Vārāṇāsī. They tried to starve themselves to death, but SKINNER's Brahmin informant assured him that nobody would be allowed to die in such a holy place. So the sādhus were carried away or fed by force in order to maintain Gaṅgotrī's quality of not being connected with death.

The temple Brahmin related a story to SKINNER which I would like to categorize as a 'myth of legitimation'. It is based on the brahmanical notion of Yugas[52] and legitimizes Gaṅgotrī as an important pilgrimage site during the present Kali Yuga[53]: in the golden age (kṛta yuga) it was easy to worship the source of the Gaṅgā since it was in Vārāṇāsī. In the following lower age (treta yuga) the source retreated to Haridvār, in the second lowest (dvāpara yuga) back to Barahat, and finally, in the lowest (kali yuga), to the heights of Gaṅgotrī. To relate such stories, myths, or legends to pilgrims is a fundamental service rendered by temple Brahmins.[54]

The Brahmin FRASER met in Gaṅgotrī in 1815 told him that most pilgrims hold the idea of the river originating from a rock resembling the mouth of a cow, as coming directly and visibly from the sky, or the leaves of a sacred birch tree. Furthermore, the Brahmin asserted that these notions were wrong, and instead the river originated from the snow masses![55]

V. Dwellings of the Sādhus

There are two major types of dwellings, huts (kutīr) and caves (kūpa). The huts are often built in a solid way, of mortar, loam, and are frequently timber-framed; the roof is often of corrugated iron sheet as is usual in this area, like the doors that can be closed with a lock from the outside. Eight sādhus live in such huts, five have more than one hut. Another type is built from natural stone with loam or cement. Such huts tend to be smaller, usually not bigger than 3 – 5 m^2 and are often built as an extension of a cave behind it. Three sādhus live in places of this type. They are usually lockable, too. Another variety is the cave with its opening closed by stones, or loam/cement. There were two uninhabited caves of this type. Finally there is the natural cave, either rather open, sometimes only formed by overhanging rocks, or deep, with a small opening.

VI. The Survey

Aim of the survey is to classify the sādhus in some fundamental categories of their religious affiliation, practice, and motivation and thus to supply some ethnographic data of this Hindu pilgrimage site and a group of its sacred specialists[56], to show their composition in 1986 as a base for further research. The data are new as far as I know[57] and there is no publication on this pilgrimage place so far.

Only sādhus who live permanently and solitarily in and around Gaṅgotrī have been included in this survey. 'Permanently' denotes more than a year (or season), 'solitary' separates them as a group from other sacred specialists like mahantas, monks, and nuns living in āśramas. Eight of these sādhus live completely alone, three have disciples living with them: Daṇḍiswāmi Haṃsānand (one sādhvī), Gaṅgā Dās (two disciples, one servant), No. 1 (one disciple).

However, the lifestyle of the three sādhus and their own definition make them part of the solitary group. Three of the sādhus (Nos. 1, 2, 3) must remain anonymous because they were against being photographed or published.

I would like to mention a possible influence, a structural parameter in the empirical situation that may have blurred the data to a degree: the factor of mystification. Since I find it extremely difficult to prove its influence, and degree of influence, I endeavor to delineate the phenomenon and its tendency in general only.

One of the intentions of the Mythological is mystification. Mystification effects veiling, disguising, obscuring — of a god, a process etc. It should produce awe, reverence and the like in those people that are being influenced to these ends. This is to generate distance – by the sacred specialist — between him and the outsider (here the lay pilgrim) in order to make it necessary for the pilgrim to seek out the specialist to remove again the distance that he can have contact with the god or other object of mystification. Amongst other results, this operation of the sacred specialist creates the base for his livelihood. This is easily proven by the circumstance that 'insider training', i.e. esoteric training of nuclear groups of the brahmanical religion, especially in 'extreme' groups like different Śaiva sects, Tantra sects, and Śākta sects, but also in 'regular' brahmanical circles like the temple priests of the Jagannāth temple in Puri[58], includes the *removal* of mystification that basically goes back to the Upaniṣadic finding that brahman equals ātman. To exemplify it in the present setting: the mūrti in Gaṅgotrī's Gaṅgā temple is not to be approached too closely. It is not to be photographed, the visitor is not allowed to enter the temple — gifts for the goddess are given to her through the medium of the temple priest. Likewise, a sādhu or other 'sacred' specialist is not to be questioned 'profanely' too much, otherwise he or she may inhibit the flow of information to the questioner — even of certain categories of religious teaching. But more often the data concerned relate to material conditions, or power (see the cases of Gaṅgā Dās, Nos. 1 – 3).

To sum up: distance (as created by mystification, non- or misinformation) creates uncertainty, prevents "exact investigation" — to say it in Western words. Mystification serves to enhance the sacral element, veiling increases fascination whereas exact investigation (e.g. historical) is profane and contradicts mystification. The foundation of the import of India's classical pilgrimage places is of a mythological nature; potentially Gaṅgotrī is one of them, but only the (profane) condition of road construction and means of transport made it a (quantitatively noticable) manifest one. But road construction again is partly motivated by the myth of Gaṅgā's descent, and, as a next move, myth overtakes, or incorporates, the present condition, as is illustrated by the 'myth of legitimation' of the nineteenth century when Gaṅgotrī started to become a pilgrimage center.

As I said before, the data of the survey represent a few very broad categories only, and maybe some subtleties, tendencies of behavior in the sādhus. Since the content matter of such categories has been dealt with before[59], and, I believe, the individual religious experience cannot be 'extracted' and communicated easily, this study does what remains. It would take a long stay in the field to describe life style and opinions of the sādhus minutely and would come close to biographies. Also, it might create resistance as the aim is to generate 'profane' data contradicting 'mystification.' In the case of Gaṅgā Dās a conversation was interrupted by a disciple when I posed the question of Gaṅgā Dās' number of disciples. From this moment the disciple prevented further detailed questioning; No. 1 reacted to questions in that he resisted a direct interview situation by only accepting me as the seeker to be instructed.

My informant, Ravindra Prasad Semwal, with whom I visited the sādhus except Swāmi Sundarānanda, Nos. 1 and 3, mainly functioned as translator (Hindi/English) and answered questions that were relevant for the study. He was born in a village about fifty kilometers upstream from Uttarkāśi, belongs to the gotra of the temple priests, graduated in law, and runs a shop with souvenirs and devotional articles in Gaṅgotrī. Presently he has a small Hotel constructed and believes tourism should be promoted here. Besides his business ambitions he writes and composes folk songs in the tradition of Garhwal, plans to study history, and intends to write a history of Garhwal. I had expressed the wish to visit and talk to all permanently and solitarily living sādhus of Gaṅgotrī. He agreed to translate and according to him we met all except "one or two". He had a way to select: first, only the "important" ones. Here, the foremost criterion for "important" was duration of stay in the village and the resulting degree of veneration (as with Gaṅgā Dās who is considered the most venerable sādhu; his stay of 46 years is the longest); but generally the mahantas of the āśramas as a group are considered higher in the hierarchy, according to Ravindra.[60] Furthermore, life style in accordance with the precepts of religious literature (like epics, Purāṇas, Dharmaśāstras) is important. These are criteria of formal and ritual character; Ravindra did not mention charismatic qualities.

The cases that have been labeled "not important" by Ravindra are not included in the study; they were: — one saṃnyāsinī; he did not want to meet her because of the rumour of her visiting the mahanta of one of the āśramas after dark[61]; — the second case was a saṃnyāsin who lived in a simple cave, suffered from rheumatism, often sat on the steps of the temple begging, and seemed somewhat demoralized. Ravindra said he came to Gaṅgotrī only recently, and mainly to collect money by begging. A conversation with him centered around his health problems, acquired by living in the cave. Together with Abdhūt Rāmānand, who could not be traced during the survey, they might be the "one or two" sādhus in Gaṅgotrī who were not included.

The conversations took place in the huts or caves of the sādhus. Usually we were served tea or coffee, sometimes sweets, and it was customary to leave a donation of a few Rupees after the meeting. The donation was rejected by some sādhus. The interviews were not strictly standardized but had a similar structure, and a fixed catalogue of questions. Ravindra first introduced himself, (the older sādhus knew him from childhood), talked about his family that was known to many sādhus, his business, and problems of the sādhus. Here, as often in India the importance of social mediation by a relative or otherwise related person, or by a letter of introduction, became visible. He then introduced me and stated my intention "to write something on Gaṅgotrī and to take photographs". After an agreement we started with questions.

Daṇḍiswāmi Haṃsānand

The Swāmi has lived in Gaṅgotrī for thirty years, upstream on the Northern side in two spacious huts. With him is a 63 year old nun, his disciple, who took saṃnyāsa from him in 1985. Of his disciples, she alone is allowed to stay with him. Other disciples, followers, and visitors may see him during the summer. He loves solitude and considers this period as disturbance, but in interacting with him he is friendly, courteous, and gentle. He is frequented often by visitors in comparison with the other sādhus. He stays in Gaṅgotrī during the winter, together with his disciple, and says he spends most of the time in meditation. He stressed that Daṇḍiswāmis venerate nirguṇa brahman[62] and love isolation. Haṃsānand practices Mantra-Yoga since he considers the other classical branches of Yoga, Rājā and Laya[63], unsuitable at the altitude of Gaṅgotrī — and said that he was too old for Hatha. It happened to him (probably in the beginning) when he practiced prāṇayama exercises, that prāṇa concentrated in his head and he was unable to bring it back and neutralize it. Thus he practices Mantra- Yoga (he apparently implies here that mantras do not have a physiological effect as strong as prāṇa exercises).

Haṃsānand was born in the District of Gorakhpur, Uttar Pradesh, but his Guru is from the Paṇjāb. The Swāmi is a saṃnyāsin, sees himself as a teacher, and has many disciples and followers. He lives by donations, is here for the solitude, and intends to remain here in the future.

Most Daṇḍi ascetics are initiated in the fourth life stage, i.e. are rather old. When I took his photographs the Swāmi had his 100th birthday, as people told me later on. Sinha and Saraswati mentioned a 113 year old Daṇḍi.[64] However, such statements often cannot be verified, for lack of documents or records. The interviews were in English, without Ravindra's help. The Swāmi's statements on philosophical concepts and Yoga practices, his knowledge of English etc. identify him as educated, a quality described as widespread with Daṇḍi ascetics by Sinha/Saraswati.[65] Daṇḍis are recruited from the highest varṇa (Brahmins), other saṃnyāsins also from Kṣatriyas and Vaiśyas, Nāgas may even be Śūdras. This fact, and their old age may account for the Daṇḍis' educational level.

Gaṅgā Dās

He lives about two kilometers upstream from Gaṅgotrī on the Northern banks of the river in three buildings, and with three disciples. One of the huts, a rather small one, is for the reception of visitors who will sit on the floor, facing a small altar with an idol of Gaṅgā in the middle, and a few other deities. Between the altar and the visitor, on the left side, sits Gaṅgā Dās, answering questions.

He has been in Gaṅgotrī for 46 years without interruption, longer than any other sādhu, which makes him the most venerable. As can be inferred from his name, he is a Vaiṣṇava; he is a Bhakta devoted to Rāma, and mostly studies the Bhagavatam. His Guru is Śrī Rām Balak Dās Mahārāj. He sees himself as a teacher and has many followers. He lives by donations and grows some vegetables in his garden. The sādhu is rather old and became blind a year ago. During this (first and last) conversation two of his disciples were in the room, too. One of them, when the question on the number of disciples was asked, intervened with the argument that it would not be necessary to ask such specific questions. From there on, an atmosphere of tension and mistrust prevailed that prevented further meaningful conversation.

Govind Dās Mahārāj

lives alone in a small hut in the village, on the Northern banks of the Bhāgīrathī. He came here 29 years ago, but for the last three years he has not been here exclusively any more but occasionally visits other pilgrimage sites, and also does not spend every winter in Gaṅgotrī any more.
He was born in a Brahmin family in Kānpur and had concentrated on "God and Gaṅgā" since childhood. He said that he had a holy mother and an educated father who instructed him. He was never married. His Guru was Swāmi Śrī Tapovan Mahārāj who used to live in this area of the Himālayas, which is also a reason for Govind Dās' presence here. Śrī Tapovan is also Sundarānanda's Guru and was an admirer and explorer of these mountain regions; he published a book on this subject. Govind Dās does not claim to be a teacher, has no

disciples but many followers. He lives by donations, is a Vaiṣṇava, Bhakta, and practices havan. He is devoted to goddess Gaṅgā and is considered a specialist on the Rāmāyaṇa (which means knowledge of the epic and its interpretation for the public). My informant also stressed Govind Dās' local popularity — the sādhu himself mentioned his intent not to create conflicts between him (a sādhu) and temple priests (pāṇḍas); due to their respective characteristics there is a latent tension between these two groups of sacred specialists. Another characteristic situation came up in a discussion when Govind Dās mentioned that a sādhu, whom he had allowed to stay in his hut during the winter, had smoked caras there, which Govind Dās disapproved of (caras is smoked by a part of the Śaiva renunciants) — he regarded it as a defilement. The majority of 'serious' sādhus will probably disapprove of the use of caras. The derogatory term "Hashish-Baba" is occasionally used for caras smokers.

Ravindra related a legend about the sādhu that exists elsewhere with some variations — that he is a siddha and, through application of mantras, is able to intervene in cases of snake bite by forcing the snake to return, within seven days, and to suck in the venom again.

Kapilānand Paramahaṃs

This saṃnyāsin has been in Gaṅgotrī for four years and lives on the Southern side of the river in a lot with a few small huts. He grows flowers (to enjoy them) but no vegetables or fruit, i.e. nothing that produces worldly gain. Communication with him was in Hindi and, on his part, in writing, as he has been a Mauni for two years now and intends to continue his vow of silence indefinitely. He wrote his answers on a small piece of slate he always carries with him. He lives alone and stays here in the winter as well. He does not teach and has no disciples. The reason for him being here is "śānti" and goddess Gaṅgā. Earlier, he lived in the Kailās āśrama[66] of Uttarkāśi, his Guru is Mahāmaṇḍaleśvar 108 Swāmi Vidyānand Giri (the mythologically founded number 108 has, as part of monastic names, the meaning of "special venerableness, attainment of a high spiritual level"). He is a Śaiva Bhakta, practices havan, and mostly reads mythological scriptures: epics and Purāṇas, but added: smṛti as well as śruti literature.

My informant had mentioned a group of sādhus who are supposed to live in the environment of Gaṅgotrī but does not appear in public. They would work not for their own liberation (mokṣa) but for the good of all people (the thought is based on the transferability of karma and appears both in Hinduism and Buddhism — e.g. in the mahāyānistic ideal of the Bodhisattva). Asked whether these sādhus exist, Kapilānand said he does not know them, they might be Gandharvas perhaps (it didn't become clear though, whether he meant the class of heavenly beings, or the "race of people dwelling in hills and wilds" mentioned in Dowson's dictionary). On the question whether he is a siddha, the sādhu said that nobody except Śiva is a siddha. As most of the others, the Paramahaṃs lives by donations.

Lakṣmī Prapannācārya

This Vaiṣṇava lives on the Southern banks, a little beyond Kapilānand in a hut surrounded by a small lot. In winter he goes to Govardhan, the Vaiṣṇava pilgrimage center 25 kilometers west of Mathurā, where he has six disciples and many followers. He performs pūjās in temples there and receives small fees, presents, and also lives by donations. In Gaṅgotrī he has no disciples. He was born in the District of Arrah in Bihar, his Guru's name is Basudevācārya. Prapannācārya's daily religious practice includes havan (agnihotra) and he describes himself as a Bhakti Yogi, studies the Rāmāyaṇa and Siddhānta (astronomical works), and generally "metaphysical principles of the mythological books", i.e. the Purāṇas. He is a devotee of the deity of Shaligram (śālagrāma). The reason for his being here is the peace, and he wants to stay in Gaṅgotrī.

Swāmi Gaṅgeśvarānand

He occupies a room in a newly built two-storey building in the center of the village. This Śaiva came here six years ago, lives alone, and stays through the winter. He was born in a Brahmin family of the gotra of the temple priests in this area. His Guru is Daṇḍiswāmi Pūrṇānand Tīrtha, head of an āśrama in Gaṅgotrī. The saṃnyāsin is a Bhakti Yogi and concentrates in his religious literature on the Rāmāyaṇa and Purāṇas, does not regard himself as a teacher, does not have disciples, but is open to "metaphysical needs of seekers". He lives by donations. His stay here is partly due to his Guru living here and also due to his local origin. He plans to stay in Gaṅgotrī.

Swāmi Sundarānanda Giri

The meetings with the Swāmi took place without Ravindra's introduction. It is easy to approach him since he lives centrally in a small lot with two huts which he decorated with many objects from the natural environment. He is visited by many people. One of the huts was built by his Guru Swāmi Śrī Tapovan Mahārāj between 1925 – 30 whose love of nature is present in Sundarānanda also: he is a photographer — the hut is full of pictures from his wanderings in the Himālayas. Additionally, he occasionally writes short articles on this subject in journals. He is rather one of the "simple" sādhus of a contemplative nature, than one of the "educated", and more intellectual (such

as No. 1 or Haṃsānand, who shows both traits). So Sundarānanda in general criticizes contemporary sādhus: they are not "simple". Moreover, there are no mahātmas any more, they entered (mahā-)samādhi by now, today everything would be business — a real saint would be very simple. Regarding nature he's pessimistic, too — formerly there were flowers everywhere in Gaṅgotrī, today everything is being cut (to have wood for construction and fireplaces). His pessimism is enhanced through a theft a year ago when several photo albums and camera equipment were stolen from his hut. He suspects the thieves have done it out of jealousy because of his popularity.
The Swāmi has lived in the Himālayas for 38 years, in Gaṅgotrī since about 1950. In winter he usually travels and gives slide lectures on his wanderings in the mountains. He lives alone, grows vegetables and fruit in his garden, and lives partly by the payments from his lectures and articles. The Swāmi is a Bhakta, says he is not a teacher, does not have disciples, but many visitors, who will be exposed to a little Hindu lecturing also. He wants to stay in Gaṅgotrī, for love of nature which is part of his sādhana, and because he received the hut from his Guru. In a leaflet he distributes, with information on himself, it is stated that between 1950 – 54 he practised tapas and Kuṇḍalinī Yoga and, as a Karma Yogi, sought god in nature. He is originally from Anantpuram, District Nellore, Andhra Pradesh. The Swāmi spoke in broken English.

Swāmi Yogānanda Sarasvatī

The Swāmi lives in the village, directly on the Northern banks, in a small combined hut and cave (the hut being attached to the cave). He has been here for sixteen years, although he spends the winter time in Uttarkāśi, for health reasons. The talks were in Hindi, with English scraps. He is from Kerala, his Guru is Swāmi Niṣkalānanda. Yogānanda is a Rājā Yogi, practices prāṇayama and dhyāna. He studies the Bhagavadgītā and Yoga treatises (Patañjali's Yogasūtras and others) and describes his sādhana as the "study of the inner body" — all characteristics that are Rājā-yogic. He lives in the hut and meditates in the cave, which is very cold; he says, he sits here in mirvikalpa samādhi. He does not teach, has no disciples, and lives by donations from visitors and seekers. He is here because of the peace he finds here. The Swāmi appears happy, free and easy. When I took photographs he asked for copies and complained about Western tourists who had taken pictures but did not send them to him as promised.

No. 1

This Swāmi (like Nos. 2 and 3) was against photographs and publication plans, so he must remain anonymous. But some of their opinions and characteristics might be interesting — especially in regard to the motivation of their refusal, and to have a glimpse of the whole spectrum of renunciants; the negation of these three represents one end of this spectrum and shows some aspects of the sādhus' self-image and role prescriptions.

He is comparatively young and seems to have been in Gaṅgotrī only for a few years. He has a well-built hut in the village, and a cave with a hut outside the village by the river, where he is often, to be undisturbed. He has a disciple, who also functions as a servant. The Swāmi speaks good English, and the conversation was without Ravindra. First, he gave a good lecture on Karma Yoga, in conformance with general hinduistic teachings. Afterwards he introduced his Yoga book (written in Hindi) to me. He wants to establish his own Yoga school; in the book he combines Sāṃkhya, Yoga, and Vedānta teachings with his own 'therapeutic' plans and wants to institutionalize it in the form of "therapy āśramas". His therapy concentrates on a mixture of physical and mental diseases that are commonly treated by ayurvedic physicians and Yoga therapists: back-ache, rheumatism, impotence, sexual weakness, weak memory etc. Thus, in combining Yoga teachings with this type of therapy he is within the boundaries of a folk tradition of healers.
When it came to the topic of my plan to publish, he reacted negatively: that books are not necessary, they would create confusion only. This thought can be found in the teachings of many Indian religious teachers (saints, Gurus etc.); the idea is that intellectual matters distract the seeker from his religious goal. When I asked about the sādhu's own book he reacted the same way, but somewhat softer, more indirect and brief: it seemed, primarily not to contradict himself. It became clear that he accepted me only in the role of a 'seeker', the one to be taught, and himself only as the teacher. He allowed no change or reversal which showed each time I tried to break through his line. But it was possible to discuss some of his future plans (as above). So there are only a couple of data, to be inferred indirectly: from his book that he adheres to Sāṃkhya-Yoga (probably Rājā-Yoga) and Vedānta. He said that he mostly studies the Veda, likes to live in isolation, meditates much, and works on a book (the continuation of the first). He spends the winter in Delhi, mainly to write. After his second book he wants to go further up in the Himālayas. The Swāmi wants to remain unknown because he does not want that people who seek him out 'don't find him and are disappointed'. His name, garment, and other attributes identify him as a Śaiva saṃnyāsin.

No. 2

This sādhu is young, perhaps under twenty. He lives alone outside the village on the Southern banks upstream in two small huts built with stones against the rocks. He did not want to participate because he sees a commercial undertaking here, and as a renunciant he is not supposed to get involved in such

matters. He also explained the processes of pollution and confusion of the mind that go with it, e.g. the generation and effects of greed etc. He seemed somewhat annoyed, and it can only be guessed whether it was because we disturbed him, or because of my plan. He considers this activity "unnecessary" for sādhus and criticized in this respect the commercialization of āśramas.
He is from Garhwal and a Śaiva according to his attributes (triśul, kamaṇḍalu, gerrua). He rather gives the impression of a Yogi than a Bhakta, or ritualistically inclined sādhu.

No. 3

Since he speaks English I saw him without Ravindra's introduction. The sādhu lives outside Gaṅgotrī, downstream on the Southern side, and is alone. His dwelling is built under an overhanging rock and closed by natural stones. He has been here for four years, including the winter, which he spends in the village itself. He is not a teacher and mainly wants to reach higher spiritual levels here. This, in his opinion, is the main reason for sādhus to go to solitary places like this one. After this attainment he wants to live "in the world" again.
The Swāmi is a Śaiva and a member of an international religious organization with its own monastic order, although he has to support himself. He says his material situation, food provision for the winter etc. is "difficult", yet he refused to take a donation after the interview. He is quite hospitable but at the same time introvert and suspicious — of spies for instance; such suspicion is fairly widespread in India. He probably mentioned it because of my being a foreigner and doing fieldwork. He disapproves of a publication, as it is a business undertaking which is not in accordance with activities of renunciants. Also, some French people had promised to send him photographs which they did not. He was concerned that photographs might be used for business purposes.
The Swāmi may be called educated, but some times confuses facts with concepts of a mythological nature, a phenomenon I regard as widespread among orthodox Hindus (cf. note 24); so the Swāmi put the old sciences of India (jyotiṣa, ayurveda etc.) on the same level as present Western sciences. Elsewhere, an educated Brahmin, a scientist himself, assured me that the knowledge for the construction of a television set is contained in the Mahābhārata because Vyāsa invested the charioteer of the blind king Dhṛtarāṣṭra with the ability to see everything, so the king would be able to follow the whole battle between Pāṇḍavas and Kauravas.

VII. Discussion

Eight out of eleven sādhus agreed to be interviewed and photographed for a publication, three refused. One sādhu, Gaṅgā Dās, in the course of the interview, refused to be interviewed in a detailed way. If we consider the language of the interviews we notice that two of the refusing sādhus spoke English, of the remaining eight also two (if we include Gaṅgā Dās). Of the three refusing sādhus, I visited two without Ravindra's introduction; i.e. in those two cases his absence and hence the lack of social mediation may have been a negative factor. In the case where he was present (No. 2) the sādhu, who was very young, did not know Ravindra and his position in the village. The three negatively reacting sādhus were rather young (ca. 20 to 35 years), whereas Gaṅgā Dās, who refused in the process, was probably the oldest — but the refusal here was initiated by his young disciple (who didn't know Ravindra as well!) so that we can conclude that in all cases where sādhus showed a negative attitude to interviews, young age and ignorance of Ravindra (and his position) played a major role. In two (of the altogether four) cases of refusal Ravindra was not present, so his social mediation could not become effective, and the other two sādhus did not know his position — so in all four cases a lack of social mediation was there.

Qualitatively speaking, the refusing sādhus were motivated by their monastic rules, plus the case of Gaṅgā Dās' disciple who did not permit too exact questioning.

I consider their reasons to be authentic and do not think they were reacting to my person (the coincidence of refusal and young age corroborate this view. I am inclined to interpret it as the young following the rules more rigidly and dogmatically than the old), although, as a questioning stranger I naturally provoke suspicion and distrust. However, this is the same with Indians not known in the locality — another expression of the closedness of the group (jati, gotra, joint family) towards outsiders. Intruders are perceived to cause something negative — and often it is based on experience, too. On the other hand it may well be that my initial statement concerning photographs and a publication moved them in the other direction, caused or increased their agreement, i.e. it may have been welcome for those who wanted publicity. In general I think there is no tendency in the interview questions that make a change of behavior (in the interviewee) likely. This is the approximate frame, I suppose, within which the interactive processes of the interviews took place if one considers DEVEREUX' conception of the reciprocity between observer and object.[67]

The sādhus who consented to be interviewed are all older, except Yogānanda (ca. 30 years). The refusing sādhus all live outside of the village, a possible indicator for a 'seclusive' attitude; two of them (Nos. 1, 3) explicitly stated that they were here for seclusion and higher development, No. 2 didn't want to be questioned. All three are Śaivas and have been here for a short time as compared to the others. Of the eight consenting sādhus six have been in Gaṅgotrī for more than ten years. Ten sādhus live in huts resp. buildings, five have more than one hut. Only one (No. 3) exclusively lives in a hut, and two have a hut and a cave. Often the sādhus demarcated a small lot around their dwellings. They came here and occupied it. Presently they fear the government might take it from them, because there have been changes already to develop the village. Therefore, the conversation between the sādhus and Ravindra in the beginning often centered on this topic, and several appeared to be worried. In the winter time, six remain in the village, two visit holy places, the rest travel or spend the winter in the plains.

Most sādhus originally come from Northern India, in two cases from the present area (Garhwal). Only two are from the South (Kerala and Andhra Pradesh). In three cases the birthplace could not be determined. Regarding the Gurus the only point worth mentioning in our context is that in Govind Dās' case there is a discrepancy, since he is a Vaiṣṇava and his Guru a Śaiva. But in Hinduism one is often confronted with deviations from the rule, so after some experience, nothing seems impossible. The contradiction only appeared while evaluating the data, so it couldn't be clarified in the field.

Another general point showed in the case of Govind Dās (q.v.), the conflict between sādhus and other more institutionalized religious specialists such as temple priests, which, according to his remark, seems to exist in Gaṅgotrī also: such conflicts are widespread and are due to the different functions and goals of these two groups of sacred specialists, despite similarities and points of contact: both 'live' by religion, though in different ways. The brahmanic temple priest administers a place granting grace and religious merit, for which function he indirectly, via the gifts for the deity, is paid, in important pilgrimage centers often substantially. The lucrativity of his benefice influences his behavior vis-à-vis his grace-seeking clients insofar as he tries to move them to higher and more frequent donations (cf. RÖSEL 1980:161–75; for the opposition between ascetics and Brahmins cf. note 56). The sādhu on the other hand also lives by gifts and donations of his followers (not his disciples!) as has been shown in most cases of the interviewed sādhus, but here the practice is not as institutionalized and rather voluntary — with individual deviations of course. So five of the sādhus in Gaṅgotrī refused donations, one seemed to appreciate it, the others behaved neutrally. The attitude on donations may change with increasing institutionalization, say, when a sādhu strives to establish an āśrama, which is considered a promotion. But the saṃnyāsin is superior to the Brahmin in content matter, modification, and innovation of the administered knowledge (which of course the client does not notice necessarily). Also, according to his teachings, the saṃnyāsin is traditionally not donation-oriented. Thus a field of tension between the two is generated which is enhanced by the circumstance that the renouncer is better able to offer 'living' charisma (i.e. himself) to the client, than the pāṇḍa (to a degree the mahanta, too) who can offer only 'ritual' charisma (mūrti, ritual actions). Even if one presupposes a 'mythological consciousness' in the client, who sees the mūrti as the actual deity which it is by definition, a higher grade of flexibility in the interaction with a 'living' deity (the sādhu) can be assumed.

The sadhāna of the ascetics shows that five of the nine sādhus where these data are available, are Bhaktas. This obviously correlates with their sects: all three Vaiṣṇavas are Bhaktas (which corresponds with Vaiṣṇavism in general), of the Śaivas only two are Bhaktas, the other Śaiva ascetics more often apply Yogas in the direct sense in their sādhana. This is explicitly the case with Haṃsānand, Sundarānanda, and Yogānanda. Accordingly, the scriptures they use show this clearly: Vaiṣṇavas study Purāṇas and/or epics without exception while the Śaivas also use more 'specialized' texts (e.g. yogic). If we consider this structure in order to correlate it with the meaning of the place we may first delineate three major factors of 'meaning': 1) the natural setting, which is a remote and solitary mountain area, the ideal 'habitat' for ascetics doing tapas; 2) the specific scriptural myth of the incarnation of the river goddess, which is circulated mostly in 'mythological' scriptures: Purāṇas, epics (cf. note 6); 3) the place is created through Śiva, letting Gaṅgā flow through his hair and releasing her at Gomukh. It seems obvious that by factor 3) Śaivas should be drawn to Gaṅgotrī, and also by factor 1) since Śiva's abode is in the Himālayas, he is the Lord of the Yogis (who are more often Śaivas); esoteric practices that require retreat are more often connected with Śaivism. Only factor 2) may also draw Vaiṣṇavas since with them 'mythological' texts are somewhat more prominent. Another factor, holiness of the Gaṅgā, may be considered universal, i.e. drawing both Śaivas and Vaiṣṇavas. In our case, nine out of twelve sādhus are Śaivas which seems to be in proportion with the religious meaning of Gaṅgotrī.

Five of the eight agreeing sādhus do not regard themselves as teachers, or Gurus; three considered themselves to be teachers, two of them being Vaiṣṇavas. Of the three refusing sādhus, who can be regarded as Śaivas only one sees himself as a teacher (No. 1). These answers correlate with those for disciples and followers. Govind Dās was the only one who specified that he is visited by followers from all over India. So only four of eleven sādhus act as teachers which seems consequent if most of them came here for peace and seclusion (see below), and it also corresponds with the structure of the village which is frequented by regular pilgrims for the benefit of a ritual bath in the Gaṅgā, not for esoteric teachings. Peace was the major reason for the sādhus to be here, seclusion and striving for higher development may be subsumed under it, since they are related, resp. peace is the precondition. Hence most sādhus don't function as teachers. If they wanted publicity, or were intent on gathering disciples, a place like Rishikesh would be more appropriate. So their statements seem to correspond with the outer conditions of the place.

The sādhus' contact with the public, i.e. pilgrims, is not very intense: they are frequented by those few only who do not seem to be average pilgrims coming in large groups, but rather individuals, or families, coming here on their own. They may have known the sādhu they visit for a long time. This much can be said from personal observation and on the basis of remarks by sādhus themselves. For more specific data, more research needs to be done. This is also true for inquiring into the sādhus' role as 'innovators' (cf. note 56), which would require further work, e.g. on the basis of the present study. Such an investigation would include the sādhus' visitors, their motivation, their position and influence in their worldly life, the contents and influence of the sādhus' teachings, perhaps their opinion on the effects of their teaching etc. In general, it can be said that the sādhus' data clearly show a mixed but accentuated structure that seems to be in conformity with the pilgrimage place.

The means of livelihood of all saṃnyāsins should be through begging (or donations), but two sādhus are (at least in part) self-sufficient through agricultural work which may be an indicator that rules can be relaxed in extreme situations of climate and infrastructure where subsistence is difficult, although there is the opportunity for the sādhus to get free food from the āśramas of the village. Swāmi Sundarānanda and No. 1 have some income through royalities, and slide presentations also.

Notes

[1] Gaṅgā + uttṝ, uttṝ meaning "to pass out of, come out of, disembark, to come down, to descend". HAMILTON (1828, I:560) explained it thus: Gaṅgā avatārī (descent of the Gaṅgā); The ENCYCLOPEDIA OF RELIGION AND ETHICS (1913, VI:180): "probably Gaṅgā-avatāra-purī (Gaṅgā-descent-city).

[2] The exact date of construction up to Gaṅgotrī couldn't be detected. Long stretches have been built in the 1940s: "Since the 1940s, the Indian government has developed long stretches of the road, but the last few miles to Gangotri are still done on foot." (DARIAN 1978:3); so the rest must have been built after 1978.

[3] according to my informant.

[4] Cf. DUMONT 1980, esp. Chapter II and VI.

[5] HODGSON (1822) gives an extensive, mostly geographical description of the area.

[6] Cf. KEILHAUER 1983:176 f.; BOCK 1984; some important passages on Bhagīratha and the myth of Gaṅgā's descent: Mahābhārata I, 226, 2112, 7001; II, 67; III, 9918 ff.; VII, 2249 ff.; XII, 956 ff.; Rāmāyaṇa I, 43, 8 ff.; I, 70, 37 f.; II, 100, 27 f.; Viṣṇupurāṇa III, 79; Bhāgavatapur. IX, 9,2; Mārkaṇḍeyapur. 56, 11; 101,6.

[7] DARIAN 1978:3.

[8] BHARDWAJ 1973:86.

[9] HODGSON 1822:117 f.: "The Gangotri Brahmin who came with us, and who is only an illiterate mountaineer, observed, that he thought these icicles must be Mahadeva's hair, from whence, as he understood, it is written in the Shástra, the Ganges flows."

[10] "But Gaṅgotrī itself is regarded as the source of the river, and few pilgrims venture higher up its course, though it is a popular error to suppose that the route is impracticable." ENCYCLOPEDIA OF RELIGION AND ETHICS, (1913, VI:180. HODGSON (1822:104) and SKINNER (1832, II:70) hold the same view.

[11] DARIAN (1978:9) also mentions the river goddesses Yamunā and Sarasvatī. HODGSON says (1822:97) the temple is dedicated to "Gangá Máí and Bhágirat'hí" and the IMPERIAL GAZETTEER OF INDIA, 1908, XII:139 states that it "[...] contains small statues of Gangā, Bhāgīratha and other mythical personages".

[12] Gaṅgā Daśaharā is not an all-India festival but only local; at Haridvār it is celebrated for five days. It falls on the tenth day of the light half of the month of Jyeṣṭha (May/June) and celebrates the descent of Gaṅgā from the ear of sage Jahnu, who held her up temporarily. It is a fertility and river festival; as the name suggests, the five greater and five lesser sins of body, mind, and soul are washed away by a bath in the Gaṅgā on this day (WALKER 1968, I:380).

[13] HAMILTON 1828, I:560: "The water taken from hence is drawn under the inspection of a Brahmin, to whom a trifling sum is paid for the privilege of taking it, and much of it is offered up by, or on the part of the pilgrim at the temple of Baidyanath in Bengal. The specific gravity of this river is said to exceed that of its neighbour the Alacananda, according to Hindoo belief, and is so pure as neither to evaporate, or become corrupted by being kept and transported to distant places." Cf. also v. GLASENAPP (1928:22); ENCYCLOPEDIA OF RELIGION AND ETHICS (1913, VI:180).

[14] SALOMON (1979:120). SALOMON's survey (to supplement BHARDWAJ 1973) deals with two medieval texts on pilgrimage (smṛtiarthasāra of Śrīdhara and Madanapāla's madanapārijāta) that have this succession of rivers: Gaṅgā-Sarasvatī-Śoṇā-Godāvarī-Yamunā... It is based on the notion of differing karmic indulgence (according to place) by visiting the place, or river, and through performance of the prescribed rituals there.

[15] V. GLASENAPP (1928:22 f.)

[16] E. g. Garuḍa- and Matsyapurāṇas; cf. BHARDWAJ (1973:63 ff).

[17] BANDHYOPADHYAYA (1983:1); JOSHI (1986:194).

[18] DASGUPTA (1975, I:432).

[19] SALOMON (1979:123).

[20] Rivers are considered superior among tīrthas, other physical places are often connected with them, like these four most important sites on the banks of the Gaṅgā (SALOMON 1979): Vārāṇāsī, Prayāga (Allahabad), Gaṅgāsāgara (the mouth), Gaṅgādvāra (Haridvār). They earn the pilgrim a merit of 360 kṛcchras each. A ritual bath in Gaṅgā's waters at any place earns 180 kṛcchras, to do it at a sacred place earns twice as much.

Kedarnāth and Badrīnāth have been pilgrimage sites long before the Middle Ages (see notes 16 – 19). They are mentioned in Sanskrit sources and are connected with Śaṃkara (788 – 820): his temple in Kedarnāth and the fifth jyotirliṅga. Today, Yamunotrī, Gaṅgotrī, and the other two are the most important pilgrimage centers for Hindus in the Kumaon Himālaya and are similar in importance. Badrīnāth is one of the four dhāms of the Hindus (the northern one of Śaṃkara's māthas — BHARDWAJ (1973:169 f.).

In the myth, Gaṅgā, emerging from Śiva's hair, falls into lake Bindusaras (= Vindu Sarovara, ALI (1966:68), RĀMĀYAṆA I, 42, 6) which is created by a few drops of water falling from Śiva's hair in this process (BOCK 1984:76). ALI (1966:68 f.) devotes a few interesting thoughts to Bindusaras' physical location. In the Purāṇas, according to him (ibid.: 61 f.), rivers always originate from a lake (1); and (2) continue to flow under-ground to overcome hindrances such as mountains, so, as a consequence, all river sources are taken to be rivers coming to the surface again, not that they originate here; a river and its tributaries are seen and described as *one* river. ALI differentiates three stages of cosmographic development in the descent of the Gaṅgā

(1966:63 ff.; cf. also v. GLASENAPP 1928:21 f.): (1) identification of the 'heavenly' Gaṅgā with the Milky Way; (2) the river's identification with the snow masses of the Pāmir mountains (in the myth: the obstruction in Śiva's hair); (3) from here Gaṅgā starts to melt and as four rivers, flows in four directions. ALI implies that all rivers from the snow masses are identified with the Ganges (ibid.: 64), and in fact many rivers bear her name, like Kṛṣṇagaṅgā, Viṣṇugaṅgā, Kālīgaṅgā etc. The seven Gaṅgās, identified with the seven mothers (saptamātṛkāḥ), are mentioned in SALOMON's texts (111:3). Despite this universal mythological importance of the Gaṅgā, that river originating at Gomukh is revered as the original and holiest.

Also purāṇic is the classification of tīrthas in BHARDWAJ (1973:97): Daiva tīrthas (created by Brahmā, Viṣṇu, or Śiva), Asura tīrthas (by Asuras), Ārṣa tīrthas (created by saints), and Manuṣa tīrthas (by rulers of solar and human dynasties). Gaṅgā, being created by Śiva, is of the first group. KANE names those six rivers that originate in the Himālayas and are considered Devatīrthas: Bhāgīrathī, Narmadā, Yamunā, Sarasvatī, Viśokā, Vitastā (1953, IV:567) and concludes: "It is clear therefore that it was recognized early that tīrthayātrā was a popular way for redemption of sins in the case of all classes of men and women." (ibid.: 569).

The Sanskrit sources show that their cosmographic ideas are of a mythological nature rather than geographical, and, where geographical aspects appear their meaning is universalistic rather than 'detailed'. The reason that the geographical Ganges source is not mentioned in the texts lies certainly in the fact that it is difficult to approach, too: whether it was completely unknown can be conjectured only. Well known and revered was the "Gate of the Gaṅgā", Gaṅgādvāra (Haridvār, — SALOMON 1979:111:4), the place where she leaves the hills. It is not quite clear whether "Gaṅgodbheda" (in the Agnipurāṇa) designates Haridvār, it can mean break-through, appearance, spring, or the source of the Gaṅgā. Since for Haridvār usually "Gaṅgādvāra" is used, it may be a different place. BHARDWAJ, in his map (1973:69), places it approximately at Gaṅgotrī but doesn't refer to it explicitly. Since the source is not referred to in almost all texts, and considering the statements in early British reports, it can be assumed that very few people had seen the area before the early nineteenth century, and that they probably were ascetics (cf. note 56). DARIAN's comment on the age of the village: "Considering its age, the town seems almost makeshift." (1978:8) doesn't seem to be founded, and probably cannot be proven, except by "old" he implies about 1750.

The Bhāgīrathī river though appears in the texts: for instance MATSYAPURĀṆA (121,38–41), in the description of Jambūdvīpa; in the Brahmapurāṇa as part of the classification of tīrthas. Here the river is a devatīrtha, one of the six rivers of this type originating in the Himālayas. BHARDWAJ established a sequence of Hindu pilgrimage sites (1973, chapter 5:80) on the basis of present literature by counting the occurrence of places in seven authors: of 142 places, 28 are mentioned by 6 – 7 authors, 26 by 4 – 5 (among them Gaṅgotrī), 30 places by 3 authors, and 58 by 2 authors, which shows the relative importance of Gaṅgotrī.

[21] Cf. JOSHI (1986) for the history of religion in this area.

[22] AMADO (1978:66). The reason for the high percentage of Rājasthānis cannot be due to the assignment of different parts of the country to Śaṃkara's four māthas: Bādarikāśrama (jyotirmātha) serves the North and North West, whereas Rājasthān and Mahārāṣṭra belong to the Śāradāmātha in Dvārakā (cf. GHURYE 1964:88 f.). According to TATTVANANDA the percentage of Śaivas is high in Rājasthān, which may be an explanation for them to come to this Śaivic place; also, touristic motivations may be there (which are actually not separated from religious ones, in this society), like the relative proximity, or the possibility to flee from the hot desert climate — especially in May and June, the time of the yātrā.

[23] E. g. BANDHYOPADHYAYA (1983). A kind of 'ritual and mythological' guidebook is Śrī Gaṅgā Mahātmya... (n.d.); on 63 pages it contains a succession of quotations from the Padma- and Skandapurāṇas pertaining to Gaṅgā, and several small prayers, songs, and ritual hymns. Ravindra told me that the publisher of this booklet has produced one for each pilgrimage site, in other words, it would be a pure business undertaking. Mahātmyas (a kind of local Purāṇas)

exist for many pilgrimage sites and are of no great literary importance.

[24] This mechanical exactness of some brochures can be met elsewhere in Indian everyday life — where something has an official character, for instance in the bureaucratic machinery which, although established by the British, is nevertheless perpetuated with devotion by Indians. And since its aim and meaning in India seems to be somewhat different from its Western counterpart, sometimes unusual applications occur, because besides this drive to exactness, to follow rules literally, there is a drive to the informal, or vague, and non-committal which makes exactness a farce again.

In the Indian case, the trait may have been influenced — among other factors — by a ritual practice in Vedic religion for more than 3000 years: the Vedic sacrifice, if it is to be successful, has to be applied minutely; several priests participate in it with a strict departmentalization of duties. If this structural feature, that played a prominent part in its process for such a long time, then started to bear upon social life, it would mean that a deeply internalized characteristic of the religious subsystem, here a structural, or formal characteristic, influences everyday life behavior. Another instance of this transference from the religious subsystem to other areas may be the increasing differentiation of the caste system: one of its principles being separation of its groups from each other as well as their interdependence — another analogon in regard to the sacrifice. In a different context, MICHAELS recently stressed societal effects of ritual (sacrificial) gifts and other elements of Vedic sacrifices on Hindu society (1986:106 ff., esp. 110 f.): "Diese Problematik der Opfergaben und rituellen Geschenke führte unter den brahmanischen Priestern und Gelehrten im Laufe der Zeit zu unterschiedlichen Ritualkonzepten: von einem ursprünglich auf Rivalität und ritualisiertem Kampf beruhenden wechselseitigen Tausch des Übels zwischen den am Opfer beteiligten Parteien bis hin zu einer Form des rituellen Spezialistentums, in der das Übel und die Unreinheit in erblichen Berufen erstarrten und das eine Grundlage des hierarchischen Kastenwesens bildet." (1986:110) For MICHAELS, invading Indo-Aryans found themselves in a situation where they had to protect themselves culturally and politically vis-à-vis the autochthonous tribes, and developed, in the structure of the sacrifice, mechanisms of exclusiveness, and, out of the sacrifice, caste structures (111 f.).

So the observation of exactness, practiced in the Vedic sacrifice (exact division of labor of the priests, exact observation of each ritual element) may have influenced and enhanced the formation of present caste differentiation. In this formation process, the brahmanical group has the major role — a typical one as described by DUMONT (1980:275; cf. also note 56), in distinction to the renouncer who operates on the meta level. KAKAR found a connection between religious, mythical consciousness and profane behavior (1982:5 f.) in his psychoanalytical research on the Indian socialization process: "The role of myths, especially those of religious derivation, in defining and integrating the traditional elements and the common features of identity and society in Hindu India — certainly in the past, and in most parts of the community till today — cannot be over-estimated." and: "Animistic and magical thinking persists, somewhat diluted, among many Indians well into adulthood." (ibid. 105). It seems justified to me to speak of a "mythical consciousness" regarding this phenomenon. RUBEN elaborated on the relation between philosophy and Indian mythology/Indian mythical thinking and gave an overview of the reception of Indian mythology and philosophy with Western philosophers and scholars 1971:1 ff.). To follow up this thought on mythical thinking, and to put it in an even wider context, I would like to quote from HORKHEIMER/ADORNO who wrote, from the philosophical angle and without considering the Indian context, on mythology/mythical thinking, from where enlightenment (and with it rationality and science) emerged, and which finally becomes 'mythological' again:

"Je mehr die Denkmaschinerie das Seiende sich unterwirft, um so blinder bescheidet sie sich bei dessen Reproduktion. Damit schlägt Aufklärung in die Mythologie zurück, der sie nie zu entrinnen wußte. Denn Mythologie hatte in ihren Gestalten die Essenz des Bestehenden:

Kreislauf, Schicksal, Herrschaft der Welt als die Wahrheit zurückgespiegelt und der Hoffnung entsagt. In der Prägnanz des mythischen Bildes wie in der Klarheit der wissenschaftlichen Formel wird die Ewigkeit des Tatsächlichen bestätigt und das bloße Dasein als der Sinn ausgesprochen, den es versperrt. Die Welt als gigantisches analytisches Urteil, der einzige, der von allen Träumen der Wissenschaft übrig blieb, ist vom gleichen Schlage wie der kosmische Mythos, der den Wechsel von Frühling und Herbst an den Raub Persephones knüpfte." (1986: 27 f.)

25 The profane, or historical information value of the guide books is negligible, which is true in regard to Sanskrit sources also. BHARDWAJ (1973:16): "However, almost no details are given either in the *Mahābhārata* or in the *Purāṇas* about the physical setting of these places, their population, or relative distances in any form. In this respect these descriptions are indeed disappointing." But it seems consequent for mythology that it doesn't supply geographical data.

26 COLEBROOKE (1810).

27 TIEFFENTHALER (1785-7).

28 FRASER (1820).

29 HODGSON (1822).

30 RAPER (1810:483 f.)

31 HAMILTON (1828, I:560).

32 RAPER (1810:485).

33 HODGSON (1822:104).

34 At the point where the river emerges from the ice: 27 feet breadth, ca. 12 inches deep; in Gaṅgotrī 43 feet breadth, 18 inches deep.

35 1828, I:556.

36 HODGSON (1822:104); HAMILTON (1828, I:560); cf. FRASER (1820).

37 HODGSON (1822).

38 HAMILTON (1828, I:560).

39 1832, II:42.

40 Ibid.:67, on the road conditions in Gaṅgotrī: "There is no road beyond; and, with all the effort possible, I question whether a traveller could penetrate much more than a mile further. The river about a quarter of a mile beyond Gangotri winds to the east, towards the high mountains of the Rudru Himmalch, in which it is believed to have its source."

41 IMPERIAL GAZETTEER OF INDIA (1908, XII:139 f).; HODGSON (1822:98); HAMILTON (1828, I:560); v. GLASENAPP (1928:22) took his description almost literally from the Imperial Gazetteer.

42 IMPERIAL GAZ. ibid. HESKE reports in his travel account (1937:301) that according to statements of inhabitants the old temple was replaced by the present one in 1923 through the Mahārāṇī of Jaipur.

43 HODGSON (1822:98); HAMILTON (1828, I:560).

44 SKINNER 1832, II:56.

45 1820:223 f.: "[...] just above this bridge, in a bay formed in this stringly space, is situated the small temple or *Mat*, dedicated to the goddess *Ganga* or *Bha'gi'rat'hí*. In former days, there was no temple made with hands for her worship; but within these few years, as has been observed above, the piety of *Amer Sinh T'happa*, chief of the *Gorc'ha* conquerors, provided a sum of money (from 400 to 500 rupees) for the erection of this small building."

46 1822:104. HAMILTON's account (1828, I:556) suggests that the Munshi nevertheless reached Gomukh because here the data of 1808 appear (cf. note 34). From this point several reports

seemingly have been mixed up in HAMILTON's account: he says there is no practicable route along the Gaṅgā (obviously he means the Bhāgīrathī since he specifies the latter's co-ordinates) as along the Jāhnavī, otherwise the natives would have found it prior to 1808, and that this path hasn't been explored by Europeans during the rainy season, when the snow masses are probably reduced noticeably. Then the somewhat misplaced sentence follows: "But certainly the Dauli, and not the Bhagirathi ought to be considered the main stream of the Ganges" (556). The Dhauli Gaṅgā originates about thirty kilometers east of Joshimāth and confluences here with the Alaknandā). The altitude of the source is 13,800 feet (4527 m) in HAMILTON, in HODGSON 12,914 feet (4236 m — 1822:112); actually it is 3892 m.

47 Although birch trees (Bhojpatra) = bark of the birch tree) are found only below Bhojbāsā today.

48 HODGSON (1822:109–21). For a long time, Gomukh was described as a rock in front of a high mountain, resembling a cow's head from which the water came. It seemed impossible to go beyond, its location must have been between Srīnagar (in Garhwal) and Gaṅgotrī, not beyond Gaṅgotrī, as is indicated by several statements — like COLEBROOKE's (1810:434), or AMADO, who refers to an expedition under Akbar's reign at the end of the sixteenth century that ended at this place (1978:56). So it may be assumed that "Gomukh" was used to identify the river source at the glacier only from the beginning of the nineteenth century.

49 FRASER (1820:225).

50 ibid.: 232: "The truth is, that though the shrine of *Gangotrī* is the holiest of those to be met with in this sacred range, it is the least accessible, and consequently has fewer votaries; for those coming from the low country choose rather to take a comparatively easy road, and proceed to a more splendid and better frequented shrine, that of *Badarīnát'h* which is thus far better endowed, and the officiating priests of which are in much better worldly circumstances, than those of *Gangotrí*."

51 1832, II:57 f.

52 Cf. KIRFEL (1967:91 f., 334 f.)

53 1832, II:70.

54 Cf. RÖSEL (1980:215 f.)

55 FRASER (1820:229): "The old popular idea, that the *Ganges* issues from a rock like a cow's mouth (*Gae Muk'h*) did not fail to occur to me, and enquiries were made into the origin of this fable. When it was mentioned, the pundit laughed and observed that most of those pilgrims who came from the plains put the same question in several shapes; one asking whether it did not take its rise from the leaves of a sacred birch, (*Bhojpatr*;) others from its roots: and others again supposing, that the stream really and visibly came down from heaven. But he gravely assured us that no such thing happened, and that the river, in truth, came from the snow as above mentioned."

56 I would like to separate solitarily living sādhus from the Brahmins of a temple (pāṇḍas) and mahantas and monks/nuns of āśramas because I postulate them to be closer to the ideal of separation from the world, and consider them to be closest to the "individual-outside-the-world" as DUMONT named it (1980:275); āśrama- and temple organization are necessarily closer to society. DUMONT (who doesn't differentiate between sacred specialists such as sādhus and renunciants in āśramas) sees the renouncer as the major creator in religion and philosophy, and, since social life in India is widely influenced by religious principles, also as creative in this aspect: "Is it really too adventurous to say that the agent of development in Indian religion and speculation, the 'creator of values', has been the renouncer? The Brahman, as a scholar, has mainly preserved, aggregated, and combined; he may well have created and developed special branches of knowledge. Not only the founding of sects and their maintenance, but the major ideas, the 'inventions' are due to the renouncer whose unique position gave him a sort of monopoly for putting everything in question." (1980:275). DUMONT concludes "[...]

that hierarchy in actual fact culminated in its contrary, the renouncer!" (ibid.:194). The renouncer, according to Dumont, lives in a society where the "individual" in the Western sense is unknown, a society that is marked by hierarchy and, therefore, mutual dependence, and separation of the groups. In this society, or at its fringe, the renouncer, or "individual-outside-the-world", strives for salvation. In this process he has to get rid of the ego (in order to overcome reincarnation), and, as a first result, is confronted with it and has to recognize it first. This type of "socialization" generates a different consciousness from that of the person in the world, whose life is governed by regard for family, clan, and obedience to these values; where action that enhances and promotes the group is rewarded, and individual achievement is rather discouraged, as KAKAR has found (1982). DUMONT thinks that "[...] the presence of the individual- outside-the-world and his immemorial action was truly decisive for the permeability of Indian society to individualistic ways of thought." (1980:235).

[57] I.e. data of a structural kind on the sādhus of a given place, esp. of an important pilgrimage site. SINHA and SARASWATI (1978) concentrated on āśramas in Vārāṇāsī only, their mahantas, monks, and nuns, and didn't include the sādhus. They also give an account on the organization of Śaiva- and Vaiṣṇava sects in general, but it doesn't come up to GHURYE's excellent treatise on the organization of Hindu monastic sects (1964). So they state (to name a case) that daśanāmis are divided in three groups, Daṇḍi, Paramahaṃsa, and Nāga (1978:63), an error, resp. misconception already GHURYE pointed to (1964:71). Two other works of this type, written by Swāmis (SADĀNANDA 1976; TATTWANANDA 1984) are too brief, and often not exact, or faulty. Explicitly historical, and including Buddhist and Jain monasticism, is CHAKRABORTI (1973). Furthermore there are works on particular sects, of which I would like to mention only BRIGGS' classic on the Kānphaṭa-Yogis (1982).

SHARMA, a disciple of Śivānanda in Rishikesh, has given biographical sketches of 41 Swāmis and other celebrities (1982) mainly persons he personally met. BHAGAT's book (1982) also contains religious, biographical sketches, but of sixteen well-known Indian saints of the past. GREVIS (1970), in the journalistic style of his time (the book was written around 1946 - 7), writes on sādhus in and around Rishikesh. Also in a journalistic manner is STÜRMER (1980); he deals with rumors, intrigues and the like among sādhus and āśramas in Rishikesh.
A different category are those studies, initiated by Vidyarthi, on Hindu sacred complexes, i.e. famous temples and their (mainly religious) infrastructure, including sacred specialists, pilgrims etc. (VIDYARTHI 1961, 1979; VIDYARTHI and JHA 1974; UPADHYAY 1974). A later monograph of this type deals also explicitly with the economic side of such a complex (CHAKRABARTI 1984). An interdisciplinary project concentrated on the temple of Jagannāth in Puri and its organization from several angles (ESCHMANN et al. 1978, RÖSEL 1980). A short, analytic treatise on Indian asceticism is contained in MICHAELS' essay on "Ritual und Gesellschaft in Indien" (1986:116–24).

A number of Master's theses of the University of Ranchi in the tradition of Vidyarthi (who taught at Ranchi), investigate on the sacred complexes of Kedarnāth and Badrīnāth. They were prepared following a mutual "field work excursion"; their scientific standard is not satisfactory, though.
This survey shows that the concentration so far was on a religious center, its structure and importance, or on monasticism, either as a whole or on particular sects, or on hagiographies of different type. The present study though aims at the religious-ethnographic structure of the sādhu population of a place, as has been stated in the introduction.

[58] RÖSEL reports a process of "mystification" (1980:185–200) that connects the hitherto autochthonous village god (i.e. Jagannāth) without a heaven, but ruling over territory, with the brahmanical deity, lacking territory, but commanding a heavenly sphere. The brahmanical ritual consists of the esoteric connection of the two types in the ritual of "delocalization" of the god to unite it with the brahmanical pantheon. Here the priest creates, during a pūjā, the god in his heart and transfers him to the wooden idol for the period of feeding only; so the priest

is made the creator of the god, which I interpret as an essentially demystifying process when seen as an event within the structure of religion and in comparison to what the pigrim is told: it is kept secret from him — he is told instead that during the ritual food is presented to the god (who for him always resides in the wooden image) secretly, and hence, ritually pure. This, for the knowing Brahmins, intrareligiously "enlightening" process *increases* the total amount of mystification that 'religion' creates in the pilgrim. RÖSEL also remarks, however, that there is a rather blind execution of rituals on the brahmanical side, without any esoteric knowledge (ibid.:186 f.) which certainly diminishes the 'enlightenment' again. The degeneration of the esoteric brahmanical ritual would speak for DUMONT's argument (see note 56), because it can be argued that this type of esoteric process fits the renouncer better.

[59] E.g. the elaboration of mythological topics from the Purāṇas etc., descriptions of sects or their socio-cultural portrayal (cf. note 57).

[60] This higher plane in the hierarchy of sacred specialists, attributed to mahantas by Ravindra, probably has its main reason in the fact that the sādhu in his development first strives for a higher state of consciousness or englightenment, and in this stage preferably lives in solitude, so this stage comes before he can become a mahanta. In that position he may want to teach his insights within the setting of a monastic organization. But the succession sādhu/mahanta cannot be made a rule since many sādhus always remain solitary, or teach without an organizational frame, or do not settle down.

[61] Saṃnyāsins have to follow the rule of celibacy in general, but even excepting it, segregation of the sexes common in the Hindu cultural area would be reason enough to judge this behavior negatively.

[62] Although it is valid in principle for all saṃnyāsins (those belonging to Śaṃkara's daśanāmis), it is especially stressed for Daṇḍis: "We may note here that though the Dasanāmi Samnyāsis, who are followers of the monastic Vedānta of Śankarācārya, accept for worship various aspects of the Deity in more or less human forms, in theory they are expected to meditate on the formless Supreme Soul." (GHURYE 1964:87 — on Daṇḍis), and "The realisation of the Absolute [i.e. nirguṇa brahman] is their goal." (TATTWANANDA 1984:78 — on Daṇḍis).

[63] YOGATATTVOPANIṢAT: 19, in: ĪŚĀDYAṢṬOTTARAŚATOPANIṢADAḤ (1983:255).

[64] SINHA/SARASWATI (1978:71 f.)

[65] ibid.

[66] It is one of the āśramas having a rich tradition in Northern India (e.g. Haridvār, Rishikesh, Uttarkāśi), where learning plays an important role. Cf. SADĀNANDA (1976:80–2).

[67] DEVEREUX (n.d.: 40–54).

Table 1: Ethnographic data of the sādhus in Gaṅgotrī

Name	talks in	place	dwelling	in Gaṅgotrī since	in winter
Daṇḍiswāmi Haṃsānand	English	outside, upper Northern banks	2 buildings	30 years	Gomukh
Gaṅgā Dās	Hindi	dito	3 buildings	46 years	Gaṅgotrī
Govind Dās Mahārāj	Hindi	in the village	hut	29 years, since 3 years with interruptions	sometimes G. or visits holy sites
Kapilānand Paramahaṃs Puri	Hindi; written, since he is a Mauni	dito	3 buildings	4 years	Gaṅgotrī
Lakṣmi Prapannācārya	Hindi	outside, upper Southern banks	hut	14 years	Govardhan
Swāmi Gaṅgeśvarānand	Hindi	in the village	room in a building	6 years	Gaṅgotrī
Swāmi Sundarānanda Giri	English (broken)	dito	2 huts	36 years	travels and gives slide shows
Swāmi Yogānanda Sarasvatī	Hindi some English	dito	hut with a cave	16 years	Uttarkāśi
Nr. 1	English	in the village and outside, upper Southern banks	building, and hut with cave	several years	Delhi
Nr. 2	Hindi	outside, upper Southern banks	2 huts		
Nr. 3	English	outside, lower Southern banks	hut with cave	4 years	Gaṅgotrī

Name	alone resp. no. of disc.	origin	guru	sect	sādhana
Daṇḍiswāmi Haṃsānand	one sādhvī	District Gorakhpur		Śaiva (saṃnyāsin)	Mantra-Yoga, Meditation on Nirguṇa Brahman
Gaṅgā Dās	3 disciples		Śrī Rām Balak Dās Mahārāj	Vaiṣṇava	Bhakta
Govind Dās Mahārāj	alone	Kānpur	Swāmi Śrī Tapovan Mahārāj	Vaiṣṇava	Bhakta; havan, agnihotra
Kapilānand Paramahaṃs Puri	alone	earlier: Kailāsāśrama. Uttarkāśi	Mahāmaṇḍaleśvar 108 Swāmi Vidyānand Giri	Śaiva (daśanāmi saṃnyāsin: Puri)	Mauna
Lakṣmi Prapannācārya	alone	District Arrah Bihar	Basudevācarya	Vaiṣṇava	Bhakta; havan agnihotra
Swāmi Gaṅgeśvarānand	alone	Garhwal	Daṇḍiswāmi Pūrṇānand Tīirtha	Śaiva (saṃnyāsin)	Bhakta
Swāmi Sundarānanda Giri	alone	Anantpuram, District Nellore	Swāmi Śrī Tapovan Mahārāj	Śaiva (daśanāmi saṃnyāsin: Giri)	Karma-Yoga; 1950-4: Kuṇḍalinī-Yoga, tapas
Swāmi Yogānanda Sarasvatī	alone	Kerala	Swāmi Niṣkalānanda	Śaiva (daśanāmi saṃnyāsin: Sarasvatī)	Rāja-Yoga; prāṇayama, dhyāna
Nr. 1	1 disciple			Śaiva (saṃnyāsin)	probably Yogas, Meditation)
Nr. 2	alone	Garhwal		Śaiva	
Nr. 3	alone			Śaiva	

scriptures studied	venerated deity	teacher?	disciples/followers	livelihood	reason for being here	future
	(nirguṇa brahman)	yes	many/yes	donations	solitude	Gaṅgotrī
Bhāgavatam	Gaṅgā	yes	at least 3/yes	donations, some agriculture	śānti	dito
Rāmāyaṇa	Gaṅgā	no	no/from all over India	donations		
epics, Purāṇas; generally śruti as well as smṛti	Gaṅgā	no	no/	donations	Gaṅgā, śānti	
Rāmāyaṇa; (Siddhānta)	Śālagrāma	yes	6 (in Govardhan)/ many	gifts in return for pūjās	śānti	dito
Rāmāyaṇa, Purāṇas		no	no/yes	donations	origin and guru are local	dito
		no	no/yes	in part self-sufficient: agriculture, royalities	tapas, śānti	dito
Bhagavadgītā, Yogatexts		no	no/no	donations	śānti	
mainly the Veda; teaches Sāṃkhya Yoga			/yes	in part royalties from publications	in part: seclusion	the inner of the Himālayas
		no		"difficult"	to reach higher stages of development	G. only for a few years

Glossary

(If not indicated otherwise, the words are in Sanskrit)

Agnihotra — fire sacrifice for Agni, mostly of milk, or oil.

Āśrama — 1) hermitage: place, where ascetics live; rarely: hut of an individual ascetic. 2) āśramadharma: the four life stages of a Brahmin: brahmacārin, gṛhastha, vānaprastha, saṃnyāsin.

Avadhūta — (lit.: shaken off, removed, expelled, disregarded) — related to wordly obligations etc.: ascetic, who reached this state, having no obligations, not being subject to conventions, limitations. A title often used with Kānphāṭa-Yogis and Rāmānanda Vaiṣṇavas.

Avatāra — descent, especially manifestation of a deity on earth.

Bhakta — a person who practices, cultivates bhakti.

Bhakti — religious love, surrender, devotion (as a religious method or path to reach salvation).

Caras — (Hindi) a drug prepared from the flowers of the Hemp plant; comparable to Marihuana. Often smoked by Śaiva sādhus; its use (mythologically) goes back to Śiva.

Daṇḍa — staff, stick; a staff given to the saṃnyāsin at his initiation.

Daṇḍi — a person, carrying the staff. Special group among the daśanāma saṃnyāsins recruited from Brahmins only, having special rules. They additionally belong to one of the ten subdivisions (daśanāmis).

Daśanāmi saṃnyāsins — (also: daśanamis. Hindi: dasnami) grouping of Śaiva ascetics dating back to Śaṃkara, consisting of ten (daśa) monastic orders (Araṇya, Āśrama, Bhāratī, Giri, Parvata, Puri, Sarasvatī, Sāgara, Tīrtha, Vana.).

Dharmaśālā — rest house for pilgrims, mostly free of charge, at almost all pilgrimage places, famous temples etc.

Dharmaśāstras — group of law-giving works, also in a wider sense extending to moral and ethical behavior.

Dhyāna — meditation, esp. abstract, religious. Seventh step in Patañjalis eightfold Yoga path.

Fakir — (arab.) Muslim ascetic, esp. juggler.

Gaṅgā — here: eldest daughter of Himavat and Menā, incarnated as river (Ganges).

Gerrua — orange colored robe of the saṃnyāsins.

Giri — see daśanāmi saṃnyāsins.

Gomukh — (Hindi) mouth of the cow. Location where the river Bhagīrathī emerges from the glacier.

Gotra — here: exogamous group within the endogamous sub-caste (jati); has been described as clan and lineage as well. A gotra goes back to a legendary saint, or a deity, and mainly serves marriage regulations.

Haṃsa — here: type of ascetics, mainly among Śaivas, defined by qualities, spiritual attainments and behavior. A person having those qualities, is thus designated.

Havan — (Hindi) here: fire sacrifice.

Jambūdvīpa — in Hindu cosmography the central of the seven continents that surround the Meru mountain.

Kamaṇḍalu — begging bowl of saṃnyāsin ascetics.

Karma — action, activity. Here: one of the central principles of Hinduistic beliefs, saying that "normal" (i.e. deeds not free of intentions) actions will generate results, i.e. are the cause for an effect, and the causal action also is the result of an earlier action; an endless chain. This is connected with the notion of saṃsāra (cycle of reincarnations), extending over many lives.

Kṛcchra — a penance of twelve days (described in YAJÑAVALKYASMṚTI III, 318–9).

Kśetra — here: place, site (e.g. an āśrama) where sādhus beg for food (annakśetra).

Kūpa — cave, here: a cave where a sādhu lives.

Kuṭī, Kuṭīr — hut.

Mahanta — head of an āśrama (hermitage, monastery).

Mahārāj — (Hindi) lit. "great ruler, king". Honorific designation sometimes added to ascetics' names without fixed rules.

Mahātmā — lit. "great self, great soul", here: designation for completely liberated renouncers (having attained mokṣa).

Mauna — vestibule of a Hindu temple.

Maṇḍapa — here: vow of silence. Mauni: sādhu who took a vow of silence.

Mokṣa — liberation; being free from the cycle of birth and death (saṃsāra).

Muni — a wise and holy man, ascetic.

Mūrti — here: idol, statue; of deities, especially in temples.

Nāga — here: group of ascetics belonging to the daśanāmi saṃnyāsins, and whose function used to be to protect other saṃnyāsin- groups (from other sādhus, esp. Fakirs). They are usually nude and rub their body with white ashes.

Nirguṇa brahman — in contrast to saguṇa brahman (having qualities) that brahman (the impersonal supreme being) without qualities (i.e. abstract), as an object of veneration and meditation.

Nirvikalpa samādhi — samādhi (in the system of Yoga: highest state of meditation, eighth step in Patañjali's system) beyond change or difference (in contrast to savikalpa s., which still includes "change"), i.e. constant, irreversible contemplation.

Pāṇḍa — temple priest.

Paramahaṃsa — is generally described as high hierarchical level of individual spiritual achievement among sādhus and has this meaning in the Paramahaṃsa-Upaniṣad. Other Upaniṣads and the Nāradīya-Purāṇa report six hierarchical steps of spiritual attainment among saṃnyāsins: kuṭīcaka, bahūdaka, haṃsa, paramahaṃsa, turīyatīta, and avadhūta. It is difficult though, considering the different statements of authors and sources, to arrive at one succession, the qualities ascribed to each state differ too much from each other.

Prāṇayama — yogic exercises, mostly breathing exercises, to attain control over prāṇa (life force).

Prasāda — here: food dedicated to a (temple-)deity, which is afterwards distributed to the followers.

Pūjā — worship, reverence; ritual action for a deity.

Pūjāri — Brahmin performing pūjā in temples.

Purāṇas — here: category of religious, mythological texts of Hinduism.

Sādhana — here: means and methods applied to attain mokṣa, the path to this end.

Sādhu — saint, sage, ascetic etc. Used as a generic term for renouncers, in a special sense those who don't live in āśramas. For a good definition and discussion of comparative terms see MICHAELS 1986:116 f.

Śaiva — follower of Śiva, also ascetics belonging to Śaiva monastic orders.

Śalagrāma — (Hindi: Shaligram) a black ammonite, found in Mount Gandakī (Nepal), which is considered an incarnation of Viṣṇu by Vaiṣṇavas according to a legend of the Bhāgavata-Purāṇa.

Samādhi — see nirvikalpa samādhi.

Śaṃkara — (788 – 820) teacher of Vedānta philosophy and founder resp. organizer of the daśanāmi saṃnyāsins.

Saṃnyāsa — putting down, or aside, giving up; here: renunciation of the world, ascetic life.

Saṃnyāsin — renunciant; more particularly a designation for the daśanāmis.

Śānti — peace, stillness, tranquility, absence of passion.

Sarasvatī — second-holiest river of the Hindus. Identical with the goddess, consort of Brahma: her domains are wisdom, learning, music, and the arts.

Siddha — success, attainment; ascetic who has attained supernatural powers (siddhīḥ).

Śivaliṅga — phallus of Śiva; object of adoration for Śaivas as a symbol of fertility and potency.

Smṛti — what is remembered; that part of Hindu religious literature of secondary importance (the recollection is by earthly teachers).

Śruti — what is heard; Hindu religious literature of primary importance (heard by the ṛṣis = sages, seers).

Tapas — different types of rigid exercises to attain body control, supernatural powers, or karmic merit.

Tīrtha — here: pilgrimage site and one of the ten names of Śaṃkara's monastic order.

Vaiṣṇava — follower of Viṣṇu, also ascetics belonging to such monastic orders.

Yātrā — here: pilgrimage journey.

Yoga — yoking, joining, union (of powers, efforts, and with a religious goal). One of the six systems of Hindu philosophy (darśanas), consisting mainly of practical methods to attain the goal (liberation).

Yuga — here: an age of the world, consisting of four periods: kṛta (satya), tretā, dvāpara, and kali.

Summary

Gaṅgotrī is the closest village to the source of the Ganges river and an important Hindu pilgrimage site. A group of its sacred specialists, sādhus living here solitarily and long term, have been interviewed on religious and ethnographic categories such as sect, sādhana, guru, scriptures studied etc., in order to attain a basic picture of their composition, motivation etc. Also, a portrait of Gaṅgotrī is given (present appearance, history, importance as a pilgrimage site) in order to correlate these data with the composition of the sādhus, and several theoretical points pertaining to sādhus, Hindu society, and mythological consciousness are discussed. The data show that the composition and orientation of the sādhus correlates with the religious meaning of the village. Furthermore, they can serve as a basis for future studies comparing pilgrimage places of this kind, groups of sacred specialists etc.

Zusammenfassung: Die Sādhus in Gaṅgotrī

Gaṅgotrī ist das letzte Dorf vor der Gangesquelle und ein wichtiges hinduistisches Pilgerzentrum. Eine Gruppe seiner religiösen Spezialisten, solitär und langfristig hier lebende sādhus, wurden zu religionsgeschichtlichen und ethnographischen Kategorien wie Sekte, sādhana, Guru, studierte Schriften usw. befragt, um ein grundlegendes Bild ihrer Zusammensetzung, Motivation usw. zu erhalten. Außerdem wird Gaṅgotrī dargestellt (gegenwärtige Erscheinung, Geschichte, Bedeutung als Pilgerort), um diese Daten mit denen der sādhus zu korrelieren; auch werden einige theoretische Fragen zu sādhus, hinduistischer Gesellschaft und 'mythologischem Bewußtsein' angesprochen. Die Daten zeigen, daß die Zusammensetzung und Orientierung der sādhus mit der religiösen Bedeutung des Ortes korreliert. Sie können darüberhinaus als Basis für weitere Untersuchungen vergleichender Art zwischen verschiedenen Pilgerorten, oder etwa für weitergehende Untersuchungen am Ort dienen.

Bibliography

ALI, S. M.: The geography of the Puranas. New Delhi 1966.

AMADO, Pierre: Les sources sacrées du Gange. In: L'histoire 7. 1978: 53 – 66.

ATKINSON, Edwin Felix Thomas: Notes on the history of religion in the Himalaya of the N. W. P., India. Allahabad 1883.

BECHERT, Heinz: Zum Ursprung der Geschichtsschreibung im indischen Kulturbereich. In: Nachrichten der Akademie der Wissenschaften in Göttingen, I: Phil.-hist. Klasse, 1969, No. 2: 36 – 58.

BHAGAT, Manu G.: Ancient Indian ascetism. Delhi 1976.

BHAGAT, Manu G.: Sages and saints of India. Bombay 1982.

BHARATI, A.: Pilgrimage sites and Indian civilization. In: Elder, J. W. (ed.): Chapters in Indian civilization. Dubuque 1970.

BHARDWAJ, Surinder Mohan: Hindu places of pilgrimage in India. (A study in cultural geography) Berkeley 1973.

BOCK, Andreas: Der Sāgara-Gaṅgāvataraṇa-Mythus in der episch-purāṇischen Literatur. Stuttgart 1984. (Alt- und Neuindische Studien. 27).

BRIGGS, George Weston: Gorakhnāth and the Kānphaṭa Yogīs (1938). Reprint Delhi 1982.

CHAKRABARTI, Profulla: Social profile of Tarakeswar. Study of a pilgrim town in West Bengal. Calcutta 1984.

CHAKRABORTI, Haripada: Ascetism in ancient India. In Brahmanical, Buddhist, Jaina and Ajivika societies (from the earliest times to the period of Śaṅkarācharya). Calcutta 1973.

COLEBROOKE, H. T.: On the sources of the Ganges, in the Himádrior Emodus. In: Asiatick researches 11. 1810: 429 - 45.

DARIAN, Stephen: Gaṅgā and Sarasvatī; an incidence of mythological projection. In: East and West, N. S. 26.1976: 153 - 66.

DARIAN, Stephen: The Ganges in myth and history. Honolulu: 1978.

DASGUPTA, Surendranath: A history of Indian philosophy. Vol. 1 (1922). Reprint Delhi 1975.

DEVEREUX, Georges: Angst und Methode in den Verhaltenswissenschaften. München n.d. (after 1967).

DEY, Nundo Lal: The geographical dictionary of ancient and medieval India. London 1927.

DOWSON, John: A classical dictionary of Hindu mythology and religion, geography, history, and literature. Twelfth ed. London 1972 (Repr.).

DUMONT, Louis: Homo hierarchicus. The caste system and its implications. Complete rev. Engl. ed. Chicago 1980.

DUMONT, Louis: Essays on individualism. Modern ideology in anthropological perspective. Chicago 1986.

DU PERRON, Anquetil: Historische und chronologische Abhandlungen von Indien, und Beschreibung des Laufes der Ströhme Ganges und Gagra ... In: Tieffenthaler 1785 - 7.

ENCYCLOPEDIA OF RELIGION AND ETHICS. Vol. VI. Edinburgh 1913.

ESCHMANN, Annecharlott, H. KULKE and G. C. TRIPATHI (eds.): The cult of Jagannath and the regional tradition of Orissa. New Delhi 1978.

FRASER, J. B.: Account of a journey to the sources of the Jamuna and Bhagirathi rivers. In: Asiatick researches 13.1820: 171 - 249.

GERVIS, Pearce: Naked they pray. Delhi 1970 (Reprint).

GHURYE, G. S.: Indian sadhus. 2 ed. Bombay 1964.

GLASENAPP, Helmut v.: Heilige Stätten Indiens. Die Wallfahrtsorte der Hindus, Jainas und Buddhisten, ihre Legenden und ihr Kultus. München 1928.

HAMILTON, Walter: The East-India Gazetteer; 2. ed. Vol. I. London 1828.

HESKE, Franz: Im heiligen Lande der Gangesquellen. Neudamm 1937.

HODGSON, J. A.: Journal of a survey to the heads of the rivers Ganges and Jumna. In: Asiatick researches 14.1822: 56 – 175.

HORKHEIMER, Max, and Theodor W. ADORNO: Dialektik der Aufklärung. Philosophische Fragmente. Frankfurt 1986. (Fischer-Taschenbücher .6144.)

THE IMPERIAL GAZETTEER OF INDIA. Vol. XII: Einme to Gwalior. New ed. Oxford 1908.

ĪŚĀDYAṢṬOTTARAŚATOPANIṢADAḤ (One hundred & eight Upanishads) ... [Skt.] Vārāṇasī 1983.

JOSHI, M. P.: The religious history of Uttarakhand: sources and materials. In: Vidyarthi, Lalita Prasad and M. Jha (eds.): Ecology, economy and religion of Himalayas. Delhi 1986:193 – 216.

KAKAR, Sudhir: The inner world. A psycho-analytic study of childhood and society in India. 2. ed. Delhi 1982.

KANE, P. V.: History of Dharmaśāstra. 2. ed. Vol. 4. Poona 1953.

KEILHAUER, Anneliese and Peter KEILHAUER: Die Bildsprache des Hinduismus. Die indische Götterwelt und ihre Symbolik. Köln 1983. (dumont taschenbücher. 131.)

KIRFEL, Willibald: Die Kosmographie der Inder. Nach Quellen dargestellt (1920). Reprint Hildesheim 1967.

KUTZSCHENBACH, Gerhard v.: Feldforschung als subjektiver Prozeß: ein handlungstheoretischer Beitrag zu seiner Analyse und Systematisierung. Berlin 1982 (Diss.)

The Matsya Puranam. Pt. 1. Translated by a Taluqdar of Oudh (1916). Reprint New York 1974. (The sacred books of the Hindus. 17,1.)

MICHAELS, Axel: Ritual und Gesellschaft in Indien. Ein Essay. Mit Photos von Niels Gutschow. Frankfurt 1986.

MONIER-Williams, Monier: A Sanskrit-English dictionary [...] New ed. (1899). Reprint Oxford 1979.

OMAN, John Campbell: The mystics, ascetics, and saints of India. A study of sadhuism, with an account of the Yogis, sanyasis, Bairagis, and other strange Hindu sectarians. London 1903.

RAPER, F. W.: Narrative of a survey for the purpose of discovering the sources of the Ganges. In: Asiatick researches 11.1810: 446 – 563.

RÖSEL, Jakob: Der Palast des Herrn der Welt. Entstehungsgeschichte und Organisation der indischen Tempel- und Pilgerstadt Puri. Diss. Freiburg 1976. München 1980.

RUBEN, Walter: Die Entwicklung der Philosophie im alten Indien. Berlin 1971. (Veröffentlichungen des Instituts für Orientforschung. Deutsche Akademie der Wissenschaften zu Berlin .67.)

SADANANDA Giri, Swami: Society and sannyasin: a history of the Dasnami sannyasins. Rishikesh 1976.

SALOMON, Richard: Tīrtha-pratyāmnāyāḥ: ranking of Hindu pilgrimage sites in classical Sanskrit texts. In: Zeitschrift der Deutschen Morgenländischen Gesellschaft 129.1979: 102 – 27.

SARKAR, J. N.: A history of Dāsnāmi Nāga sanyāsis. Allahabad 1958.

SHARMA, A. N.: Modern saints and mystics. Sivanandanagar 1982.

SINHA, Surajit and BAIDYANATH SARASWATI: Ascetics of Kashi: an anthropological exploration. Varanasi 1978.

SKINNER, Thomas: Excursions in India: including a walk over the Himalaya mountains, to the sources of the Jumna and the Ganges. 2 vols. London 1832.

SPROCKHOFF, Joachim Friedrich: Saṃnyāsa; Quellenstudien zur Askese im Hinduismus. I. Untersuchung über die Saṃnyāsa-Upaniṣads. Wiesbaden 1976. (Abhandlungen für die Kunde des Morgenlandes. 42.)

Śrī Gaṅgā Mahātmya aur Gaṅgotrī Mahātmya. Gaṅgā avataraṇ kī kathā, Gaṅgā kī mahimā, Gaṅgā vandnā, Gaṅgā stuti, Gaṅgā calīsā, āratiyām va bhajan. Saṃgrahkartā: Srī Gaṅgotrī dhām ke prasiddh Pāṇḍā. [Hindi u. Skt.] Haridvār: n.d. (ca. 1975 – 85).

STÜRMER, Ernst: Paradies Rishikesh. Die Hochburg der Gurus — einst und jetzt. Salzburg 1980.

TATTWANANDA, Swami: Vaisnava sects, Saiva sects, mother worhsip. Calcutta 1984.

THAKUR, U.: The holy places of North India as mentioned in the Skanda Purāṇa. In: Purāṇa 15.1973: 93 – 120.

TIEFFENTHALER, Joseph: Historisch-geographische Beschreibung von Hindustan. ...Bd. 1; II, 1; II, 2. Berlin 1785 – 7. [Bd. II, 2 under the title: Description historique et géographique de L'Inde...]

UPADHYAY, Vijay Shankar: The sacred geography of Dwarka. In: Vidyarthi, L. P. and M. Jha (eds.): Symposium on the sacred complex in India. Ranchi 1974:52 – 74.

VIDYARTHI, Lalita Prasad: The sacred complex in Hindu Gaya. 2. ed. Delhi 1978.

VIDYARTHI, Lalita Prasad: The sacred complex of Kashi. A microcosm of Indian civilization. Delhi 1979.

WALKER, Benjamin: Hindu world. An encyclopedic survey of Hinduism. Vol. I, II. London 1968.

WILKINS, W. J.: Hindu mythology, vedic and puranic (1882). 2. ed. Reprint Calcutta 1983.

Surinder M. Bhardwaj and Madhusudana Rao

EMERGING HINDU PILGRIMAGE IN THE UNITED STATES: A CASE STUDY

I. Introduction

Pilgrimage (tīrtha yātrā) to the holy rivers, hallowed shrines and temples has long been a popular Hindu religious activity in India (BHARATI 1963, STODDARD 1966; SOPHER 1968, BHARDWAJ 1973, MORINIS 1983). However, many of the *"overseas" Hindu communities* of the Caribbean, South Africa and other areas, established during the Nineteenth Century, were relatively isolated from the Indian mainstream and generally developed local cult centers of worship rather than long distance pilgrimages. Hindu Pilgrimage activity has been observed to the Urban temples of Malaysia (SANDHU 1969, 233), beaches in Trinidad (KLASS 1961, 162; BRYANS 1967, 188), certain caves in Malaysia (ARASARATNAM 1970), and a sacred lake in the mountains of Mauritius (TINKER 1974, 211). These observations have been mostly of a casual nature. In fact, the pilgrimage practices of the overseas Hindus have been largely ignored (BHARDWAJ and RAO 1983; PROROK 1982).

Although several scholars of overseas Hinduism (KUPER 1960, SCHWARTZ 1967, SPECKMAN 1965) have noted in some detail the religious practices and rituals of the expatriate Hindus, pilgrimage activity *per se* has not been prominently treated. A reason for such de-emphasis has been suggested by ARASARATNAM (1970, 165). He posits that the domiciled Indians in Malaya (now West Malaysia), before the end of the Second World War, tended to ignore certain aspects of their religious and cultural heritage. He goes on to suggest that a revival of the traditional Hindu practices is now taking place among the overseas Hindus, and that it may have to do with the rejection of cultural westernization, and the revival of indigenous culture in India itself after Independence.

This study of the evolving Hindu *religious circulation* in an alien environment has been carried out from the eclectic perspective of cultural geography. We examine some spatial and cultural dimensions of *pilgrim circulation,* focused upon a Hindu temple and emanating from the patronage and support of its *cultural hinterland;* the latter defined by the distribution of donors to this temple. Our pilgrimage and donorship data provide clues to the linkages of this overseas *religious circulation* with the historically deep rooted role of the iconic temples (temples with images of deities) in Dravidian India. Thereby, it helps us to suggest some reasons why the South Indian cultural pattern having been transposed into the new environment may have formed the basis of the primary religious circulation above and beyond the local metropolitan level. Following the cultural geography mode we have tried to relate the developing spatial structure of Hindu pilgrimage of the Sri Venkateswara Temple (Pittsburgh) to the Indian cultural anchor.

The post Independence era of India witnessed the out-migration of relatively affluent Hindus to the major industrial English speaking nations, among them, United States and Canada. It is within the last fifteen years that the building of authentic Hindu temples has begun in these countries, and the process of pilgrimage to some of these developing religious centers has already started. Leaving aside the temples of the Hare Krishna movement, the chief *iconic centers* of Hindu pilgrimage at the present time in North America are the recently completed Minakshi Temple in Houston, the Hindu Temple of Flushing, New York, the Balaji Temple (Chicago), Shiva- Vishnu Temple of Livermore (California), and above all, the Sri Venkateswara Temple, Pittsburgh. In this study we examine some facets of the developing pilgrimage process centered on the S. V. Temple.

Religious institutions have usually provided an important framework for the regrouping and acculturation of many immigrant groups in the United States (ABRAHAM et al., 1983, 171 – 175; ABRAMSON 1980, 869 – 875; CONSTANTINOU 1982; SMITH 1981). Hindus are no exception. Several mutually interactive modes of religious activity can be identified among Hindus in the United States. Although our main concern here is to examine the religious circulation focused on the S. V. Temple, it is necessary to place it in the context of other modes of Hindu religious activity in the United States.

II. Modes of Religious Activity

1. The Family Altar

At the family level most Hindu households abroad, as in India, maintain some form of an altar as a religious focus for the family (WOOD 1980). The *family altar* serves as the first imprint of Hinduism on the children of the immigrants.

The family altar also serves as the axis of the Indian *cultural timeclock* in the newly adopted culture. It provides the immigrant the 'sense of place' while thousands of miles away from the Hindu world.

2. The Interfamily Religious Meetings

The interfamily religious meetings are one of the most prevalent religious mechanisms among the Hindus in most American cities. Whether it is to give thanks to a deity, to invoke the blessings of one's favorite deity, or to conduct the study of scriptures such as the Bhagavadgita, Indian Hindu families invite other Hindu families to participate in prayers, singing of hymns and worship. On an average most families participate in the religious meetings once a month. However, increasingly, the interfamily religious groups in larger metropolitan areas are beginning to be defined by Indian regional languages. Thus, there is clear indication that as the Hindu population increases, linguistic and regional ties will reassert (FISHER 1980, 55 – 76). In any case, each Hindu household in turn becomes a sacred center drawing other worshippers from the town. The ubiquity of this mode of interaction shows a high degree of Hindu religiosity in America perhaps even greater than among similar social strata in India.

3. The Prayer House Focus

The increasing numbers of Asian Indians, the growing size of the interfamily worship groups, coupled with the concern for the growing children of the young immigrants has precipitated a trend to establish prayers houses and community centers. Even a casual perusal of the major ethnic newspapers, such as *India Abroad, India West* or the *Overseas Times*, will show this trend. In several large cities such as New York, Chicago, Cleveland and Houston, the community organizational level has reached the point where buildings have been purchased or built by Indian community for its social educational and cultural needs.

Perhaps the most important way in which an Indian community center plays a religious role is by bringing together the local Hindu population of different linguistic origins, and thus possibly generating some pan-Hindu identification — at least among children of the immigrants. Popular Indian festivals held at these centers also provide a religious flavor and generate some ethnic identification.

4. The Visiting Guru

The visiting holy person, *guru* or *swami* from India is a potent, if occasional, religious focus for the Hindu families. Quite frequently, the visiting spiritual figures are representatives of the well- developed "segmental" religions — some wishing to establish 'missions' and spiritual centers in the United States. The *Nirankari Mission* of Chicago is one of the busiest in this activity. Periodic convergence of families for spiritual communion with the visiting holy person seems to be psychologically and socially rewarding. The Indian ethnic newspapers frequently publish itineraries of the visiting spiritual *gurus* as a matter of community service.

5. Linkage With Sacred Centers in India

Although a cluster of reasons occasion the visits to India by the Hindu residents in the United States, once in India, they may tend to visit sacred centers. Since many Indian families in the United States are in the relatively high income brackets, it is not unusual for them to take their parents for visits to Hindu sacred sites. This may have been a latent desire on the part of the parents and their now affluent children. Such religious experience tends to feed back into the Hindu communities in North America.

6. Linkage With Non-Iconic Hindu Philosophical Centers

Some centers of philosophical, as contrasted with iconic and ritualistic Hinduism have existed in North America since the early decades of this century (MELENDY 1977, 184), and some new ones are beginning to take root (BHASHYANDA 1981). Whereas the early centers of Hindu philosophy were patronized almost exclusively by the mystically inclined Americans (JENSEN 1980, 300), the recent centers, e.g., the Vivekananda Monastery in Ganges, Michigan (Southwest of Grand Rapids, MI), are beginning to attract ethnic Indians — especially the philosophically oriented modernized Hindus, who are *less* inclined toward the traditional iconic ritualistic Hinduism. In general, the *Vedanta* philosophical centers seem to be gaining in popularity in the larger cities such as New York and Chicago.

7. The 'White Hindu' Iconic Connection

Before the mid-sixties, mostly Americans were the object of 'conversion' to or attraction by the spiritual purveyors of Hinduism inspired religious movements such as the International Society for Krishna Consciousness, popularly known as "Hare-Krishna", and Transcendental Meditation. Due to the highly theistic nature of the "Hare-Krishna" movement based on *bhakti* (devotion) focused on the popular Hindu deity Krishna, many Hindus, especially immigrant Hindus from North India are beginning to seek association with the Hare-Krishna temples. These temples purport to provide a traditionally 'authentic' form of worship by the "White Hindus" to the amazement and pride of many immigrant Hindus. The New Vrindaban Palace of Gold (West Virginia) has already become an important tourist attraction. New Goloka (North Carolina), has also become another popular center for many Hindus living in the famous "Research Triangle".

8. Religious Camps and Retreats

Extremely concerned about the possible cultural drift of their children, the Hindu organizations in North America are beginning to emphasize summer youth camps to provide a Hindu atmosphere for the children for at least some days in the year. Religious 'camps' for the adults also have been started in the hope of maintaining some semblance of detachment from the material world. Youth camps have been organized by the S. V. Temple, Pittsburgh, The *Vishwa Hindu Parishad of America*, and the Center of the Holy Sankaracharya Order of the Pocono Mountains.

9. The Hindu Iconic Temple

In the short history of the Hindu people in the United States since the mid-sixties, the last decade has been characterized by fervent iconic temple building activity. Iconic temples are those in which the images of specific deities (female or male), have been duly installed for authentic Hindu worship. Among the major architecturally and ritualistically authentic Hindu temples already completed are in New York, Pittsburgh, Houston, Livermore (California), Los Angeles and Chicago. Some of the temples have already become important centers of worship, pilgrimage and cultural activities. It seems that the ancient institution of Hindu pilgrimage may take root in the new cultural setting of North America, centered on some of these iconic temples.

Among the various modes of Hindu religious regrouping briefly stated above, the last — the iconic temple — is the most conspicuous symbol of Hindu identity on the New World landscape. Hinduism, however, is an extremely syncretic religion, and has been characterized as a "complex ethnic" religion (SOPHER 1967). The complexity is not only due to its great iconic and philosophical heterogeneity, but also because the Hindus in North America represent many languages.

At the broadest level, however, Hinduism may be dichotomized into the Northern and Southern Indian cultural traditions represented by the speakers of the various Indic and the Dravidian languages respectively. Considering the iconic Hindu temples, it is intriguing to note that although a number of temples are in the process of being constructed by various local Hindu communities, the major temples in operation, and planned on the basis of authentic Hindu tradition of temple architecture and worship have been organized by the Hindus from the South Indian cultural region. The grand conception of Hindu temple building by the Hindu Temple Society of North America in various parts of the United States, and basing it on the local and regional Hindu immigrants' resources for the actual construction, has not been achieved by any other 'overseas' Indian cultural group. On the other hand, virtually all the 'temples' organized under the aegis of North Indian Hindu groups, so far as we are aware (on the basis of our experiences of the last twenty-five years), are in response to the needs, wishes and resources of local communities. Here is a point of some theoretical interest which was first brought to the geographer's attention by CHANDRA JAYAWARDENA (1968, 446). He observed, in reference to overseas Hindus of West Indies, that the *South Indian* ceremonies rather than those of North Indian origin have provided the foci for the development of cult centers. He suggested that such religious foci in the West Indies may be due to the position of a distinctive South Indian culture in a wider community that is predominantly North Indian.

We examine below some of the spatial and historical-cultural aspects of pilgrimage to the S. V. Temple, and suggest that vigorous Hindu temple building activity currently taking place in the United States could lead to a large scale pilgrim circulation.

III. Hindu Pilgrimage: The Case of S. V. Temple

1. Survey Data

In order to examine some facets of the developing process of Hindu pilgrimage in the United States, we carried out a survey of the visitors to the Sri Venkateswara Temple, Pittsburgh (hereafter referred to as the S. V. Temple), during 1981 – 82. Survey Questionnaires were placed in the S. V. Temple so that those who wished could fill them and return them in a prepaid envelope. On one religious occasion, the questionnaires were hand distributed to the pilgrims. The process of survey was stopped when 300 questionnaires had been received, representing approximately ten percent of the visiting 'families'. It was estimated by a member of the board of trustees of the temple that approximately 3000 "families" visited the temple during 1980 – 81. Rarely does an individual alone visit the temple, even unmarried adults such as students come in as a 'group'. Thus, the total number of pilgrims during the 1980 –

81 (estimate year) was probably about ten thousand. Not all questions were answered by each responding pilgrim. Our emphasis is, however, not on the statistical analysis of the data; rather it is on the portrayal of an empirically derived spatial pattern and to account for this pattern using some of the cultural aspects of the South Indian Hindu tradition.

2. The Indian Roots of S. V. Temple Pilgrims (Fig. 1)

Of the responding pilgrims who revealed their Indian roots, over 75% had migrated to North America from the four Dravidian language states of India (Table 1), viz., Tamil Nadu, Andhra Pradesh, Karnataka and Kerala. Although the rest of the pilgrims were immigrants from the non-Dravidian language states of India, it is possible that some of them had Southern Indian roots. It is well-known that some families from the Dravidian language region have migrated to the major Indian industrial commercial centers such as Bombay, in Maharashtra, or have found employment with the Central Government in Delhi. Both of these areas of non-South stand out (Table 1) as significant sources of S. V. Temple pilgrims (Maharashtra 7.3%, and Delhi 4.7%). However, Kerala, even though a Dravidian language state, is represented by very few pilgrims to the S. V. Temple. In part, this may be due to the fact that Hindus back in Kerala form a much smaller proportion (60%) of the total population, as compared to the three other Dravidian language states in each

Table 1: Indian Roots of the S. V. Temple Pilgrims*

State/Territory	Number	Percent of Pilgrims
Tamil Nadu	69	29.6
Andhra Pradesh	56	24.0
Karnataka	40	17.2
Kerala	10	4.3
Maharashtra	17	7.3
Delhi	11	4.7
Others	30	12.9
Total	233	100.00

* Those who revealed their state of origin in India

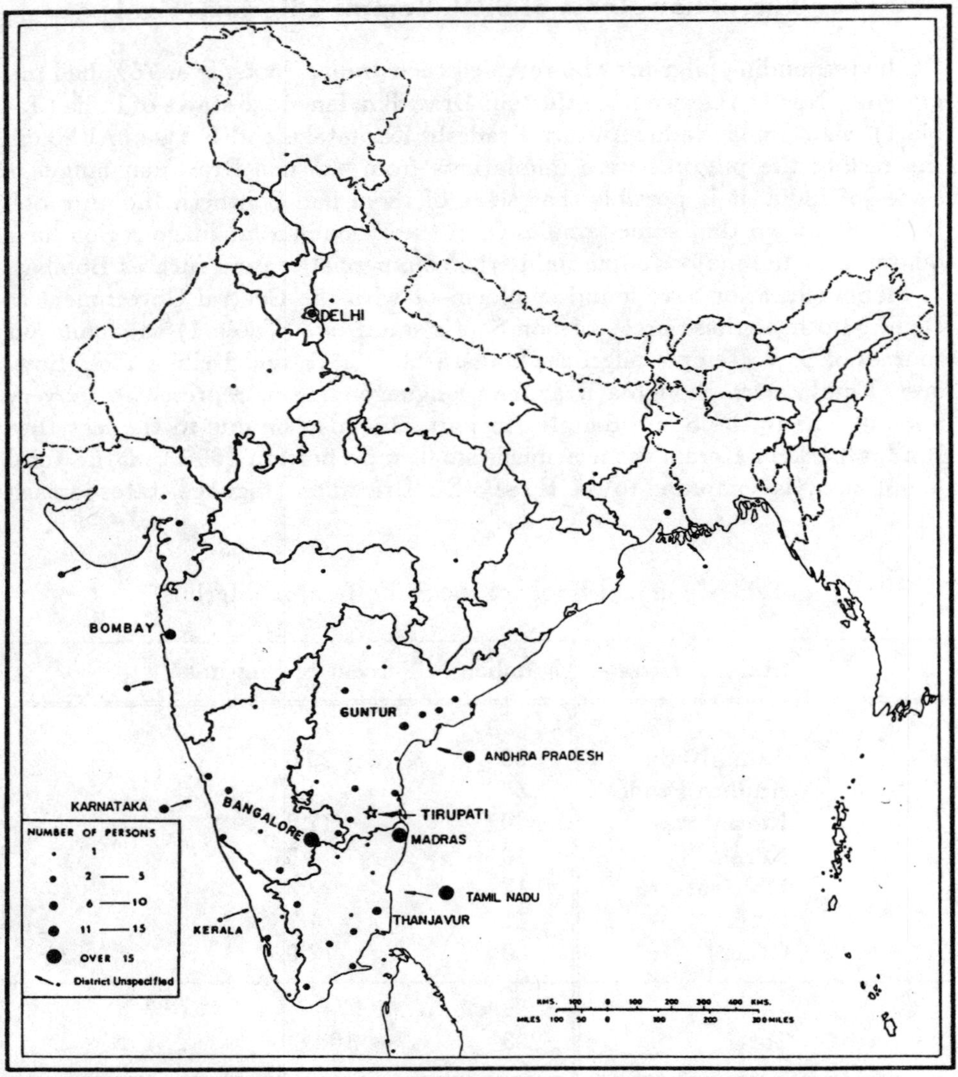

Fig. 1: Indian Roots of S. V. Temple Pilgrims
Source: Author's survey data

of which the Hindus are well over 85% of the population (SCHWARTZBERG 1983). Figure 1 portrays the Indian origin of the S. V. Temple pilgrims who stated their place of origin. This map clearly shows that the bulk of pilgrims have originated from some of the major metropolitan districts such as Madras and Bangalore. In addition, historically, Kerala (the Malabar Coast) has shown a considerable degree of political "isolation" from the rest of India (NILAKANTA SASTRI 1958, 46). This relative political isolation even from the neighbouring Dravidian states in the past possibly also meant a less intense participation in the religious circulation system of these areas. Some support for this argument is available from BURTON STEIN's map showing "Chola Macro Region" which excludes Kerala, indicating the latter to be outside the political orbit of Chola Kings of Southeast India, rulers of most of the area that currently forms Tamil Nadu, Andhra Pradesh and Karnataka (STEIN 1978, 15). Since there has been historically a close association in South India between the major temples and the rulers (SPENCER 1969), beginning with the Cholas and followed by the Vijaynagar rulers, we may propose that the areas outside of their political orbit also had limited participation in the religious circulation system of their domains. SOPHER (1968, 424) brought out a similar relationship between the *Svetambara Jain* pilgrim field and the "historical field of political organization and cultural circulation" of the Chaulukyan dynasty. Kerala, thus, occupied a 'peripheral' location in relation to the historical politico-religious symbiosis of Southeast India. Thus, the S. V. Temple at Pittsburgh seems to have become the American religious focus for the many Hindu immigrants from the old "Chola Macro-Region", which in today's India is roughly composed of parts of Tamil Nadu, Andhra Pradesh and Karnataka. Here is, then, a fascinating example of the regrouping of people mostly originating from an old politico-historical region of India; the focus for the modern linkages, being provided by the "reactualization" of their major Indian religious center (Tirupati) in the form of S. V. Temple in the United States.

3. The American Distribution of S. V. Temple Pilgrims

Over 76% of the pilgrims (who indicated their origin within the United States came from six states: Pennsylvania, Ohio, Illinois, New York, New Jersey, and Michigan (Table 2). Almost 90% of the pilgrims were from the Midwest and the adjoining parts of the Megalopolis. Figure 2 brings out this spatial distribution of the pilgrims and clearly shows that most pilgrims (in the survey data) come from east of the Mississippi. It is to be expected because of the 'friction' of distance in travel time and actual travel expenses. Overall, twenty-five states and the District of Columbia were represented from the United States, and the provinces of Ontario and Quebec from Canada. The distant California, Texas, and Florida were 'represented' by only a few respondent pilgrims. The 'pilgrim intensity' is very high for both Pennsylvania and Ohio whereas it is

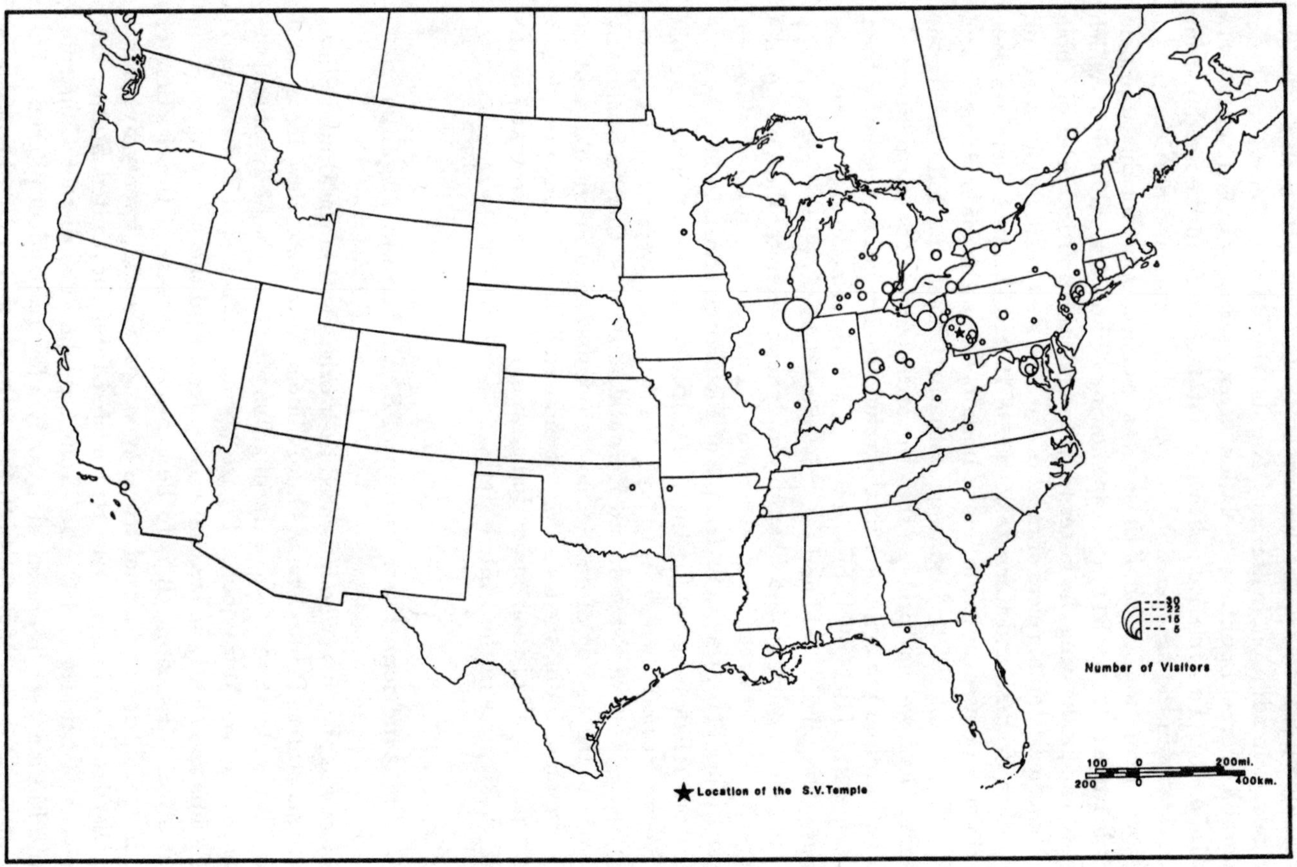

Fig. 2: Distribution of S. V. Temple Pilgrims
Source: Author's survey data

very low for New York (Table 2). Thus, relative proximity to the temple seems to have an important bearing on the pilgrim generation. However, the very low pilgrimage intensity of New York-New Jersey area cannot be explained by distance alone, especially when compared with Illinois on the west which has much higher intensity than does New York. This suggests that attraction of other temples could be a factor in pilgrimage in addition to mere distance. This hypothesis may be tested, when data from the Hindu Temple of Greater Chicago, and Balaji Temple near Chicago become available.

The median distance travelled by pilgrims to the S. V. Temple was 295 miles (475 km) and the median frequency of visit was three times. However, some devotees have visited the temple many times since its consecration in 1976. The median distance as well as the frequency of visits to some degree reflect the attractiveness of this temple to its devotees. There are, however, significant differences between the pilgrims of Northern and Southern Indian origins (Table 3). These differences are reflected in their relative proportion (about three- fourths of South Indian origin), donorship, distance travelled to the temple and the frequency of visit.

Table 2: S. V. Temple

American Origin of Pilgrims

U.S.A. N = 236*

STATE**	Number	Percent of Total Pilgrims (x)	Percent of all Asian Indians in the State (y)	Pilgrim Intensity (x/y)
Pennsylvania	58	24.6	4.2	5.86
Ohio	48	20.4	3.6	5.67
Illinois	23	9.8	9.9	0.99
New York	19	8.1	16.7	0.49
New Jersey	17	7.2	8.2	0.88
Maryland & D.C.	17	7.2	3.8	1.89
Michigan	16	6.8	4.1	1.66

* Number responding to the question about their origin in the U.S.

** Only states with over 15 pilgrims are selected.

Table 3: Cross-Classification of Dichotomous Variables*

Variable	Dichotomous Variables	Region of Origin		Donor		Pilgrim Distance		Number of Visits	
		South	North	Yes	No	Less than 295 miles	More than 295 miles	Less than Three	More than Three
Region Origin	South			48.4	25.8	33.8	40.4	38.5	35.7
	North			11.2	14.6	15.0	10.8	18.8	7.0
Donor	Yes	103	24			30.0	29.6	26.7	32.9
	No	55	31			18.8	21.6	30.5	9.9
Pilgrim Distance	Less Than 295 miles	72	32	64	40			20.2	28.6
	More Than 295 miles	86	23	63	46			37.1	14.1
Number of Visits	Less Than Three	82	40	57	65	43	79		
	More Than Three	76	15	70	21	61	30		

* To the left of the diagonal line, the numbers indicate the observed cell frequencies for each variable, while on the right side its respective percentages are shown.

The Southern Indian pilgrims form a higher proportion of pilgrims from longer (over 475 kms.) distance. They also have a higher frequency of visits from beyond the median pilgrim distance. These facts indicate a greater degree of commitment of the pilgrims of Southern Indian origin to the presiding deity of the S. V. Temple. However, this pattern is *not* unexpected in light of the greater historical cultural association of the S. V. Temple with the Dravidian region of India, especially with the Telugu speaking people.

4. Donorship Trend of the S. V. Temple

Donorship from the devotees is the chief source of revenue of the S. V. Temple, and to that end the temple publishes lists of donors in its official journal *Sapthagiri Vani.* The donorship lists are apt to be the longest in the last quarter of each year, possibly because more devotees have a tendency to think about making donation toward the end of the year for tax deducation purposes. In the last quarter of 1977, about nine hundred donors were listed (SAPTHAGIRI VANI 1978). This number greatly increased by the end of 1980 when over 2200 donors were listed (*Sapthagiri Vani* 1981). The number of donors in most of the states (and Ontario province of Canada) substantially increased between 1977 and 1980 (Table 4). There are, however, a number of donors who do not wish their identity revealed, and are not included in the preceding table. The number of donors in 1980 more than doubled for most of the states that had over fifteen donors to the S. V. Temple in 1977. The increase in the number of donors from Ontario and Texas was even greater. This number could further increase in the case of Ontario as information about the S. V. Temple spreads among the Indian community there. Similarly the distant California registered major increases compared to 1977. The diffusion of donorship has been, to some extent, accompanied by small relative decline in the percentage of donors from certain states. This was to be expected as more people began to learn about the S. V. Temple in areas farther away from the Midwest and the adjoining areas of Canada. The increase in the number of donors is reflected also in the amounts of donations to the temple. In 1977, donations from all sources were less than $200,000, climbing to over $854,000 in 1986 (SAPTHAGIRI VANI 1978 and 1987).

5. Donor Distribution of the S. V. Temple

Over 60% of all the S. V. Temple's donors in 1977 and 1980 were from the Middle Atlantic and the East North-Central regions (Table 4). Since over half of all the Asian Indians (total 361,544) of the United States live in this region (U.S. CENSUS 1980), it is only to be expected that a majority of the Hindu donors to the S. V. Temple will be from this region.

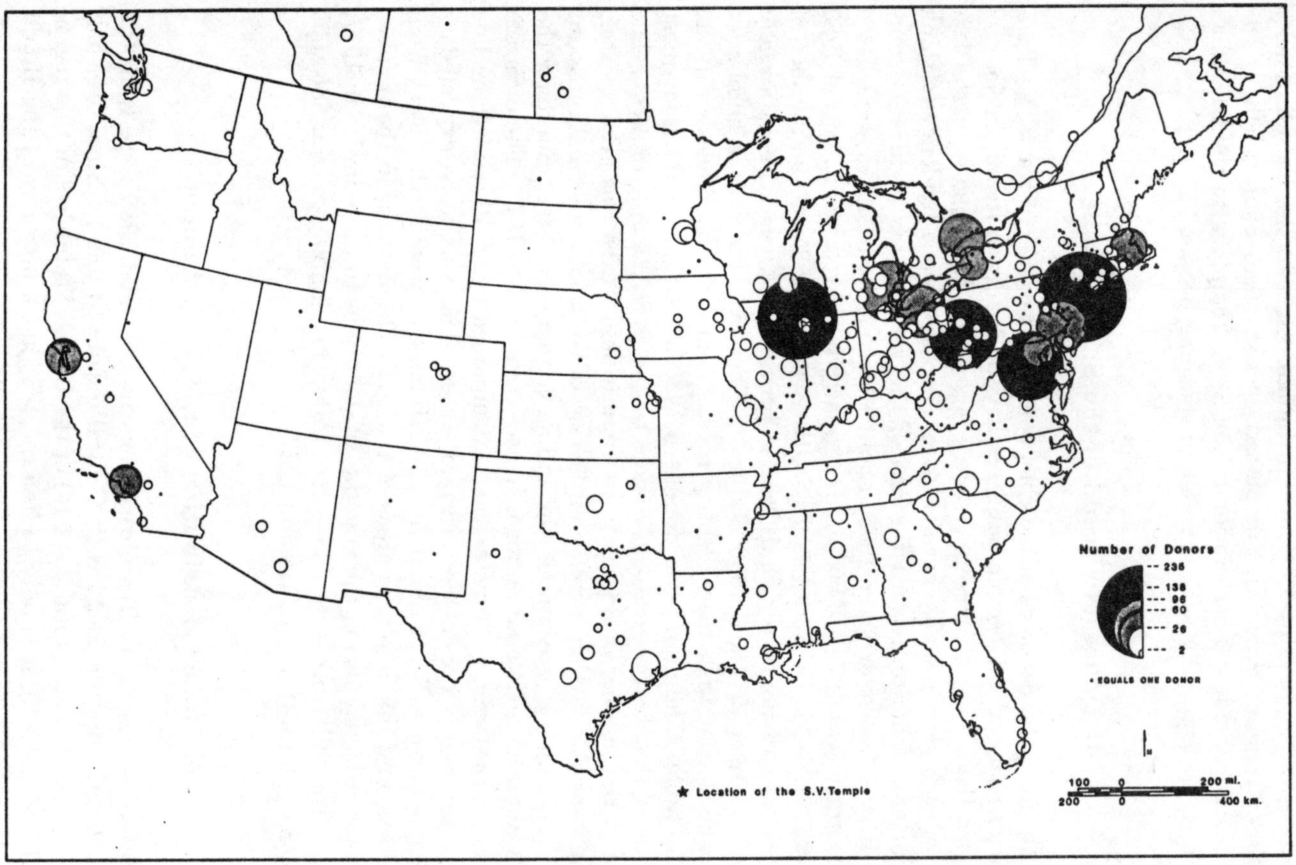

Fig. 3: Distribution of S. V. Temple Donors
Source: SAPTHAGIRI VANI, 1981

Table 4: S. V. Temple Donorship Intensification

STATE/PROVINCE*	1977 4th Qtr. Donors N=908		1980 4th Qtr. Donors N=2281		Percent Increase 1977 – 80
	No.	%	No.	%	
1. Pennsylvania	113	12.5	261	11.4	230
2. Illinois	104	11.5	228	10.0	220
3. New York	104	11.5	227	10.0	220
4. Ohio	99	10.9	228	10.0	230
5. Maryland	56	6.2	153	6.7	270
6. Michigan	55	6.2	153	6.7	280
7. New Jersey	52	6.1	142	6.2	270
8. California	29	3.2	86	3.8	300
9. Virginia	27	2.9	51	2.2	190
10. Massachusetts	26	2.8	56	2.5	210
11. Ontario (Canada)	22	2.4	103	4.5	470
12. West Virginia	21	2.3	30	1.3	140
13. Indiana	20	2.3	48	2.1	240
14. Texas	17	1.9	78	3.4	460

* States in U. S. and Province of Canada with over 15 donors in 1977.

Source: SAPTHAGIRI VANI 1978 und 1981.

In order to get a somewhat better idea about the distribution of the donors, the 1980 Fourth Quarter list of donors was mapped (Figure 3). Donor locations within each "Ranally Metro Area" were grouped for mapping convenience (RAND MCNALLY 1982). The four top ranking states in donorship are also the same in pilgrim generation, although donorship is much more widespread compared to that of pilgrims (compare Figures 2 and 3).

The distribution of the S. V. Temple donors seems to be clearly associated with large industrial commercial centers (Figure 3). The contrast between the Northeast and the South, and between the Eastern and Western United States is quite obvious. Since the majority of the immigrant Asian Indian families are of professional orientation, their concentration in the major metropolitan areas may be expected.

A closer examination of the distribution of the S. V. Temple donors, however, suggests that their number in each state is not necessarily proportional to the state's Asian Indian population (Table 5). Donation rates were calculated per 1000 for 1980 Asian Indian population. However, the "Asian Indians" ethnic group includes all the religions represented in this group, whereas we are concerned only with Hindu population. Thus, the donation rates calculated on this basis are understated. Additionally, our scrutiny of the surnames of the donors, available in the published lists, shows that only 80% of the donors are of Southern Indian origin. Although the donation rates of the Northern Indian visitors are lower than of the Southern Indian devotees, the former are beginning to donate. The lower donation rates of North Indians are at least partly reflective of the fact that many of them are first time visitors and indeed many of them do not fully understand the predominantly South Indian ritual. The S. V. Temple has yet to expand its appeal to the entire Hindu community — especially those from Northern India.

Donation rates by state vary widely from less than 2 to over 17 per 1000 Asian Indians. It can be immediately noticed (Table 5) that whereas New York and New Jersey together have about a quarter of all Asian Indians in the U. S., their donation rates are much lower compared to the Midwest states. New York State's low donation rate of only 3.7 may be contrasted with Ohio (17.4) and Michigan (10.4). This contrast cannot be due to 'distance decay' effect only. A possible explanation, still to be investigated, might lie in the 'intervening opportunity' which the Hindu Temple in Flushing, New York, provides for the Hindu population of the Megalopolis. On the other hand, the S. V. Temple (Pittsburgh) had the same locational advantage for donorship as long as there was no other major Hindu temple west of Pittsburgh possibly competing for donations. Iconic temples have developed in Chicago. In fact, plans for the construction of "Hindu Temple of Greater Chicago" were already underway in 1982 as evidenced by the pledges of $20,000 in donations on the 30th of October, 1982 (INDIA ABROAD 1982, 11). In April 1983, "The Shree Rama Temple" committee of Chicago had already in hand $70,000 for the beginning of the temple construction (INDIA ABROAD 1983, 8). This temple has already been consecrated after the laying of the foundation stone (June 17, 1984) by N. T. Rama Rao, the Chief Minister of Andhra Pradesh. In addition, another large temple — The Balaji Temple — was also consecrated in the vicinity of Chicago in July, 1986.

Although the deity Sri Venkateswara commands the greatest popularity in the United States, temples with other presiding deities are being developed. For example, the chief deity at the Houston Temple is the goddess Minakshi, at the New York Temple, it is the god Ganesa, and at the Hindu Temple of Greater

Table 5: S. V. Temple Donors Compared With the Population of Asian Indians: (United States Only)

STATE (Excludes those with less than 10 donors)	Asian Indians*: Number (US total) = 361,544)	Percent of U.S.	Number of Donors**	Percent of all donors (N=2130)	Donation Rate: Donors per 1000 Asian Indians
Pennsylvania	15,212	4.2	261	12.2	17.2
Ohio	13,105	3.6	228	10.7	17.4
Illinois	35,711	9.9	228	10.7	6.4
New York	60,511	16.7	227	10.7	3.7
Maryland	13,705	3.8	153	7.2	11.2
Michigan	14,680	4.1	153	7.2	10.4
New Jersey	29,507	8.2	142	6.7	4.8
California	57,989	16.0	86	4.0	1.5
Texas	22,226	6.1	78	3.7	3.5
Massachusetts	8,387	2.3	56	2.6	6.7
Virginia	8,483	2.3	51	2.4	6.0
Indiana	4,290	1.2	48	2.3	11.2
North Carolina	4,718	1.3	35	1.6	7.4
Missouri	4,099	1.1	31	1.4	7.6
West Virginia	1,641	0.4	30	1.4	18.3
Florida	9,138	2.5	25	1.2	2.7
Wisconsin	3,657	1.2	25	1.2	6.8
Alabama	1,992	0.5	23	1.1	11.5
Kentucky	2,226	0.6	22	1.0	9.9
Minnesota	3.669	1.0	22	1.0	5.5
Tennessee	3,195	0.9	21	1.0	6.6
Georgia	4,347	1.2	19	0.9	4.4
Connectitcut	4,995	1.4	18	0.9	3.6
Louisiana	2,873	0.8	15	0.7	5.2
Oklahoma	2,879	0.8	15	0.7	5.2
South Carolina	2,143	0.6	13	0.6	6.1
Kansas	2,357	0.7	12	0.6	5.1
Washington	4,002	1.1	12	0.6	3.0
Iowa	2,147	0.6	11	0.5	5.1

* U.S. Department of Commerce, Bureau of the Census, 1980 Census of Population, Supplementary Report, No. PC 80 S1-3, July 1981.

** SAPTHAGIRI VANI, vol. 6, No. 1, 1981, "Contributors Listening 4th Quarter, 1980." U.S. Average 5.89

Chicago, it is Rama. Whereas it is too soon to empirically demonstrate, it can be argued that irrespective of other Hindu iconic temples emerging in the United States, the attraction of the S. V. Temple's chief deity will continue to command spatially most widespread allegiance of donors, just as in India. This is, then, tantamount to implying that an Indian religious pattern may be transferred to the United States virtually intact. This is expected because the presiding deity at the S. V. Temple at Pittsburgh (as the deity in India's Tirupati Temple) is particularly renowned in South India for the fulfillment of the devotees' wishes. It can be further posited that since the donation rates among Hindus as yet are fairly low (Table 5), there is room for their substantial intensification in the future. In such a case, the number of donors could increase for some time to come for the S. V. Temple as well as for other iconic temples yet to be built, before competition for donations becomes consequential.

Nevertheless, eventually the American temples of different Hindu deities will draw upon the regional financial patronage, and thus affect the current pattern of donorship. It is not yet clear whether the emergence of new iconic temples in different regions will mean a corresponding "fission" of the devotees, or whether they will be willing to donate more money as new temples arise. The donors may reduce the amount of donation to one temple in order to spread their donation around to more. In the latter case, the number of donors could increase without a significant addition to the donation amounts. As yet, however, the S. V. Temple remains the primate sacred center of the Hindus as a whole and of the Southern Indian Hindus in particular throughout North America. The donorship pattern may change as new temples emerge. There is some likelihood, however, that the S. V. Temple, may retain *the* widest donorship due to geographically more central location in the nation's heartland, its proximity to a major East-West highway system, its temporal precedence over other temples, and, not the least, its special attraction rooted in the enormous popularity of Sri Venkateswara (Balaji) in India. In any case, it should be possible to monitor changes in the spatial pattern of donorship through the donorship lists in the coming years, if these lists continue to be available.

Donorship distribution suggests the potential hinterland from which immigrant Hindus, especially from South India are currently associated with the S. V. Temple (Figure 3). This seems to include virtually all of the United States and the adjoining areas of Canada. The widespread pattern of donorship to the S. V. Temple is clearly an expression of the Hindu religious linkage with their Sacred Center. In fact, the iconic temples have played a pivotal role in the South Indian Hindu cultural tradition. It is necessary to briefly explain this role because only in that context can be appreciated the significance of the iconic temple, especially the S. V. Temple, in the United States.

IV. The Significance of the S. V. Temple In the Context of the South Indian Temple Tradition

Literature related to the role of temples in India suggests that the iconic temple has traditionally played a far more pivotal role in the Southern Indian culture than in the life of Northern India. In North India, the larger, wealthier temples were repeatedly destroyed or pillaged through centuries by foreign invaders resulting also in the weakening of the related institutions (INDIA, REPUBLIC 1962, 9 – 12). *The Report of the Hindu Religious Endowments Commission* stresses that Hindu temples especially in South India were not merely centers of religion, but served as active repositories and transmitters of the many institutions of Hindu culture (INDIA, REPUBLIC 1962, 13 – 14). In fact, the famous Tirupati temple of South India which inspired and supported the construction of S. V. Temple of Pittsburgh, was itself a major redistribution center of *economic* resources during the medieval times in addition to being a major center of worship (STEIN 1958). More recent studies of the South Indian temples further emphasize their important role. According to BURTON STEIN (1978, 43), "historiography gives deserved prominence to the importance of temples: to temples as a manifestation of the devotional faith of the time; to the variety of social, cultural, and even economic functions which temples carried out." APPADURAI (1981, 18) views the South Indian temples' importance from three facets, as "sacred space", as a "process" of redistribution of resources, and as a system of symbols with a "meta social" quality. He argues that the South Indian temple "serves to dramatize and define certain key South Indian ideas concerning authority, exchange and worship" (APPADURAI 1981, 18). In fact, the existence of a close relationship between the South Indian temples and the ruling kings has been brought out by several scholars (NILAKANTA SASTRI 1963; STEIN 1960, 1978; APPADURAI 1981, 63 – 104).

The centrality of the temple in the South Indian culture has meant an accumulation of management experience and a long tradition of structured relationships between the various institutional components of the temple. During the British Raj, and following it after independence, the South Indian temples further developed a system of relatively efficient endowment and management under boards of trustees supervised by the government civil authorities (INDIA, REPUBLIC 1962, 61). Such organizational and institutional experience has been very limited in North India (OVERSEAS HINDUSTAN TIMES, March 10, 1983, 10). Thus, the South Indian overseas Hindu communities are more apt to organize the building and maintenance of major temples. Dominated by Islamic rule for almost a millennium, the North Indian Hindu religious centers did not develop a close system of mutual relationship with the government. Thus, temples in Northern India, in general, did not achieve the symbolic centrality of power and prestige they did in Southern India. Perhaps then, the leading role played by the South Indian community in the conception and execution of major iconic temples in the United States is a reflection of their traditional relationship with temples.

The distinctiveness of the South Indian Hindu iconic temple tradition, in addition to serving as a focus for the Hindus from South India, already, though slowly, seems to have begun to provide a religious nexus for Hindu immigrants from North India, the West Indies, Surinam, Guyana and other overseas sources. This latter trend may possibly intensify among the coming generations of Hindus for whom specific Indian regional linguistic roots may be less meanigful. It is possible that a sense of Hindu identity transcending original linguistic differences will develop in North America centered on the common religious symbols of Hinduism although the normal process of ethnic fusion and fission cannot be expected to end. But our experience about the current acculturation process of the Hindus in North America lends only partial support to JAYAWARDENA's thesis that among the overseas Hindus, there is a tendency to accept a more universalistic definition of Hinduism transcending local, regional and linguistic differences (JAYAWARDENA 1968, 446).

The extent to which a pan Hindu tendency will develop in the United States, is not clear because frequent family visits to India help maintain regional cultural distinctiveness. Such was not the case with most overseas Indian expatriates of the nineteenth century to the "sugar colonies" because they became isolated from India. In the latter situation, even such fundamental aspects of Hindu social structures as caste hierarchy weakened or altogether disappeared (SCHWARTZ 1967; TINKER 1977; LEMON 1980, 229), since institutional reinforcement from homeland was limited due to lack of opportunity and ability to keep in touch with the homeland.

V. The Cultural Significance of the S. V. Temple

The symbolic importance of the S. V. Temple to the Hindu devotees especially from Southern India may be judged from the fact that the presiding deity in this temple is the same as in the famous Tirupati Temple in the state of Andhra Pradesh in India. In fact, the S. V. Temple is viewed by the devotees as the American homologue of the Tirupati Temple in India. The images of the various deities, including the imposing black image of the presiding deity enshrined in the temple, were carved in India. The architecture of this temple is patterned after one of the popular South Indian styles. It is also noteworthy, in light of the major significance of the temple in the South Indian culture, that joint planning of the S. V. Temple and the New York Hindu Temple in Flushing was done in cooperation with the Endowments Department of the Government of Andhra Pradesh in India (ALAGAPPAN 1978, 28). Several masons, artisans and stone sculptors, were brought from South India to insure authentic construction. These artisans continue to be in demand for helping in the construction of more temples since they have learned new construction techniques and concepts in the United States. Several modifications in the traditional methods of temple architecture and construction had to be made to incorporate heating, insulation, indoor washroom facilities, and other aspects unfamiliar to Indian temple architecture.

The worship and the various religious ceremonies are conducted by the priests who have been brought from India for this exclusive purpose. The language of the worship is Sanskrit although several specific ceremonies and recitations are done in the Dravidian languages such as Telugu, Tamil and Kannada. The priests are polyglot because they have to communicate with Hindus coming from different language areas of India, especially during the regional religious festivals. Unlike the Christian churches, the priests are employed ritualistic functionaries, and not part of the "management" which is done by a highly motivated board of trustees, an executive committee and the managerial staff of the temple. The S. V. Temple is conceived to be "more than a religious institution! It is a cultural center — a place of dialogue — for Indian adults to reaffirm their heritage — for their children to discover who they are — for all Americans as a reminder of the diversity that has shaped this country" (SAPTHAGIRI VANI 1979, 3).

We may ask whether the S. V. Temple with its roots in Southern India Hindu culture will help only to reaffirm the Indian pattern of cultural identification based on the Southern Indian tradition, or whether it is likely to generate a broader pan-Hindu appeal throughout the United States. As yet, there is no clear answer to this or similar questions. Interestingly, this question did become prominent when, in May 1984, the "Hindu-Jain Temple", still under construction, was consecrated also at Pittsburgh. This temple, under one large roof, has the *separate* temples of not only the major Hindu deities (Shiva, Krishna, Rama, Durga) for theistic worshippers (*Sanātandharma* followers), but also has the sacred sacrificial fire spot (*havan kuṇḍa* for the preformance of vedic *yajñas*, and even a Jain temple! This 'temple complex' reflects both the great diversity of Indian Hinduism as well as its broader syncretism. There is no particular "chief" deity at this new temple in contrast with the S. V. Temple where Sri Venkateswara (also called Balaji) is the presiding deity. These two temples in effect also bring out the fundamental variations of Northern and Southern Indian Hindu religious ambience. Such pairs of temples, expressing the two major Hindu traditions are found in several other cities of America.

One thing is clear, however, that in his New World home, the presiding deity at the S. V. Temple in Pittsburgh commands the allegiance of a geographically much more widespread population of his devotees than he did even in his Old World home. Thus, in a very real sense, Sri Venkateswara of Pittsburgh has already become a widely known Hindu deity at the national, if not international, level for the American and Canadian Hindus. Additionally, since several Hindus from the previous British possessions including West Indies, and Guyana have also migrated to the United States and Canada, they find the S. V. Temple an exciting new religious center. Thanks to the immigration policies of the United States which favor the entry of professionals, and the process of internal migration, there is a much greater spatial proximity and greater degree of social interaction between the Hindus of diverse Indian regional- linguistic and religious backgrounds than was ever possible in India. Thus, there may be a greater chance for the presiding deity of this iconic temple in America to become more 'generalized' as a symbol for all Hindus. The traditional Indian regional roots of this deity and of the devotees will perhaps never be lost, but the American born (English speaking) future generations of the Hindus may be somewhat less prone to form their linkages based on Indian languages or the North/South Indian dichotomy, than the immigrants themselves. Thus, it appears that while the presiding deity at the S. V. Temple at Pittsburgh has a South Indian cultural anchor, some North Indians have begun to accept him as an incarnation of *Vishnu* in spite of their unfamiliarity with the South Indian temple ritual. It is our impression that few temples in South India are visited by as high a proportion of pilgrims from North India as is the case with the S. V. Temple. Will this New World religious center become equally attractive to the North Indian Hindu immigrants as pilgrims? Perhaps a future generation of Hindus shall determine the answer. The mere visiting of this temple by the Northern Indians is not the issue here because the pilgrims from one linguistic region of India have, over centuries, been visiting the sacred places located in the other linguistic regions (SOPHER 1968). However, it is one thing to make a pilgrimage once in a lifetime (to a sacred place situated in a different linguistic region), but it is quite another to begin to accept a culturally distinct deity. That seems to be in the *initial* stages of development in the American context. This process is perhaps being helped by the numerous social and cultural activities such as concerts, teaching of Indian dances and languages, performance of marriages and even the crucial funeral assistance being provided by the S. V. Temple to the Hindu community.

The fact that the S. V. Temple is situated close to a major East-West circulation corridor, the Pennsylvania Turnpike, is locationally advantageous for pilgrim visits. In addition, the beautiful New Vrindaban "Palace of Gold" of the late founder of the International Society for Krishna Consciousness (Iskcon) in neighbouring West Virginia, has become a tourist attraction with a convenient drive from the S. V. Temple. Thus, several Hindu visitors who come to the S. V. Temple as pilgrims for *darshan* (sight) and worship, religious rites, or fulfillment of vows, proceed to the New Vrindaban Community as 'tourists'. Among the Indian visitors, the peoplel of North Indian origin seem to be more prominent there (PROROK, personal communication). An enterprising New York travel agency has already begun to conduct bus tours to the S. V. Temple and New Vrindaban. It is possible that a circuit pilgrimage will develop based on the Hindu temple of New York, the S. V. Temple of Pittsburgh, the New Vrindaban in West Virginia, the Minakshi Temple at Houston, the two large temples at Chicago and, perhaps, other temples in the process of active development.

VI. Conclusion

Religion seems to be an important force in the regrouping of American Hindu immigrants in spite of their Western scientific orientation. Our observations generally support the recently begun sociological inquiry which suggests that ethnic Hindus in America have become more conscious of their religious identity (SARAN, VARMA and EMBREE 1980, 216 – 232) and actually exhibit a greater degree of religiosity than they would even in India. Our observation specifically supporting such a view is that a great variety of religious modes can be identified among the Hindus in North America. One of the most distinctive modes is the development of iconic temples with specific presiding deities. The leadership in Hindu iconic temple organization at the continental scale has come mostly from the Southern Indian culture due to the pivotal role played by the iconic temples in that culture over a long period of time. Temple building in Indian style is not only an overt expression of Hinduism in the American landscape, but also a signal of its "permanence" and of its desire to remain distinctive.

The centrality of the iconic temples of Hindus, especially of Southern Indian origin, is clearly manifested in the rapidly evolving donation and pilgrimage pattern of the S. V. Temple. The great popularity of the presiding deity of the S. V. Temple in India, and among domiciled American Hindus, will likely insure its preeminent position as a sacred center. The construction of other major iconic temples may affect the donation patterns within North America in the future, but religious circulation will surely intensify as other iconic temples emerge and develop. Even at present, the donation pattern of the S. V. Temple shows that the whole of United States and Canada have become a potential pilgrim field of this temple. Pilgrimage circuits have begun to evolve, and the "transference" of Hindu pilgrimage system from India is in progress. Conscious of its linguistic and regional cultural roots in India, and a desire for cultural authenticity spurred by heightened religiosity, the Hindus of America are busy importing and developing traditionally correct Hindu institutions and rituals including iconic temples such as the S. V. Temple. It is almost inevitable that Hinduism in America reflects the cultural-linguistic regionality and ethos. It is not as yet clear whether a wider Hindu identity is effectively in the process of being forged through pilgrim circulation. Nevertheless, American born Hindus of today and tomorrow may look upon the regional roots of the present iconic temples in a different light than their immigrant parents, thanks to their linguistic uniformity. It is crucial, then, to study the second generation — now in the process of development in the kindergartens, schools and colleges of America, a generation whose religious attitudes and interests are not necessarily the same as of their parents. RAITZ (1979) has correctly emphasized such a need in relation to ethnic groups, in general.

To the extent that a wider Hindu religious cultural identity is being forged, the iconic temples may have a crucial role through the religious circulation focused on them. It appears from our study that the South Indian iconic temples may provide the nuclei for such a future pan-Hindu identity at a theistic and ritualistic level. Among the chief reasons underlying this possibility is that the Southern Indian iconic temples have historically provided a highly organized institutional framework transcending localism. Iconic temples have been historically symbols of spatial Hindu integration. With the benefit of such history, they are providing religious centrality for the Hindu (especially Southern Indian) population of the United States and Canada. We could hazard the guess that unless an American Hindu iconic temple has well-developed organization and deep tap roots in India (and a popular deity), there is limited chance that it will develop (in North America) into a focus of any significant supralocal Hindu identification based upon pilgrimage even if it becomes a popular *local* religious center.

Although JAYAWARDENA's (1968) study of overseas Indians did not include Hindus in North America (because there were relatively few Indians as permanent residents then) some of the observations of that study seem to be valid here as well, especially that the Southern Indian iconic temples have generally provided the ritual focus for overseas Hindu communities. A caveat, however, is the development of the iconic temples of the Hare Krishna sect. Using as they do a predominantly Northern Indian religious symbology, it is possible that the Hare Krishna temples may provide a devotional focus primarily for the immigrants from Northern India. If such a close relationship indeed develops, we could see two very distinctive religious regroupings going on parallel to each other — one representing the Southern Indian cultural ethos and the other the "North" Indian — each, however, focused on iconic temples.

As in India, sacred centers are likely to play a significant role in Hindu reaffirmation and identification in North America. The role of the sacred centers could be even more crucial in the regrouping of the New World Hindus. Certainly, it will be fascinating to watch whether or not the Hindus who migrated from diverse linguistic and regional backgrounds have finally found the Zangwillian "melting pot" for themselves in the New World. Either way, religion is likely to continue to play an eminent role in this regrouping process. Already, the outlines of some patterns of religious circulation are evident. Undoubtedly, spatial changes in pilgrimage and donation patterns will take place as new iconic temples with pilgrimage oriented tradition develop.

Summary

Hindu immigrants to the United States have developed a variety of religious modes which are helping to regroup them in their adopted country. In the past fifteen years they have built many *iconic temples* (temples with the idols of deities). Some of these iconic temples are developing into Hindu *pilgrimage places.* We find that most of the iconic temples which have a potential for becoming pilgrimage centers, have Southern Indian roots because of the centrality of the temple in the Dravidian cultural tradition. Our study is focused on SRI VENKATESWARA TEMPLE (S. V. Temple) in Pittsburgh, Pennslyvania. This temple has the same presiding deity as the Tirupati temple in Andhra Pradesh, India. This temple has become a major focus for Hindu *religious circulation* in the United States. Survey data of about three hundred pilgrims showed that most of them have their roots in the Southern part of India and represent the Dravidian Hindu cultural-linguistic tradition. Donorship pattern of the SRI VENKATESWARA TEMPLE was also examined. Donors of this temple are from all parts of the United States and adjoining areas of Canada, although they are mostly from the Midwest, and the Megalopolis. The *cultural significance* of the S. V. Temple seems substantial, because it may become a symbol of Hindu religious and *cultural identity* in the United States. We point out, however, that differences between the Northern and the Southern Indian cultural and linguistic traditions of the immigrants do not make it easy for a pan-Hindu identification based upon iconic temples.

Zusammenfassung: Zur Entwicklung Hinduistischer Pilgerfahrten in den Vereinigten Staaten: Eine Fallstudie

In die Vereinigten Staaten eingewanderte Hindus haben eine Fülle religiöser Verhaltensweisen entwickelt, die ihnen helfen, sich in ihrer Wahlheimat zurechtzufinden. In den letzten fünfzehn Jahren haben sie eine Vielzahl *ikonischer Tempel* (Tempel mit Abbildungen von Gottheiten) errichtet. Einige dieser Tempel entwickeln sich bereits zu *Pilgerorten* der Hindus. Wie die Untersuchung zeigt, gehen die meisten ikonischen Tempel mit Ansätzen der Entwicklung zu einer Pilgerstätte auf südindische Wurzeln zurück, welches auf der zentralen Bedeutung der Tempel in der drawidischen Kulturtradition beruht.

Die Studie betrachtet den SRI VENKATESWARA TEMPEL (S. V. Tempel) in Pittsburgh, Pennsylvania. Dieser Tempel ist derselben Gottheit geweiht wie der Tirupati Tempel in Andhra Pradesh/Indien. Er ist ein Hauptziel hinduistischer *Pilgerfahrten* in den Vereinigten Staaten geworden. Wie im Rahmen der Arbeit ausgewertete Daten von etwa 300 Pilgern zeigen, sind die meisten dieser Pilger kulturell im südlichen Indien verwurzelt und repräsentieren die drawidische Sprach- und Kulturtradition.

Weiterhin wurde die Herkunft der Spender des S. V. Tempels untersucht. Sie kommen aus allen Teilen der Vereinigten Staaten sowie den angrenzenden Gebieten in Kanada. Die meisten leben jedoch im Mittleren Westen und in der Megalopolis.

Die *kulturelle Bedeutung* des S. V. Tempels erscheint beträchtlich, da er ein Symbol der religiösen und *kulturellen Identität* der Hindus in den Vereinigten Staaten werden könnte. Dennoch machen es Unterschiede zwischen den kulturellen und sprachlichen Traditionen der Einwanderer aus Nord- und Südindien nicht leicht, eine Identifikation aller Hindus auf der Basis ikonischer Tempel zu bewirken.

Bibliography

ABRAHAM, S. Y., et al. (1983): "The Southend: An Arab Muslim Working Class Community." In: S. Y. Abraham and N. Abraham, eds., Arabs in the World, Wayne State University, Center for Urban Studies, Detroit, 171 – 175.

ABRAMSON, H. J. (1980): "Religion." In S. Thernstrom, ed., Harvard Encyclopedia of American Ethnic Groups, Harvard University Press, Cambridge, 869 – 875.

ALAGAPPAN, A. (1978): "Links With Andhra Pradesh." In: Commemorative Souvenir, no ed., The Hindu Temples Society of North America, 27 – 29.

APPADURAI, A. (1981): Worship and Conflict Under Colonial Rule: A South Indian Case Study. Cambridge University Press, Cambridge.

ARASARATNAM, S. (1970): Indians in Malaysia and Singapore. Oxford University Press, Bombay.

BHARATI, A. (1963): "Pilgrimage in the Indian Tradition." History of Religions III, 135 – 67.

BHARDWAJ, S. M. (1973): Hindu Places of Pilgrimage in India: A Study in Cultural Geography. University of California Press, Berkeley.

BHARDWAJ, S. M. (1985): "Religion and Circulation: Hindu Pilgrimage." In: R. M. Prothero and M. Chapman, Circulation in Third World Countries, Chapter 12: 241 – 261, Rowledge and K. Paul, London, Boston, Melbourne and Henley.

BHARDWAJ, S. M. and RAO, M. N. (1983): "Religious Reknitting of Ethnic Hindus of the 'New World'." Paper presented at the 79th annual meeting of the Association of American Geographers, Denver.

BHASHYANANDA, S. (1981): Vedanta in Chicago: Golden Jubilee Souvenir. Vivekananda Vedanta Society, Chicago.

BRYANS, R. (1967): Trinidad and Tobago: Isles of the Immortelles. Faber and Faber Limited, London.

CONSTANTINOU, S. T. (1982): A Geographic-Systems Approach to Ethnicity: The Greek Americans in Northeastern Ohio. Ph. D. thesis, Department of Geography, Kent State University.

FISHER, M. P. (1980): The Indians of New York City: A Study of Immigrants From India. South Asia Books, Columbia.

GLAZER, N. (1980): Foreword. In: P. Saran and E. Eames, eds., New Ethics: Asian Indians in the United States. Praeger, New York, vi-ix.

INDIA ABROAD. (1982, 1983, 1984).

INDIA, REPUBLIC. (1962): Report of the Hindu Religious Endowments Commission 1960 – 62. Government of India, Ministry of Law, New Delhi.

JAYAWARDENA, C. (1968): "Migration and Social Change: A Survey of Indian Communities Overseas." Geographical Review 58: 426 – 450.

JENSEN, J. M. (1980): "East Indians." In: S. Thernstrom, ed., Harvard Encyclopedia of American Ethnic Groups. Harvard University Press, Cambridge, 296 – 301.

KLASS, M. (1961): East Indians in Trinidad: A Study of Cultural Persistence. Columbia Press, New York.

KUPER, H. (1960): Indian People in Natal. Natal University Press, Natal.

LEMON, A. (1980): "The Indian Communities of East Africa and the Caribbean." In: A. Lemmon and N. Pollock, eds., Studies in Overseas Settlement and Population. Longman, London, 225 – 241.

MELENDY, H. B. (1977): Asians in America: Filipinos, Koreans, and East Indians. Twayne Publishers, Boston.

MORINIS, E. A. (1983): Pilgrimage in the Hindu Tradition. Oxford University Press, New Delhi.

NILAKANTA SASTRI, K. A. (1958): A History of South India. Oxford University Press, London.

OVERSEAS Hindustan Times. (1983): Weekly Newspaper.

PROROK, C. Personal Communications.

RAND McNALLY (1982): Commercial Atlas and Marketing Guide: 113th Edition. Rand McNally & Co., Chicago.

RAITZ, K. B. (1979): "Themes in the Cultural Geography of European Ethnic Groups in the United States." Geographical Review 69: 79 – 94.

SANDHU, K. S. (1969): Indians in Malaysia: Some Aspects of Their Immigration and Settlement (1786 – 1957). Cambridge University Press, Cambridge.

SAPTHAGIRI VANI. (1978): 3(1).

SAPTHAGIRI VANI. (1979): 4(3).

SAPTHAGIRI VANI. (1981): 6(4).

SPATHAGIRI VANI. (1987): 12(1).

SARAN, P. and EAMES, E. eds. (1980): The New Ethnics: Asian Indians in the United States. Praeger, New York.

SARAN, P., VARMA, B. N., and EMBREE, A. T. (1980): "Hinduism in a New Society." In: P. Saran and E. Eames, eds., The New Ethnics. Praeger, New York, 216 – 232.

SCHWARTZ, B. M. ed. (1967): Caste in Overseas Indian Communities. Chandler Publishing Company, San Francisco.

SCHWARTZBERG, J. E. (1983): Comment on an earlier version of this paper delivered at the A. A. G. Annual meetings in Denver.

SMITH, M. K. (1981): "The Arabic-Speaking Communities in Rhode Island: A Survey of the Syrian and Lebanese Communities in Rhode Island." In: J. H. Rollins, ed., Hidden Minorities: The Persistence of Ethnicity in American Life. University Press of America, Washington, D. C., 141 – 176.

SOPHER, D. E. (1967): Geography of Religions. Prentice-Hall, Englewood Cliffs.

SOPHER, D. E. (1968): "Pilgrim Circulation in Gujarat." Geographical Review 58: 392 – 425.

SPECKMANN, J. D. (1965): Marriage and Kinship Among the Indians in Surinam. Von Gorcum & Comp., Assen.

SPENCER, G. W. (1969): "Religious Networks and Royal Influence in Eleventh Century South India." Journal of the Economic and Social History of the Orient 12: 42 – 56.

STEIN, B. (1958): The Tirupati Temple: An Economic Study of a Medieval South Indian Temple. Ph. D. Thesis, Department of History, University of Chicago.

STEIN, B. (1960): "The Economic Function of a Medieval South Indian Temple." Journal of Asian Studies 19: 163 – 176.

STEIN, B. (1978): "Temples in Tamil Country, 1300 – 1750 A. D." In: B. Stein, ed., South Indian Temples: An Analytical Reconsideration, Vikas, Delhi.

STODDARD, R. H. (1966): Hindu Holy Sites in India: Ph. D. Thesis, Department of Geography, State University of Iowa.

TINKER, H. (1974): A New System of Slavery: The Export of Indian Labour Overseas, 1830 – 1920. Oxford University Press, London.

TINKER, H. (1977): The Banyan Tree: Overseas Emigrants From India, Pakistan, and Bangladesh. Oxford University Press, Oxford.

UNITED STATES IMMIGRATION AND NATURALIZATION SERVICE. (1961): Annual Report. Department of Justice, Washington, D. C.

UNITED STATES IMMIGRATION AND NATURALIZATION SERVICE. (1978): 1978 Statistical Year Book. Department of Justice, Washington, D. C.

UNITED STATES BUREAU OF CENSUS. (1980): "Race of the Population by States: 1980." U. S. Department of Commerce, Washington, D. C. Table 1.

WOOD, M. R. (1980): "Hinduism in Vancouver: Adjustments in the Home, the Temples, and the Community." In: K. V. Ujimoto and G. Hirabayashi, eds., Visibile Minorities and Multiculturalism: Asians in Canada. Butterworth, Toronto.

Carolyn V. Prorok

PATTERNS OF PILGRIMAGE BEHAVIOR AMONG HINDUS OF TRINIDAD

I. Introduction

Pilgrimage behavior is intrinsically geographic in nature in that humans travel in specific ways to consecrated places. Pilgrimage is a central feature of South Asian Indian religious experience and as such has given rise to many studies by geographers. The institution of pilgrimage to holy places is embedded in the Hindu religious tradition. According to BHARDWAJ (1973, 7) the number of holy places in India is so large and the practice of visiting these sacred sites so unbiquitous that the whole of India can be regarded as one vast sacred space. Given the importance of pilgrimage in Hindu religious life, study of pilgrimage in overseas Indian communities is one of considerable interest for geographers. This paper will examine the role of pilgrimage in religious practices of Hindus in the Caribbean; more specifically on the island of Trinidad (Fig. 1). First pilgrimage behavior will be described and secondly, explained in the context of the Trinidadian experience.

Indians from South Asia, referred to as East Indians in the Caribbean, migrated to Trinidad as indentured labor for cane and cacao estates between 1845 and 1917. Many remained and, due to high birth rates, eventually comprised 40% of the population by 1980. Presently, East Indians of the Hindu faith represent about 62% of the Indian population and 25% of the total population, or approximately a quarter million adherents. The Hindu immigrants carried with them many of their religious practices, some of which have been transformed. The importance of pilgrimage has diminished to a certain degree and, in fact, island-wide pilgrimage patterns are weakly developed if not almost nonexistent when compared to the role of pilgrimage in India. Unlike India, few places have sacred significance to Hindus in Trinidad.

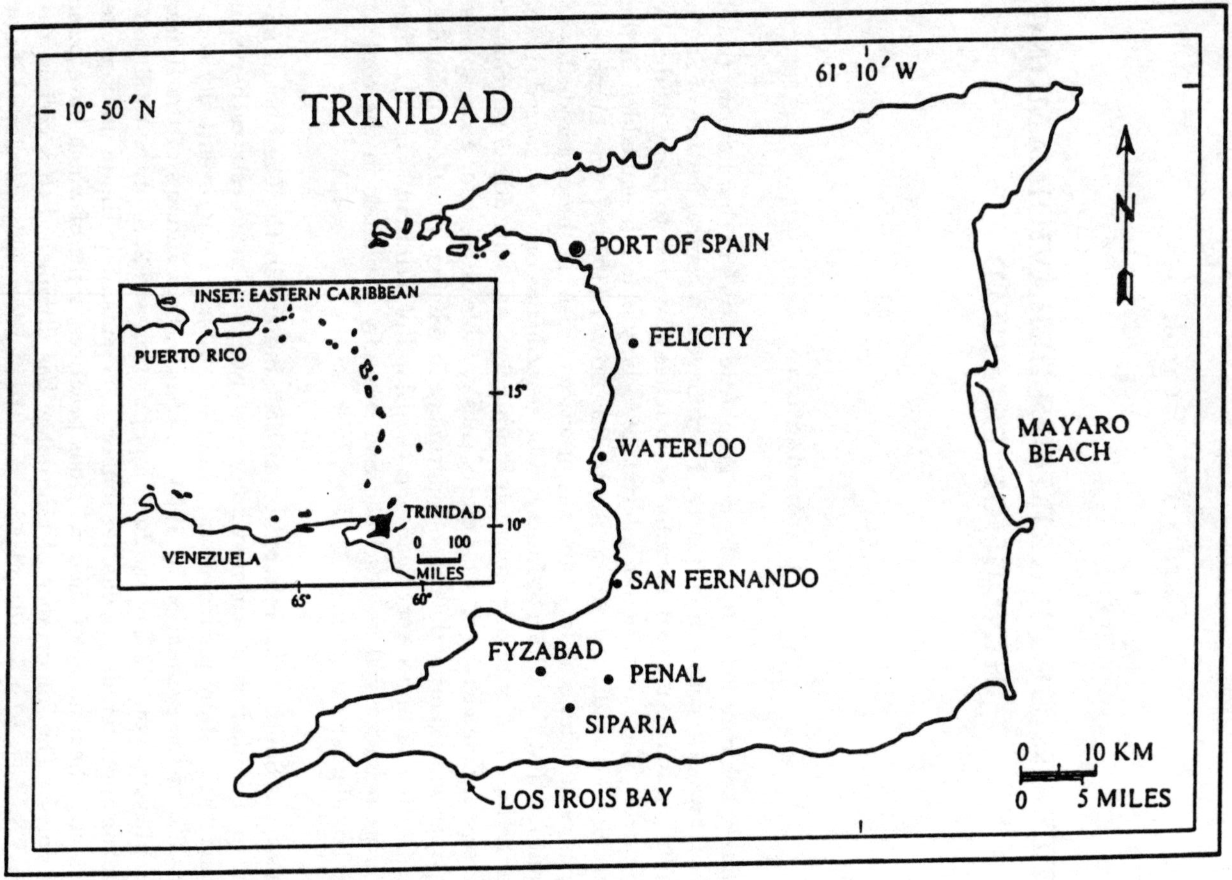

Fig. 1: Relevant place names in Trinidad
Source: Topographic maps of Trinidad

II. Hindu Pilgrimage Behavior in Trinidad

Religious activities related to the pilgrimage tradition can be divided into two basic categories. The first is time and place bound and the second is not time and place bound. In the first category a number of places and/or festivals associated with pilgrimage behavior are important in the Hindu religious calender. None of these places command the attention of Hindus on the scale that even a regional shrine would have in India and only a few Hindu festivals in Trinidad are related to pilgrimage behavior. Trinidadian Hindus have no Hardwar, Benares or a Kumbha Mela. In the second category Hindus in Trinidad have turned a traditional sacrifice ritual into a quasi-pilgrimage event.

1. Traditional Pilgrimage Behavior

Many temples in Trinidad have lingams, or phallic symbols representing Lord Shiva. Shiva is a major deity in the Hindu Sanskritic pantheon and, within the triumvirate of creation, preservation and destruction, he represents the destructive element of the universe; although other characteristics have been attributed to him. Lingam worship is a very ancient practice in India and was carried by the indentured servants to Trinidad. Lingams can be formed of any material, but they are often worshiped as stones which naturally display the phallic form.

In Trinidad, a few temples have lingams which some Trinidadian Hindus believe have grown in size since discovered. Informants claim true faith in worship causes the lingam to grow. In each case a stone protruded from the ground, a sacred event became associated with the stone, and eventually a temple erected over the stone. A sacred myth is associated with the lingam of two separate temples, both myths similar in form. At Gherahoo Trace, near Fyzabad, while a man cutlassed bush in order to plant cacao, he hit a stone. The cutlass is a sharp tool used by agricultural laborers, and some Hindus believe the cutlass used by the man "cut" the stone. Milk, a substance considered sacred by Hindus, is believed to have flowed from it. Another version explains that blood flowed from the stone. Within a short time a temple was erected. Many people in southwestern Trinidad know of the Shiva Temple at Gherahoo Trace and the story of the lingam, but few patronize it on a regular basis. A jhandi (a small, triangular flag) is raised on a green bamboo (Bambusa vulgaris, Oendre calamus giganteus, or Oendre calamus strictus) pole when people perform a puja (prayers)[1] to honor the lingam. Only 19 flags stood on the temple grounds, some well weathered. The caretaker estimates 1000 people visit the temple on Shiv Ratri, a special day in late spring dedicated to Lord Shiva and celebrated as his birthday. When one considers a population of a quarter of a million Hindus, this figure indicates only a small percentage of Hindus are traveling specifically to worship at this particular site, which is marked by a sacred event.

More popular is the Shiva Temple at Patiram Trace, near Penal, also in south-western Trinidad. Hindus of northern Trinidad know of this temple and many suggested that I visit it. Patiram's sacred story is similar to that of Gherahoo. A man hired to clear bush sharpened his cutlass on a stone protruding from the earth. As a result the stone chipped and milk flowed (again some say blood). Growing over a foot in the last 40 years, according to the informant Sanachariya, it appears that another stone is emerging out of the side. The man went blind as a result of his carelessness. He immediately erected a temple. His blindness made it difficult to take care of the lingam and so he prayed to Lord Shiva in order that his sight could be restored. Sanachariya explained that Lord Shiva gave him sight in one eye and the man devoted his life to the temple. Since his death the informant has taken care of the lingam. She is the daughter of the original owner of the property. According to Sanachariya several people visit the temple every day to perform puja, as witnessed by numerous flags which have been recently erected. She estimates over 5000 people pay their respects to the lingam on Shiv Ratri.

Even though, on the average, five times as many people are likely to visit the Patiram site when compared to Gherahoo, few Hindus are making a special effort to worship at such sacred places. Approximately half of the lingams in Trinidad's Hindu temples are man-made and formed of concrete or other material, while the other half are natural stones. If any sacred significance is attached to the natural stones, more likely than not it is a local one. Only a few stones have national or near national recognition on the part of Trinidad's Hindus and yet they are visited by only two to three percent of the population. Most Hindus who observe Shiv Ratri, the most important festival associated with lingam worship in Trinidad, go to their local temple.

Another practice that appears to incorporate some aspects of traditional Indian pilgrimage is observance of Kartik-ke-nahan in the fall. Kartik is the name of a month in the Hindu lunar calender and devout Hindus should ritually bathe every day of that month, but most Trinidadian Hindus bathe only on the last day which is the full moon. Devotees in Trinidad believe bathing in the sea will obtain almost the same spiritual merit as bathing in the Ganges (JHA 1974, 9). This practice is not unlike that of Hindus in India. The WISERS (1964, 156) describe a similar situation in the 1930s:

> Those who can afford it go to the Ganges by bus or train to bathe. Several months before our house was finished we took a load of village friends in our pick up to the nearest place of pilgrimage on the Ganges. I have never seen a happier crowd. When a group of friends and relatives can combine a picnic and a long exciting drive

> with the gaining of religious merit by bathing in the waters of a sacred river and visiting temples of favorite gods and goddesses, the experience is most satisfying.

KLASS (1961, 161 – 162) explains that many Hindus of Trinidad make a trip to the beach, perform puja, and then enjoy the day at the water's edge with a picnic dinner. Hindus in Felicity, studied by KLASS in 1960, organized an excursion to Los Irois beach, on the southern side of the island. They hired buses for women and children while men traveled in private or hired cars. The expense at the time precluded making such excursions often. It did not matter which beach was used as long as people traveled the length or breadth of the island. In Trinidad today, this activity, which is no longer cost prohibitive, is usually organized by community temple committees whereby a pundit is hired (not necessarily the local pundit) (SCHWARTZ 1963, 8) and transportation contracted with temple funds. Members of the community temple then go as a group.

Finally, in the time and place bound category, Hindus of Trinidad also pay respect to the Catholic shrine of La Divina Pastora or Black Virgin of Siparia. They call her Sipari Mai and believe she grants wishes to those who pay her homage. The statue supposedly represents appearance of the virgin in Venezuela. She was removed to Trinidad by Capuchin monks for safe keeping and the Amerindians at Siparia mission took care of her. Siparia Mai was stolen in the early 1800s and carried to Port of Spain (variously San Fernando) and found her way back to the mission where she reappeared in her shrine (ASPINALL 1910, 141 – 142). Stories of her powers spread rapidly. Hindus of southern Trinidad have visited the shrine since their arrival in the middle of the 19th century and now thousands of East Indians, including Hindus, visit Sipari Mai throughout the week leading up to Good Friday. Celebrations culminate in a special mass dedicated to her and attended mostly by East Indians. (CROWLEY 1957, 821; KOSS 1959, 149).

2. Quasi-Pilgrimage Behavior

The second category of pilgrimage behavior represents an area of religious practice that overshadows behavior associated with the first category. This activity is centered around the yagna or jag (pronounced yag) as it is commonly called in Trinidad. Traditionally the yagna is an ancient, ceremonial sacrifice, but in Trinidad it has taken on new meaning and function. Traveling to yagnas sponsored by an extended family, a priest, or a village temple is very popular. Bhagwat Jag and Ramayana Jag are the most popular types, although some jags are dedicated to specific deities. Handbills are prepared and distributed (Fig. 2). I was often asked by people I interviewed to distribute such handbills

Om Jai Shree Ram

THE JEWAN UPKRAK SABHA

of 7¼ miles Post Plum Mitân, Branch No. 76 of the S.D.M.S. Inc.
cordially invite the Public to attend a

Seven (7) Nights
Panchouti
RAMAYAN
YAGYA

to be held at their TEMPLE
Opp. Rec. Ground, Settlement Trace, Plum Mitan.
COMMENCING ON
SUNDAY 3rd NOVEMBER, 1985
& TERMINATING ON
SATURDAY 9th NOVEMBER, 1985

RAMESHWAR PUJA
on THURSDAY 7th NOVEMBER, 1985
DEVOTIONAL HOURS
6.30 p.m. to 9.00 p.m. Each Night

Officiating:

Pandit HARDATH of Cumuto
assisted by **Pandit BIMAL & Balroop Maraj**
of Cumuto

All Sadhus, Bhajan and Kirtan Groups are cordially Invited!

COMME ONE! COME ALL!

Om Shanti! Shanti! Shanti!

Ace Printery

Fig. 2: Announcement for a Jag event
Source: Personal contact

as I traveled the island. Each night of the jag puja is performed, the Ramayana or Bhagavad-Gita read, and prasad (sweets offered at the puja) distributed to the guests. On the final night a feast is served and most people attend at this time. This is an event that draws friends and relatives from remote villages and is also an occasion for reaffirmation of kin relationships. The meetings accrue merit to those who prepare them. Jag sponsors also acquire spiritual merit by feeding holy men and the poor who attend the event (KOSS 1959, 125 – 26).

Jags can be held any time of the year and some people, especially older women, make their rounds to as many as possible. Families and priests who sponsor such events do so occasionally because they are so expensive. Only the very wealthy can sponsor them on a regular basis. Jhandi (flags) are erected reflecting the family's spiritual merit and wealth to the local community. Temple committees, on the other hand, usually sponsor a jag every year since donations given at this time are significant in supporting the temple's maintenance costs. They are usually planned in such a way that the last night falls on Friday or Saturday so that people can stay late. FONAROFF (1968, 541) believes the automobile, and its easy availability in Trinidad, has been important in perpetuating some Hindu customs. Religious events like the jag, which have no special association with physical features, sacred events or distance traveled, are now more easily attended, at greater distances, and by a greater number of worshipers.

III. The Social-Historical Framework of Hindu Pilgrimage

Trinidad's Hindus were not able to preserve their religious tradition in complete isolation nor could they maintain it unscathed in the face of strong Christian proselytization and an unsympathetic, Christian dominated, social environment. Traditional pilgrimage behavior never had a chance to develop as a significant aspect of Hindu religious action in the years of identureship, and present patterns of pilgrimage behavior may be a reflection of that weak development in the early years of Hindu settlement. Several factors may be considered in understanding the nature of Hindu pilgrimage behavior in Trinidad. These include colonial policy, the geography of the island, and the nature of traditional concepts of Hindu sacred sites.

1. The Colonial Environment

British colonial policy toward Hindu religious practices was very restrictive during the indenture period and did not relax significantly until after WW II. Hindu marriage ceremonies were not recognized as legal until 1946 (CLARKE, et. al. 1984, 73) and Hindus could not build their own sectarian schools until the late 1940s (SINGH 1974, 59). Cremation was illegal until 1936 (NIEHOFF & NIEHOFF 1960, 132) and the first place designated as a legal site for cremation emerged only in the 1970s. Since national independence in 1962 Hindus have had only one of their religious events recognized as an official holiday and that is Divali, the festival of lights. Also, temples built on government land did not receive the same treatment as Christian churches. The temple at Waterloo was first built on the beach, but later demolished because the temple-builder did not own the land. Rebuilding it in the water protected the temple from governmental sanction but not from the elements or abandonment after the builder died. Since his death over 15 years ago people have illegally performed cremations at the site. It is also a popular place to perform pujas for Kartik.

Government policy restricted travel by East Indians, which also reinforced their cultural and social isolation. While indentured, Indians carried special papers and their movement was controlled by estate owners (WOOD 1968, 136). Upon completion of a contract the East Indian was free to travel, but where could a pilgrim go? Land owned by Indians bordered the estates at first and expanded into the forest much later (JOHNSON 1972). Erecting shrines on non-Indian land or in an area with a low density of Indian population doomed the shrine to destruction as the Creole population had little knowledge of Hindu practices and as much respect.

2. The Island Framework of Hindu Pilgrimage

Trinidad's location and size is not conducive to development of a strong Hindu pilgrimage tradition when that tradition is characterized by travel over long distances to remote places. The island is small (only about 1800 sq. miles). An excellent road system, developed in the last thirty years, provides easy access to any part of the island in a relatively short time. The few areas with physical features especially associated with Hindu sacred events (like higher elevations and headwaters) are either forest reserve or part of cacao plantations. Also, Trinidad is so far away from India that, until recently, only a few could afford to go to traditional pilgrimage sites, thereby limiting its role in religious life. More Hindus report visiting India today, as pilgrims and as tourists, but the cost is still prohibitive for a large percentage of the population.

3. The Framework of a Traditional Conceptualization of Hindu Pilgrimage

The nature of traditional concepts of Hindu sacred sites also does not easily fit into the Trinidadian experience. The mythical character of Indian holy sites is not easily transferred by a group of people with knowledge of and experience with such places in India. This conceptualization of sacred sites as having a mythical origin was transferred to succeeding generations of Hindus in Trinidad, not only through stories told by grandparents but also by continued usage of Hindu sacred texts. Rama did not canvas this land looking for Sita, nor did dismembered parts of Sati — consort of Shiva — fall in Trinidad. Sacred texts describe holy places of India in detail, and although places not described in the texts may become holy (BHARDWAJ 1973, 68), it is difficult to sustain their sacred significance in an alien environment. It is not suprising that early Hindu immigrants quickly recognized the efficacy of Sipari Mai, the only religious shrine in Trinidad that paralleled their own tradition. It was not until immigrants' descendants became the dominant component of the Trinidadian Indian population, that is, East Indians who had never been to India, that indiginous Hindu sacred sites began to emerge. And yet, few exist to this day. Hindus are a minority in Trinidad as well as newcomers. One hundred and fifty years may not be enough time to develop a traditional Indian sense of sacred place in a plural society such as the one in Trinidad.

Creation of sacred sites and sustaining the site's sacred significance is a natural part of the symbol making process. RICHARDSON (1981, 286) notes that in reification, which is the quintessential symbol making process, a distance is created between humans and the symbols they create to "talk" to one another. That distance increases to a point whereby the human origin is ignored and then denied. It is now possible for the "talk" to take on life and act back upon the humans that created it. Thus, symbols created and reified give off images that are hung on a material setting, thereby giving a sense of place to that place. This sense of place is both cognitive and experiential according to RICHARSON (1981). He states (1981, 287):

> "...places destined to be sacred continue, through the magic of reification, to develop until they evoke a sense of the holy, of the extraordinary, of being-in-the-world in a manner in which one is ready to suspend his disbelief in the extraordinary and is prepared to accept the out-of-place attributes of the holy — spiritual transformation ... as being common to that place."

Hindus in India have been a dominant cultural force for several thousand years and had as much time to transform the subcontinent's landscape into "one vast sacred space." Trinidadian Hindus are in the infancy of this process and must sustain it in an unsympathetic cultural milieu.

Summary

In summary, as evidenced by their pilgrimage behavior, Trinidadian Hindus do not view traditional pilgrimage in Trinidad as central to their spiritual life. Hindu shrines with a sacred origin are few and only a small percentage of

Hindus patronize them. Visiting the seashore on the last day of Kartik is only a vestige of a rich pilgrimage tradition. Traveling to other places for ritual purposes is most evident in the jag, a practice that is only quasi-pilgrimage in nature. Unsympathetic policies and the resultant social and economic isolation it fosters, lack of knowledge and respect for Hindu practices on the part of the dominant culture, lack of physical size and legal access to special places, distance from India, and finally a short history of settlement in a land without mythical ties to Hinduism has served to diminish the role of *traditional* pilgrimage among Hindus in Trinidad.

Zusammenfassung: Formen des Pilgerverhaltens bei Hindus in Trinidad

Wie an ihrem Verhalten zu erkennen ist, betrachten die Hindus von Trinidad eine traditionelle Wallfahrt nicht als Mittelpunkt ihres geistlichen Lebens. Es gibt nur wenige Hindu-Tempel heiligen Ursprungs, und nur ein Teil der Gläubigen besucht diese. Ein Besuch der Küste am letzten Kartik-Tag ist nur ein Überbleibsel einer reichen Pilger-Tradition. Reisen zu anderen Orten für rituelle Zwecke sind am besten erkennbar am Jag, was aber von Natur her nur eine Quasi-Wallfahrt ist. Die geringe Bedeutung *traditioneller* Wallfahrten bei den Hindus von Trinidad ist eine Folge verständnisloser Politik und der sich daraus ergebenden sozialen und wirtschaftlichen Isolation, mangelnder Kenntnis und Rücksichtnahme auf hinduistische Gewohnheiten von Seiten der dominierenden Kultur, mangelndem Anrecht auf Zutritt zu besonderen Plätzen, der großen Entfernung von Indien, und letztlich der kurzen Siedlungsgeschichte in einem Land ohne mythische Beziehungen zu Indien.

Note

[1] Puja is usually performed by a priest. The puja has replaced the ancient traditional sacrifice with fire which is called *yajna*, and which could only be performed by the highest caste priests (Rice 1978, 285). Puja is propitiation by symbolic sacrifice with rice, coconut, flowers, and other similar kinds of materials replacing animals as the offering to deities. Pungent odors of burning plant material, the aromatic smell of incense burning, trumpet-like blasts from the conch shell, sonorous bells ringing, and the low hum of sacred sounds chanted (*mantra*) accompany the performance of puja. Once an image has been consecrated (*prana pratistha*) puja may be performed, whether in a temple, in a home, or outside. Specific deities and specific observances of the Hindu calendar may have special puja forms associated with them.

Selected Bibliography

ASPINALL, A. (1910): The Pocket Guide to the West Indies, Chemical Publishing Co., Inc., New York, 2nd ed. 1940.

BHARDWAJ, S. M. (1973): Hindu Places of Pilgrimage in India: A Study in Cultural Geography, University of California Press, Berkeley California.

CLARKE, C. (1984): Pluralism and Plural Societies: Caribbean Perspectives. — In: Clarke, C. et. al. eds., Geography and Ethnic Pluralism, George Allen & Unwin, London: 51 – 86.

CROWLEY, D. J. (1957): Plural and Differential Acculturation in Trinidad, American Anthropologist, 59: 817 – 824.

FONAROFF, L. S. (1968): Man and Malaria in Trinidad: Ecological Perspectives of a Changing Health Hazard, Annals-Association of American Geographers, 58: 541 – 71.

JHA, J. C. (1974): The Indian Heritage in Trinidad. — In: LaGuerre, Calcutta to Caroni, Western Printing, Bristol England: 1 – 24.

JOHNSON, H. (1972): The Origins and Early Development of Cane Farming in Trinidad, 1882 – 1906, Journal of Caribbean History, 5: 46 – 74.

KLASS, M. (1961): East Indians in Trinidad: A Study in Cultural Persistence, Columbia University Press, New York.

KOSS, J. D. (1959): Hindus in Trinidad: A Survey of Culture Change and Cultural Continuity, unpublished MA Thesis, University of Pennsylvania.

NIEHOFF, A. and J. NIEHOFF (1960): East Indians in the West Indies, Publications in Anthropology No. 6, Milwaukee Public Museum, Milwaukee Wisconsin.

RICE, E. (1978): Eastern Definitions: A Short Encyclopedia of Religions of the Orient, Doubleday and Company, Inc., New York.

RICHARDSON, M. (1981): Commentary on "The Superorganic in American Cultural Geography," Annals-Association of American Geographers, 71: 284 – 287.

SCHWARTZ, B. M. (1963): The Dissolution of Caste in Trinidad, unpublished PhD Dissertation, University of California at Los Angeles.

SINGH, K. (1974): East Indians and the Larger Society. — In: LaGuerre, Calcutta to Caroni, Western Printing Service, Bristol England: 39 – 68.

WISER, W. H. and C. V. WISER (1964): Behind Mud Walls, 1930 – 1960, University of California Press, Berkeley California.

WOOD, D. (1968): Trinidad in Transition: The Years After Slavery, Oxford University Press, London.

Addresses of the editors and authors

Prof. Surinder M. Bhardwaj, Ph.D.
Dept. of Geography
Kent State University
KENT, Ohio 44242
USA

Prof. Mary Lee Nolan, Ph.D.
Dept. of Geography
Oregon State University
CORVALLIS, Oregon 97331
USA

Dipl.-Bibl. Ulrich Oberdiek, M.S.L.S.
Alemannenstr. 2
D-7800 FREIBURG
F. R. of Germany

Prof. Carolyn V. Prorok, Ph.D.
Dept. of Geography
Slippery Rock University
SLIPPERY ROCK, Pennsylvania
USA 16057-1326

Madhusudana Rao
Dept. of Geography
Kent State University
KENT, Ohio 44242
USA

Prof. Dr. Gisbert Rinschede
Math.-Geogr. Fakultät
Katholische Universität Eichstätt
Ostenstr. 26
D-8078 EICHSTÄTT
F. R. of Germany

Prof. Dr. Robert Stoddard, Ph.D.
Dept. of Geography
University of Nebraska
LINCOLN, Nebraska 68588-0135
USA

Prof. Hiroshi Tanaka, Ph.D.
School of Management
The University of Lethbridge
LETHBRIDGE, Alberta
Canada T1K 3M4